STEVE McQUEEN

THE SALVATION OF AN AMERICAN ICON

GREG LAURIE

WITH MARSHALL TERRILL

"Steve McQueen was one of my boyhood heroes. I watched his Westerns and was always excited to see his latest movie. But shortly before he was diagnosed with cancer he put his faith and trust in Jesus Christ. Four days before Steve's death, my father paid him a visit and gave his own personal Bible to Steve, who died with this Bible in his arms. Pastor Greg Laurie explores this bigger-than-life film star and shares in-depth interviews with those closest to McQueen in a fast-paced book. Don't miss Greg's riveting account of "Steve McQueen: The Salvation of an American Icon."

Franklin Graham
CEO of the Billy Graham Evangelistic Association

"When Greg Laurie shared the story with me of Steve McQueen finding faith and hope at the end of his life, I was deeply moved. Everyone knows of Steve as an American icon, but few know of this chapter in his life and I'm glad Greg is shedding light on it."

Mel Gibson
Academy Award-Winning Director and Actor

"When I first picked up this book I thought to myself, *How have I not heard Steve McQueen's story until now?!* Greg Laurie has done extensive research along with McQueen biographer Marshall Terrill, and tells a story very few people know … that Steve McQueen came to faith in Jesus Christ. You will not believe this until you read it; and it's all true!"

Bart Millard
Lead singer of MercyMe

"Greg Laurie has one of the most powerful life-change stories of anyone I know. That's why he's the perfect person to share the inspiring, yet little known story, about Steve McQueen's transformation by Christ. Greg's carefully researched book will draw you closer to Jesus and move you to share your faith with others."

Craig Groeschel
Pastor of Life.Church and New York Times Best-selling author

"A big thanks to Greg Laurie and Marshall Terrill for bringing to light this amazing story of Steve McQueen coming to faith in Jesus Christ. You will love reading this book!"

Phil Wickham
Contemporary Christian musician

"My friend Greg Laurie has written a captivating true story of Steve McQueen's spiritual journey. Greg carefully researched, interviewing McQueen's widow, friends and many others. He writes in the first-person, intertwining parallels between McQueen's life and his own. The result is a unique, personal and compelling account that kept me from putting the book down until I read the final words."

Randy Alcorn
Best-selling Author and Director of Eternal Perspective Ministries

"Steve McQueen was basically Brad Pitt, George Clooney and Johnny Depp all rolled up into one. An icon, a heartthrob and a legend. But what the tabloids never told is what happened in this movie star's heart after the cameras stopped rolling. I am thankful that Greg took the time to research and to share the legacy of the great American icon Steve McQueen. I am inspired by his fight and faith. I can't wait to meet Steve McQueen in Heaven. Do yourself a favor and read this book by my great friend, Greg Laurie, as he shares all that Christ did in the life of this Hollywood star."

Levi Lusko
Pastor of Fresh Life Church, Founder of Skull Church and O2 Experience
Best-selling author

"Greg Laurie's new book about Steve McQueen is something special. The conversion of McQueen happened when he was the number one movie star in the world. But how did this happen? Greg, in first person interviews with people who knew Steve, gives us the answers."

Chris Tomlin
Christian Recording Artist

"At the sound of Steve McQueen's name my mind breaks free and I immediately get a sense of the highway moving beneath him. Images of James Dean, John Lennon, and Ernest Hemingway join the ride as they bunch up and blend together in selfless worship of rebellion, sacrifice, heart, grit and something incredibly unique that reaches a part of us that very few people can put their finger on. It's the kind of tingle felt when God touches our heart and turns us inside out. So, in a few words it's a restless journey, a seeking heart and a loving God we are treated to here as Greg Laurie, who knows a lot about searching, heads out on the road with God at the wheel and the deep expectation of discovering Steve McQueen in his sights. What he encounters is often painful, rock bottom mesmerizing, deep down lonely, but eventually a triumphant life that touched the souls of so many on its way to spend eternity with the King of Kings."

Ken Mansfield
Former U.S. Manager Beatles' Apple Records, Producer, Author

"From the time I was a young man sitting in a dark movie theater, I admired Steve McQueen. I was taken with the way he drove cars and rode motorcycles. His daring. His style. I wanted to live with his kind of fearlessly adventurous spirit. And I remember being saddened at his death at such a young age. But until I read this book, I didn't know the remarkable story of his stepping out in faith, embracing the most important journey of his life. You will love this book."

Dr. Jack Graham
Best-selling Author and Senior Pastor, Prestonwood Baptist Church, Dallas, Texas

"An extraordinary portrait of one of the most compelling icons of the 20th century. Greg Laurie brilliantly and lovingly examines the agony beneath the surface of Steve McQueen's inimitable life, and exposes the hitherto unknown and rather shocking truth about one of our most famous American figures."

Eric Metaxas
#1 New York Times Bestselling author of Bonhoeffer,
and host of the nationally syndicated Eric Metaxas Show.

STEVE McQUEEN: The Salvation of an American Icon
By Greg Laurie with Marshall Terrill

Scripture quotations marked KJV are taken from King James Version of the Bible.

Scripture quotations marked MSG are taken from The Message, copyright © 1993, 1994, 1995, 1995, 2000, 2001, 2002, Used by permission of NavPress Publishing Group.

Scripture quotations marked NLT are taken from the Holy Bible, New Living Translation, copyright © 1996. Used by permission of Tyndale House Publishers, Inc, Carol Stream, Illinois, 60188. (Later editions copyright, 2004, 2007 by Tyndale House Foundation.)

Scripture quotations marked NKJV are taken from the Holy Bible, New King James Version, copyright © 1982, 1983. Used by permission of Thomas Nelson Publishers, Inc, Nashville, Tennessee, 37214.

Cataloging-in-Publication data on file with the Library of Congress

ISBN 978-1-94689-105-1

Published in the United States by American Icon Press™

Distributed to the general market trade by Greenleaf Book Group

For ordering information or special discounts for bulk purchases, please contact Greenleaf Book Group at PO Box 91869, Austin, Texas 78709, (512)891.6100.

www.greenleafbookgroup.com

Manufactured in the United States of America

10 9 8 7 6 5 4 3 2 1

This book is dedicated to those who had all the odds stacked against them. Those who were written off and told they would never amount to anything. Those who were abandoned by their parents, but loved by God. There is hope.

– Greg Laurie

CONTENTS

 **AUTHOR'S NOTE**

Writing a fictional book is something I've really wanted to do for a long time. But friends of mine who are very successful nonfiction authors and have made the leap to writing fiction tell me it's actually not as easy as it looks. Rocket science for the rank amateur. "Stick to nonfiction, Greg," they say. "You're a preacher with a story. Write about what you know."

Well, what I know best is my own strange, crazy life and the power of God's Word, the Bible. But I've also come to know quite a lot about something else, and he is the main subject of this book.

Terrence Steven McQueen.

Everything you're soon to read about him here is fact. And everything I've written about my own life here is also fact. For instance, I do indeed own and cherish a 1967 Bullitt Mustang—not the actual car that Steve McQueen drove in the movie *Bullitt* but what is called a "tribute car," a very close reproduction. And in this book it serves as a great vehicle—pun intended—to tell the actor's story.

The only thing in the book that's *not* true is something I wish *were* true, and possibly someday *may* be true. I'd love to actually strike out in that Mustang on the cross-country motor trip I write about. But it didn't really happen. Or hasn't happened. Not yet anyway.

Truth is, I'm the busy pastor of a church in Southern California attended by more than twelve thousand people and, at least for right now, I can't take that cross-country ride behind the wheel of this legendary car. So this part of the book, yes, is fiction—a literary device to help connect the dots between Steve McQueen's lifelong search for spiritual enlightenment and, ultimately, his eternal salvation. But by joining me on this make-believe road trip, you're about to learn things about Steve McQueen that have never before been made public.

My collaborator Marshall Terrill is a celebrated author and the undisputed "go-to" guy for all things McQueen. He has written five books on the life of the man, and this one would never have happened without Marshall's mind, his memory, and his elegance with words.

Marshall and I personally interviewed many of the people you will meet here. Some of the interviews were conducted by Marshall on his own in doing research for his previous McQueen books. And when we get down to the true story of what really happened to arguably the number-one movie star in the world, you will be surprised and inspired.

My road trip is an allegory, a metaphor. Steve McQueen's life was not. It was real. Tracing it fired me up, and I believe it will do the same for you.

Greg Laurie
June 2017

INTRODUCTION

A popular men's magazine recently posed one of the most intriguing pop culture questions of all time: "Who was cooler: Steve McQueen or James Dean?"

The question topped a *mano a mano* examination of the lives and careers of both iconic actors that rated them in a whole gamut of categories, from fashion and style sense to roguish masculinity to career accomplishments.

Dean was rightly celebrated as a pinup boy for teenage disillusionment and the archetype of disobedience for his portrayal in *Rebel Without a Cause*. He was the silver screen's first post-World War II maverick heartthrob. His squinty good looks, tousled hair, cuffed blue jeans, and white T-shirt never went out of style, and his tragic death at age twenty-four eternally cemented his youthful image and appeal in the public mind.

Interestingly, both Dean and McQueen were contemporaries, born a year apart, and were actors at the same time. But while McQueen struggled in his early career, Dean shot to success. In fact, McQueen even did mechanical work on James Dean's motorcycle, but Dean had no clue who McQueen was.

The magazine reporter deftly noted that McQueen built on what Dean accomplished in the 1950s and took advantage of the antiestablishment phenomena of the 1960s. He made rebellion a favorite pastime—both on and off the screen. He fought producers and directors, dated beautiful women, drove fast cars, and broke enough bones tumbling off his motorcycle to be considered authentic. He had the scratches on his movie star face to prove it. Yet somehow he managed to keep a low personal profile behind his massive public image.

He only made it through the ninth grade and did a stretch in reform school. His alcoholic mother abandoned him repeatedly throughout childhood, and he never even knew his father, also an alcoholic who died of cirrhosis of the liver.

So, not surprisingly—to me—the magazine's nod went to McQueen. Guess that's why he's been crowned by pop culture historians as the "King of Cool." Almost four decades after his death, people still revere the image he crafted and projected through his art. The fact is, James Dean wasn't even in the same league as Steve McQueen.

But what was this flesh and blood human being like when there was no script to read and the cameras weren't rolling? That's a much tougher question because Hollywood legends don't come more complex than Steve McQueen.

As Winston Churchill famously said, and it certainly applies to Steve McQueen, he was "a riddle wrapped in a mystery inside an enigma."

Many of the things that have been written about him seem wildly contradictory. We'll go back across a lot of them in this book. McQueen was a loving father and husband, yet he was also a womanizer and at times a shameless male chauvinist. Nobody hung on to a dollar any tighter than he did, yet he made large (and strictly anonymous) donations to charity. He was a loyal friend yet trusted nobody. He was capable of jaw-dropping cruelty to colleagues yet was a sucker for kids and old folks.

If you graduated with honors from business school, wore a suit and tie, and had a title next to your name, God help you. But his own lack of formal education was an embarrassment to him. He only made it through the ninth grade and did a stretch in reform school. His alcoholic mother abandoned him repeatedly throughout childhood, and he never even knew his father, also an alcoholic who died of cirrhosis of the liver. But McQueen rose above such desolate underpinnings through sheer force of character and determination to succeed.

Nobody in Hollywood was more disciplined and hardworking than the man whose capriciousness often made movie sets as tense and downright chaotic as war zones. He was famously antiauthority yet regularly visited the young male residents at the Boys Republic in Chino, California, and counseled them about straightening themselves out.

> McQueen was invited to Sharon Tate's house the night that she and four others were brutally murdered by the Manson Family.

Politics bored and often repelled him, but it didn't keep him off President Nixon's infamous "Enemies List" nor stop FBI Director J. Edgar Hoover from keeping official tabs on him. He made it onto another notorious list as well: Charlie Manson's celebrity hit list. In fact, McQueen was invited to Sharon Tate's house the night that she and four others were brutally murdered by the Manson Family.

The fact that he became a wildly successful actor is astonishing in itself. By all accounts, he fell into the profession in order to escape menial labor—no more, no less. He had no lofty cinematic dreams, only the desire to avoid the drudgery of a routine 9-to-5 job, plus he figured it would be a good way to "meet chicks." Even after becoming so good at it—acting, that is—he never thought of it as a "real man's job."

What McQueen really respected were cars, motorcycles, and the men who raced them at breakneck speed. His first passion was machines, and he had a natural affinity for them. He was mechanically adept, fiercely competitive, and completely fearless. No vehicle was safe as long as he was behind the wheel. On the set of *Hell Is for Heroes*, McQueen wrecked three rental cars—and the count would have been higher had the studio not made clear that the cost of anymore wrecks would be deducted from his salary. On another film he punished a brand-new rental car until the engine caught fire. When it did, he leaped out of the burning vehicle like a seasoned stuntman and laughed about it with a friend.

Steve McQueen, bottom line, was the biggest movie star in the world in the 1960s and '70s, the ultimate alpha-male of his generation.

When not making movies, he entered car and motorcycle races and held his own against the best drivers in the world. Many of these men formed McQueen's inner circle of friends, admiring and respecting him not as a Hollywood figure but as a man after their own macho hearts.

Steve McQueen, bottom line, was the biggest movie star in the world in the 1960s and '70s, the ultimate alpha-male of his generation. His tough-guy persona melded an unlikely combination of willfulness, unpredictability, strength, and vulnerability, which riveted audiences in such unforgettable films as *The Magnificent Seven, The Great Escape, The Cincinnati Kid, The Sand Pebbles, The Thomas Crown Affair, Bullitt, The Getaway, Papillon,* and *The Towering Inferno.*

That's the part most people know—as well as the fact that he lived the same way he drove his motorcycles and cars: fearlessly and at top speed.

But in December 1979, life slammed on the brakes when he was diagnosed with mesothelioma, a deadly form of cancer caused from exposure to asbestos. He would be dead before another year rolled around. Maybe you knew that too.

But there's another part of his final years that many of the idolaters, wannabes, and steadfast keepers and stokers of McQueen's eternal flame conveniently ignore, deny, or dismiss as an aberration. It is, however, indisputable fact. If I didn't know it before, I know it now. Their rabble-rousing hero reached out to God to fill the void in his heart, to find the peace that consistently eluded him throughout his pedal-to-the-metal life.

I realize I'm giving away the ending, right here in the setup. (Not a fiction writer, remember?) But I think it's important that you know where I'm headed so you can view the many details of his life I'm about to disclose through an entirely different lens.

Six months before receiving his cancer diagnosis— before being told he was on borrowed time—McQueen, in yet another seeming contradiction of his take-no-prisoners nature, quietly gave his life to the Lord on the balcony of an out-of-the-way church in Ventura, California. It wasn't a deathbed conversion.

———

What, then, would lead him to such an unlikely decision that, on its face, seems so at odds with the Steve McQueen most of us remember?

I had a personal reason for wanting to find out.

I have always admired McQueen as an actor and all-around "guy's guy." But in doing the research for this book, I was amazed to discover that our lives contained many parallels—which I surely don't mean in any kind of self-flattering sense. It's just that he and I endured similarly rocky starts and suffered many of the same bad breaks early on. Turning my life over to Christ, after enduring what my growing-up years were like, changed the entire course of my life, which was certainly headed in the wrong direction at the time. Then, to find out that a man I admired had experienced the same divinely-inspired metamorphosis, was a thrill that made me want to find out more about his long, winding journey of searching and finally finding what he was always looking for. This was something we shared too—the most important part of all.

> I have always admired McQueen as an actor and all-around "guy's guy." But in doing the research for this book, I was amazed to discover that our lives contained many parallels . . .

I told the story of Steve McQueen's unexpected conversion before a crowd of forty-five thousand people on a warm summer night recently at Angel Stadium in Anaheim for an event called "The SoCal Harvest." People young and old were riveted by the story of a troubled boy who became the number-one movie star in the world, turning to God after being disillusioned by the sheer emptiness of all he'd accumulated and accomplished.

The King of Cool laid down a typically dizzying, sometimes mazelike, spellbinding trail to follow. And in this book, I plan to do just that, tracing the woolly geography of the actor's life, his relationships, his career, and the spiritual quest that led him out onto the Damascus Road.

I'm about to head out on the road as well—a cross-country trip that will reintroduce me to our scenic and diverse country, meeting everyday people who play an extraordinary role in Steve McQueen's life. My travels will include more than four thousand miles, lots of freeways, highways, beltways, turnpikes, back roads, and a few dusty ones that no doubt will take the sparkle off my newly buffed car. It's sure to dramatically take me out of my comfort zone.

So cinch up your seatbelt. We're going on a wild ride. Steve McQueen would have us do no less.

STEVE McQUEEN

THE SALVATION OF AN AMERICAN ICON

ALL I NEED'S
A FAST MACHINE

I've been a car guy my whole life.

It started with model car kits, when I would buy the latest Ed Roth plastic concoctions, ranging from his tricked-out '57 Bel Air or the more exotic concepts like the "Beatnik Bandit" or the "Mysterion." I was never very adept at putting them together and usually got glue all over everything. When I messed up I would just go buy another model kit and try again.

As I got older I moved up to slot cars, which were very popular in the 1960s. There were even commercial track locations you could go to and race. I went with my own Batmobile based on the George Barris design from the hit TV show *Batman*, starring Adam West. The one slot car I really wanted but couldn't afford was the classic Aston Martin that James Bond drove, first appearing in 1964's *Goldfinger*, complete with ejector seat and rotating license plates.

What is it they say? The only difference between men and boys is the price of their toys.

When it came time to drive for real, my first car was a 1960 Ford Starliner. It was my mom's, and she didn't want to drive it anymore. I think a snake discovered inside had something to do with that.

One of mine.

As a kid, I liked not only cars but also reptiles. I even considered becoming a herpetologist. That's from the Greek word *herpein,* meaning "nerd." (Actually, it's from the Greek word meaning "to creep." Same difference, I guess.)

One day Mom drove me to a pet store to pick up another slithering serpent to add to my ever-growing collection. We put it in a terrarium in the trunk of the car. When we arrived back home, the snake was no longer in the terrarium. I couldn't find him, and Mom vowed never to drive that Ford Starliner again. But a few days later she had errands that couldn't be put off anymore, and with great trepidation she got behind the steering wheel and started off down the street.

At the first stoplight she felt something cold and smooth rub against her ankle. Mom leaped out of the car screaming, "There's a snake in my car!" A police officer happened to be nearby and came running. But instead of my prodigal snake, what he found in the car was a hose that had come loose from under the dash and brushed against Mom's ankle. Long story short—I got the car. And I literally drove it into the ground, eventually abandoning it in an empty field in Santa Ana.

When it came time to drive for real, my first car was a 1960 Ford Starliner. It was my mom's, and she didn't want to drive it anymore. I think a snake discovered inside had something to do with that. One of mine.

Later I drove a banged-up Corvair, the model that made consumer advocate Ralph Nader famous for decrying it as a death trap on wheels. He would've run screaming from my car. Its headlights were so far out of alignment from an accident of mine that it looked cross-eyed.

My first classic car was a 1957 Corvette in Aztec copper, with a cream insert on the side and cream upholstery. It was "art on wheels" but a mechanical nightmare, and I got rid of it with a sigh of relief. Then came a 1957 Bel Air convertible in tropical turquoise, with a gold continental kit. As beautiful as it was, no one wanted to ride with me, for reasons summed up by my wife, Cathe, when she said she felt like she was in a parade whenever we drove around town.

Anyone who loves cars knows the Bullitt, which was featured in the Steve McQueen film of the same name.

I have a longtime friend and mechanic named Don Oakes who owns quite a collection of classic cars. And on my son Jonathan's wedding day, Don told him to borrow any car he wanted for the wedding party photos. I recommended he take Don's perfectly restored Woodie, but instead Jonathan chose Don's 1967 Bullitt Mustang, a car that had been in his possession for many years and looked better than ever.

G-o-o-d choice. When Jonathan and his lovely bride, Brittni, climbed into that car, they looked absolutely stunning (though I confess, the Bullitt itself was almost as jaw-droppingly gorgeous, even without them).

Anyone who loves cars knows the Bullitt, which was featured in the Steve McQueen film of the same name. When *Bullitt* hit silver screens in 1968, theatergoers sat slack-jawed through that fourteen-minute thrill ride along the roller-coaster streets of San Francisco. Almost a half century later, it's still considered by many movie historians as the greatest car chase of all time on film.

When the movie came out, I was sixteen and driving around in that dilapidated two-hundred-dollar Corvair. But after seeing the movie, every time I got behind the wheel—even in the Corvair—I was Lieutenant Frank Bullitt, tearing through the streets of San Francisco in pursuit of bad guys.

But truth be known, I wanted the real thing. A pox on the stupid Corvair. I wanted Don's Bullitt car. But he wasn't interested in selling. And one that I tracked down in San Francisco was too expensive. I searched for two years and finally found one in Houston, where by providential coincidence I happened to be traveling on a speaking assignment. It wasn't cheap, but I bit the Bullitt (or vice versa) and got the car.

Cathe was not as excited about my extravagant purchase as I was, which was understandable. We had done little more than tread water financially since getting married. Cathe's father was a successful executive in the oil industry, and from the start he harbored strong apprehensions that I would be able to keep her up in the style to which she'd been accustomed—servants, world travel, beautiful homes. He had a lot of doubts about this young, hippie preacher his daughter had hitched up with. I'm sure some of his doubts stemmed from the fact that I had no decent role model for marriage, since my mother had been married seven times.

Cathe.

She and I had met in church. We were both strong-willed people but otherwise could not have been any more different.

She likes British shows on PBS; I like shoot-'em-ups.

She's neat; I'm messy.

She's sometimes late; I always try to be on time.

She's practical; I'm a dreamer.

Before we were married, we got into some pretty heated arguments, breaking up and vowing to never see each other again. It happened three times in three years—an annual event, like Christmas, only not as festive. After our last big fight, she and I got back together and determined to make it stick.

The jury was still out, though, on whether or not I was good marriage material. My faith in God was about the only thing I had then. Certainly it was what I cared most about and paid the most attention to. My clothes were so vintage they'd been in and out of fashion several times over. I taught a small Bible study at a church in Riverside, California, and had only been a believer myself for three years, so I hardly felt qualified to be a pastor. But I sure appreciated the regular paycheck, even if it was only a hundred dollars a week.

Steve McQueen—poster boy for a bygone macho era when men didn't complain or explain, a time when a wife greeted her husband at the door with a kiss and a martini, and a tough guy squinted at the world through the smoke from an unfiltered cigarette, plugged into the corner of his mouth.

So in an effort to allay the misgivings of her very worried father, after we'd declared our intentions to marry, she wrote him a letter cataloging what she considered my most winning attributes. After a day or two of uncomfortable silence, Cathe's mom told her, "Honey, your dad got your letter. It was beautiful. We'll give you our blessing for your wedding."

On February 2, 1974, we exchanged vows in front of five hundred friends, most of them fellow hippies (a few even wearing shoes) who had also given their lives to the Lord. It looked like Woodstock West. Chuck Smith performed the ceremony. Besides being the legendary pastor of Calvary Chapel in Costa Mesa, Chuck was a mentor and father figure. But even pastors who've performed hundreds of weddings can still make nervous, rookie mistakes, and when the time came to announce that the deal was done, he cried out: "I now pronounce Greg and Laurie man and wife!" Even my new father-in-law laughed. I got such a kick out of it, too, that I somehow found myself tangled up in Cathe's veil and almost yanked it off.

Four decades, two children, and five grandchildren later, our union remains an ongoing adventure, charted only by our enduring mutual love and respect.

But I'll be the first to acknowledge that sometimes my whims have given Cathe serious pause. The Ford Bullitt was only one of many.

It does seem now, though, that I was meant to have it.

Listen, I'm not trying to make buying a car a spiritual thing because it isn't. But this was the first piece of a puzzle that has resulted in this book and a documentary film about the iconic actor Steve McQueen, and what I believe was the most important moment of his life.

Steve McQueen—poster boy for a bygone macho era when men didn't complain or explain, a time when a wife greeted her husband at the door with a kiss and a martini, and a tough guy squinted at the world through the smoke from an unfiltered cigarette, plugged into the corner of his mouth.

Now don't jump down my throat because I'm not saying we ought to turn back the clock to those days. Despite certain losses of morality and common sense in our culture, we've picked up positive yardage over the years in a number of obvious areas. But a half century ago nobody embodied the notion of what a real man was, or made a bigger impression on adolescent males, than McQueen. I was a full-fledged member of that club. He was a mainstay of my childhood and teen years.

On the surface he cared only about himself. But McQueen's performance was infused with an unspoken compassion that spoke louder than words.

I first took notice of him in the late 1950s, when he was one of television's rising stars on the CBS show *Wanted: Dead or Alive*. Like millions of others, I stayed up late on Saturday nights, sandwiched between my grandparents on the couch, watching McQueen, as bounty hunter Josh Randall, take on some really bad Wild West hombres.

This series distinguished itself from the usual cowboy fare by making McQueen's character the heavy. Oh, he had his virtues and lived by a code as upright and sterling as Marshall Dillon's, but unlike the savior of Dodge, ol' Josh was no boy scout. He didn't wear a badge and operated by a different set of rules, so lawmen loathed him almost as much as the criminals Randall hunted down for money. Of course at five or six years old, I didn't realize the fine line his character was walking. I just instinctively rooted for the guy.

Within a few years McQueen became even bigger on the screen and in my life as he successfully transitioned to big-league movies, starting with *Never So Few* (1959). A year later came *The Magnificent Seven,* in which his portrayal of one of the gunslingers hired to protect a besieged Mexican village stamped McQueen as a rising Hollywood star. In 1963, *The Great Escape* made him a one-star constellation.

We dug and trusted him because, as the man himself once said, "I'm half farmer and half street person. I can look at both because I grew up on a farm and on the streets."

As the character Virgil Hilts, McQueen crafted one of film's greatest screen characters, transcending the prototype of the strong and silent martyr. On the surface he cared only about himself. But McQueen's performance was infused with an unspoken compassion that spoke louder than words. The character and icon he created in that role has been infinitely analyzed and deconstructed but, as with many things McQueen, it really boiled down to that old expression, "What you see is what you get." The character, the stare, the baseball and mitt, the motorcycle and the jump over the barbed-wire fence still resonate with audiences today, even ones that have seen *The Great Escape* as many times as I have.

Five years later came the defining McQueen movie, *Bullitt.* One of the big sayings in the '60s was "Never trust anyone over the age of thirty." There was one exception to that rule, however—Steve McQueen, who himself was inching toward forty. We dug and trusted him because, as the man himself once said, "I'm half farmer and half street person. I can look at both because I grew up on a farm and on the streets."

The "Age of Aquarius" was a trippy time in history, for sure, with bell-bottomed longhairs flaunting their free love, flowers, protest signs, and affection for all things psychedelic. It was also a time of massive political volatility and upheaval, including the assassinations of Martin Luther King Jr. and Robert Kennedy; the tear-gassed spectacle of the 1968 Democratic National Convention in Chicago; and the rise of groups like the Black Panthers, Students for a Democratic Society (SDS), and the Weathermen. Overhanging it all was the gruesome specter and spectacle of the Vietnam War, which sent thousands of college students into the streets to protest against their own government.

Like so many other young people at that time, my faith in our leaders and institutions was shaken. Nobody seemed to be in control of himself or events. So I preferred what I saw on a movie screen to what was broadcast on the TV news, especially when Steve McQueen, the great antihero of the era, was up there doing things his way, defying staid and rigid authority, following the dictates of his own sense of justice, and being unbelievably hip about it.

Even after God became the center of my life in 1970, Steve McQueen always rang my bell. Cathe knew that and, God bless her, she put up with it. But now—decades later—my new obsession with one of my favorite actors, fueled to the max by the discovery that he had also accepted Christ as his Savior, would really put her tolerance and understanding to the test. I wanted to find out how Steve McQueen, of all people, had come to embrace the Lord. And I was itching to take a cross-country trip in the Bullitt car to ferret it all out.

But doing so would put my wife and others who depended on me in a tough spot. I have an outreach operation that includes three churches, multiple satellite campuses, traveling crusades, television, radio, and podcasts, and more than fifty different ministries. If I was to go gallivanting around the country, the job of running everything would fall to our great staff. They're up to it, for sure, but my absence on a personal quest that strikes even me as quixotic, whimsical, and slightly weird would be a burden on them. I'd have understood, when I finally worked up the nerve to tell Cathe what I had in mind, if she had rolled her eyes and gently (or maybe not so gently) told me to get my head out of the clouds. But she just smiled and nodded, her face shining with love and understanding, and I loved her more than ever for it.

As men grow older, nature relentlessly siphons off our testosterone little by little. It's important for us to think we can do the same things we did in our teens and early twenties, despite realizing the foolishness of the notion. Laughable, we know, but common. We all grow older, softer around the middle, and, willing or not, we get in touch with our feelings. All the ingredients for a syndrome. But all it takes to reverse the process, at least in our heads, is to get together with other men to watch a football game or boxing match, look under the hood of a car, or . . . watch a Steve McQueen movie.

But it was late October when this wild hair got under my middle-aged skin. I didn't have time to analyze how or why it had me in its grip. I just knew it was time for this old dog to hit the road and start barking at the moon.

Glad to have you riding shotgun.

2

THE WIDOW AND THE PREACHER MAN

I guess this whole crazy adventure had its start on a rare lazy Saturday afternoon when I plopped down to watch some television. For months I had been pushing myself hard, as usual, multitasking, trying to do too many things at once. Now I finally had some time to myself on a crisp fall afternoon and decided to spend it sitting in one of the four well-worn leather chairs in our family room with a bowl of popcorn and the TV remote. Plenty of college football was on, but I surfed through the channels in search of something more conducive to the nap I felt coming on.

Ahh . . . what better fare to bring me in for a nice, soft landing than a boring documentary.

Only this wasn't one about the mating habits of the three-toed sloth so I got no sleep that afternoon. This documentary was about Steve McQueen, and I was hooked from the opening credits. The documentary did a decent job covering the trajectory of McQueen's life—his hardscrabble beginnings, his meteoric rise to movie stardom, then his tragic end when cancer claimed him at age fifty.

But something was missing. In early 1980, I'd heard the surprising news that the King of Cool had given his life to God. And yet this documentary never even mentioned it. Not even in passing. Seemed like a pretty glaring omission to me. How do you leave out such a pivotal event from the story about a man's life?

McQueen's momentous conversion reportedly occurred just before he released his last western film, *Tom Horn*. In fact, that's what drew me to the theater to see it, in addition to plain old curiosity. His last big hit, *The Towering Inferno*, came out in December 1974, smashing all box office records, and was then the highest grossing movie of all time. But then McQueen decided to take a break from filmmaking, except for a puzzling adaptation of an obscure Henrik Ibsen play, *An Enemy of the People*. In it McQueen grew his hair long and sported a bushy beard and granny glasses, rendering himself virtually unrecognizable. Even worse, *An Enemy of the People* had no car chases, no gunplay, nothing for McQueen's fans to sink their teeth into. Not surprisingly, studio executives hated it, and the critics who previewed it were so appalled, the movie was shelved in 1978 without being released. McQueen wasn't seen again on the big screen for almost five years, which in Hollywood qualifies as a lifetime and a career death sentence.

> In early 1980, I'd heard the surprising news that the King of Cool had given his life to God. And yet this documentary never even mentioned it. Not even in passing.

When he finally reappeared in *Tom Horn*, McQueen looked as weather-beaten as an old saddle. I wasn't exactly Peter Pan myself, but it was hard to see such a symbol of youthful rebellion looking so old. In *The Hunter*, released on July 28, 1980, McQueen seemed even more a spent Bullitt. The wear and tear on him was evident. He appeared downright lethargic. I left the theater disappointed and sad.

Not quite three months later, Steve McQueen was dead.

So his life was worthy of a documentary, for sure, and I enjoyed watching it. But why leave out the biggest, most life-changing decision he ever made? This made no sense. In fact, it bothered me so much that I got right on the Internet and typed "Steve McQueen" and "Conversion to Christianity" into the search engine. A couple of links provided a few vague clues but nothing substantial.

Yet the subject stayed on my mind. Pretty soon I ordered an out-of-print book written about McQueen by his close friend and ranch foreman, Grady Ragsdale. I was especially intrigued by the story of his fight against cancer that led him to receive rather unorthodox treatment in an obscure clinic in Mexico. I had a lot of questions about that particular time frame, but I figured I would never really know.

A few weeks later, as I mentioned earlier, I shared some of what I'd learned and been told about Steve McQueen's spiritual journey in one of my messages before a big crowd at Angel

> The wear and tear on him was evident. He appeared downright lethargic. I left the theater disappointed and sad. Not quite three months later, Steve McQueen was dead.

Stadium. Part of the evening's schedule, before my main talk, was an interview with actor Mel Gibson. And in the green room before the event, he and I talked about McQueen.

"Steve was one of these guys who seemed to be very relaxed with what he did," Mel said. "Relaxation is the key to any kind of skill at all. His performances were relaxed. They were effortless. He seemed to get his meaning across. He was magnetic. He was cool . . . . Everything about him was very considered, very economic, and he didn't waste a move."

> He also happened to be copilot of the airplane that had flown Steve McQueen to El Paso, Texas, in a last-ditch effort to save the actor's life.

I then shared with Mel the story of Steve's spiritual transformation. I could tell he was fascinated, especially when after we'd been briefly interrupted, he turned back to me and said, "Greg, finish that story about Steve McQueen."

A week later, a member of our congregation, Mike Jugan, approached and asked to speak with me in private. Mike, a friend and terrific guy, is a pilot for Alaska Airlines. For as I was about to find out, he also happened to be copilot of the airplane that had flown Steve McQueen to El Paso, Texas, in a last-ditch effort to save the actor's life.

I couldn't have been more stunned if Mike had told me he was the archangel Michael. I sat him down and urged him to tell me everything, and not leave out a single detail. Mel Gibson's admonition to finish the Steve McQueen story was taking shape.

Mike at the time was twenty-five, flying for Ken Haas Aviation, a Learjet charter company in Long Beach. On

November 3, 1980, he and Ken Haas himself went to the airport at Oxnard, California, to fly a party of three to El Paso. The group was registered under the name "Sam Sheppard," but that was an alias designed to throw off the media. The passengers were actually Steve McQueen and two medical aides.

Mike couldn't believe it. McQueen had been his hero since he'd taken up motocross racing as a boy. "Any kid who loved racing knew who Steve McQueen was," he said, "and we all wanted to be like him. We had seen *On Any Sunday* about fifty times."

When Mike and Ken got to the airport, they parked the jet far from the terminal in an effort to afford McQueen as much privacy as possible. As they sat in the cockpit waiting for their passengers to arrive, they heard a knock on the side of the plane.

"Are you with the Sam Sheppard party?" asked a tall man wearing an overcoat and hat. When Mike answered affirmatively, the man stuck out his hand and introduced himself: "I'm Billy Graham." Yes, that Billy Graham.

"Are you with the Sam Sheppard party?" asked a tall man wearing an overcoat and hat. When Mike answered affirmatively, the man stuck out his hand and introduced himself: "I'm Billy Graham."

Yes, *that* Billy Graham.

I'll explain later why Billy Graham ever happened to be a part of the Steve McQueen narrative, especially at this juncture, but suffice for now that he was there on the platform, telling the two pilots that McQueen and the others would be arriving shortly. After a few minutes, sure enough, a camper wheeled under the canopy that had been set up over the forward part of the aircraft. Out of it stepped McQueen, wearing blue jeans, a T-shirt, and a sombrero, with a bottle of soda in his hand.

"Howdy, fellas," McQueen greeted the pilots.

"I'm standing there," recalled Mike, "looking at my childhood hero, and my heart went out to him. You could see his belly was distended and swollen from the tumors." But Mike also noticed something else: "The look in his crystal blue eyes was predictably fierce. He had this indomitable spirit about him, and he seemed to be at peace."

Accompanying McQueen were nurses Teena Valentino and Annie Martell. As the trio entered the airplane, Billy gathered the folks around him and asked God to bless the pilots, the flight itself, and McQueen. Then before leaving, the famed evangelist stepped aboard for a final private word with the actor.

McQueen had made arrangements for a doctor there to excise his cancerous tumors —a nontraditional approach that would only end up igniting other complications.

Mike told me that after the plane reached cruising altitude, he went back to chat with McQueen, and found him snacking on crackers and soda.

"I wanted to talk about motorcycles," recalled Mike, "but he was more interested in the plane and asked what it was like to fly a Learjet. I told him we climbed out at five thousand feet per minute and now were cruising at forty-one thousand feet at about six hundred miles per hour. He chuckled and said, 'That's better than my Stearman,'" the World War II-era biplane he'd bought and been learning to fly in recent months.

When the jet landed in El Paso, McQueen's party was whisked off to the clinic in Juarez, just across the Mexican border. McQueen had made arrangements for a doctor there to excise his cancerous tumors—a nontraditional approach that would only end up igniting other complications. That's why four days later, on November 7, 1980, Mike and his boss were notified that McQueen had passed away and were asked to return to El Paso in *two* jets this time—one for the actor's family, close friends, and medical staff; the other to carry McQueen's body back to California.

> "There were times during the flight," Mike said, "when I looked over my shoulder at the simple wooden box and thought, *Steve McQueen's body is in there.* I couldn't believe it. It was surreal."

The scene at El Paso International Airport was sheer chaos, according to Mike. As McQueen's plain pine casket was ferried to the jet in an aged Ford LTD station wagon, news contingents raced alongside to record it all. They continued to record everything for posterity as the copilots helped Grady Ragsdale (author of the book I had read) and Dr. Dwight McKee load the coffin into the plane. An especially aggressive photographer snapping pictures of the coffin almost got punched out by a member of McQueen's party.

Mike piloted the jet that carried McQueen's casket, while Ken flew the plane with Steve's widow, Barbara; his children, Chad and Terry; Grady Ragsdale; Dr. McKee, and the other medical personnel who'd devoted months trying to save McQueen's life. "Before boarding the flight, Barbara was crying," Mike recalled. "Terry and Chad were crying, the doctors and nurses were crying. It was very sad. I remember thinking to myself that just a few days before, Steve was so positive about the whole trip. I mean, this wasn't supposed to happen. He wasn't supposed to die.

"There were times during the flight," Mike said, "when I looked over my shoulder at the simple wooden box and thought, *Steve McQueen's body is in there*. I couldn't believe it. It was surreal."

As Mike was telling me all this, his mention of Barbara McQueen made me wonder how she was doing now, and I asked if he had any idea about that. It turned out he and Barbara were friends, having met at a "Remembering Steve McQueen" event in 2008 in Santa Paula, California (where McQueen lived at the time of his death). Mike had read about the event in the newspaper, and the story mentioned that Barbara McQueen would be the guest of honor. So he decided to go and pay his respects.

These humans seemed more interested in making a buck off a dying celebrity than actually helping him.

He found Barbara and a mutual friend together at a Santa Paula hotel lobby and, upon being introduced to her, brought up that he was one of the pilots who had taken her husband to El Paso, and that he'd flown the plane that had brought his body back to California.

Mike said he'd never forget the look of total shock on her face—how she then excused herself and ran to the ladies' room. He felt terrible, afraid he had single-handedly ruined what was supposed to be a weekend-long celebration for her and her late husband. But a few minutes later Barbara reappeared, having composed herself, sat down next to Mike and said, "I have questions." They talked for hours about the two flights, as well as other matters related to McQueen's death. And as they reached the end of their conversation, Barbara slipped her hand in Mike's before saying good-bye, a quiet but powerful gesture of trust and kinship. They'd been friends ever since.

As Mike told me this, it occurred to me that if anyone would know how, if, and when Steve McQueen had given his life to the Lord, it would be the woman who was constantly at his side in his last years. Barbara McQueen was the key to the mystery, and in my growing excitement I asked Mike if he would be willing to arrange for me to meet and talk with her.

"I'll give it a try," he said. "All she can do is say no."

Barbara McQueen was known for saying "no" a lot more than "yes." Since her husband's death she had been resolutely mum about him until the publication in 2006 of her book *Steve McQueen: The Last Mile*, a memoir heavily illustrated with pictures she'd taken throughout their three-and-a-half-year union.

> "Okay," Barbara told Mike, "call the preacher man and tell him I'll meet with him. But it has to be on my turf. He'll need to come to Idaho."

While Mike went to bat for me with Barbara, I read everything I could find about her. In one McQueen biography the writer detailed the misery of McQueen's last days as he wasted away in the Mexican cancer clinic which, according to American medical experts, dispensed only snake oil and false hope. It was McQueen's choice to go there, and Barbara dutifully went with him. But what she saw there was horrifying—a constant parade of cancer-cure peddlers, doctors, and administrators. These humans seemed more interested in making a buck off a dying celebrity than actually helping him. They were faith healers and soothsayers offering high-priced mystical healing, all while straining to make themselves heard over the incessant drone of helicopters overhead, packed with camera crews hoping for a photo of the famous patient. It was like being in an anteroom of hell. Yet she stayed. For Steve.

A few days after my sit-down with Mike, he called with the news that Barbara McQueen unequivocally refused to talk to me about her husband's faith, saying it had been an intensely private matter to him and was not for public consumption, that she wasn't about to have some "preacher man" glom on to a story and exploit it for his own purposes.

That stung (especially the "preacher man" part), but I could understand how she felt. Lord knows the number of pitches she fielded from people trying to horn in on the legend of Steve McQueen, likely on a daily basis. Add to that the fact that we preachers have not always enjoyed the best reputations . . . .

I told Mike not to press the matter with Barbara. But, God bless him, he didn't listen. He suggested to Barbara that she go online to watch a sermon of mine. She did and then called Mike back.

"Okay, he's cool," Barbara said. "I liked his sneakers. He seems real. What's he like?"

Mike arranged for her to receive print and DVD copies of my 2008 autobiography *Lost Boy*. She was struck by similarities between my life story and that of her late husband. McQueen and I were each abandoned by our fathers; we had mothers who married multiple times; and we both had abusive stepfathers.

"Okay," Barbara told Mike, "call the preacher man and tell him I'll meet with him. But it has to be on my turf. He'll need to come to Idaho."

November 8, 2016, was Election Day in America, when voters would make either Hillary Clinton or Donald Trump the next president of the United States. The whole country was wrought up. Me, too, but not about politics.

This preacher man was heading for Idaho.

THE LAST CHANCE RANCH

I'm ten thousand feet above the Sawtooth National Forest in Idaho. God's artistry is breathtakingly evident as the plane winds its way through the Wood River Valley, offering a magnificent panorama of snowcapped peaks, pine trees, farms, rustic homes, and wildlife.

The jaunt from Orange County, California, to Hailey, Idaho, is surprisingly short—only about an hour and forty-five minutes. Friedman Memorial Airport is equipped to handle daily flights from half a dozen or so major cities and even includes a terminal for private jets. That's how the patrons of Herbert Allen Jr.'s annual weeklong retreat arrive, whose Allen & Company Sun Valley Conference brings together the world's top CEOs, political leaders, dot.com moguls, and philanthropists every summer to brainstorm ideas that impact the economic life of the whole planet. Oh, to be a fly on the wall . . . .

I imagine quite a few people would wish the same thing concerning my impending meeting with Barbara McQueen.

Mike Jugan told me that in the years since her famous husband's death, the former model has transformed into a very successful businesswoman, with varied real estate holdings that even include a shopping mall. Obviously she has a lot on the ball and on her plate, and for Barbara to grant me a whole day of her time to discuss my book and documentary proposal is quite generous, humbling, and frankly a little nerve-wracking.

I pull into the driveway of Barbara McQueen's house. I didn't need GPS to find it, having only to look for the artwork in the yard—a vintage leopard-skinned truck with a wild collection of skis sticking out of the cab in every direction, like Don King's hair. I love it!

The ride from the airport to her house in Sun Valley takes me fifteen miles north on Highway 75. Everywhere you look are new homes, condominiums, mountain retreats, and boutique hotels. The area is known for some of the best skiing in the world and over the past few decades has become the playground of numerous A-list celebrities and wealthy entrepreneurs. After getting their first taste of it, many of them purchase or build second homes here. A common lament of veteran local residents is that "the billionaires are pushing out the millionaires." I'll bet a lot of municipalities would love to have that problem.

Steve McQueen had plans to retire here. The story goes that he intended to open an old-time general store where folks could brew their own coffee and sit around a potbellied stove, like on that popular old TV show *Green Acres*. It's hard to picture McQueen as Sam Drucker, but who am I to quibble with another man's dream?

Sun Valley is a prosperous mishmash of both vintage and modern—saloons, mountain homes, mom-and-pop stores, ski chalets, and new age buildings. The city boasts a first-class arts scene, a comprehensive bus system, a state-of-the-art YMCA, and plenty more big-city amenities. It's easy to see why a person would want to retire here.

There are more pickup trucks than Mercedes—and there are plenty of them—on the main drag, so whichever store is selling flannel and jeans is doing a bang-up business. The one selling electric shavers, not so much. And it's not everywhere you see a gas station with camouflage painted pumps. Not sure what the message here is, but if I were driving the local Welcome Wagon, I think I'd recommend that new residents of Sun Valley keep their Gucci clothes and elitist attitudes under wraps, at least during the daytime.

On my way to my destination I drive by the private road that leads to the home and resting place of Nobel Prize-winning author Ernest Hemingway. When he first started coming here in the 1930s, he stayed at the historic Sun Valley Lodge, where I've got a reservation. Later the famous writer brought his sons here to fish and hunt, and in 1959 Hemingway plunked down fifty thousand dollars on a two-story, log cabin-style home on a dozen acres north of the downtown area. Two years later he took his life in the foyer of the house. Interesting that two of the premier macho men of the twentieth century—Ernest Hemingway and Steve McQueen—wanted to spend their final years here.

About a mile later I pull into the driveway of Barbara McQueen's house. I didn't need GPS to find it, having only to look for the artwork in the yard—a vintage leopard-skinned truck with a wild collection of skis sticking out of the cab in every direction, like Don King's hair. I love it! Tall pine trees and hedges shield the two-story, log-cabin home built in the '40s.

It's an unseasonably warm day in the mountains—seventy high-altitude, sunshine-infused degrees. Before I even step out of my rental car, a chocolate lab dog is bounding over to check me out. He's wary but friendly and accompanies me to the front door where his owner is waiting.

"Barbara?"

"My friends call me Barbi," she says with a warm smile. "Come on in and make yourself at home."

It would take a lot longer than a day for that to happen because I've never been in a home like this before. In the living room sits a king-sized bed and a dining table adorned with leather vests, cowboy hats, and Native American drums. Scattered about are mannequins sporting electric pink and green wigs, straw hats, leather saddles, antique toys, glittering skulls, Old West figurines, and Wizard of Oz dolls, a Schwinn bike wrapped in Christmas lights, a vintage cigarette dispensing machine, and lots of rock and roll photography from the 1970s.

I see numerous signs of Steve McQueen—a photo of him and motorcycle racing buddy Bud Ekins, all busted up after the 1964 Olympic trials; a Bonham's poster of Steve soaking

> In speaking with her, I can see that the sudden loss of the love of her life, despite being more than thirty-five years ago, remains devastating, still affecting her to the present day.

himself off after a motorcycle run; and a picture of him in a racing suit and foot cast after a 1970 racing victory at Sebring. McQueen's favorite antique toys and other memorabilia are displayed throughout the house. The latter includes a Native jacket he wore in Alaska for a Bob Hope USO Tour, a framed contact sheet of McQueen at Loyola Marymount discussing *An Enemy of the People*, the rocking chair where he relaxed outside his Santa Paula hangar, and the brass bed he slept in for the last year of his life.

Each day for Steve and Barbi was an adventure, whether riding his perfectly restored vintage Indian motorcycles or taking a flight in his classic Stearman biplane or looking in antique stores for discarded and hidden treasures.

We head for the four-car garage, which Barbi calls her "girl cave." It's styled as eclectically as the house, with a 1962 Ford stepside truck (with a mattress, pillows, and Steve's Navajo rug in the truck bed), a dining table and chairs from a local thrift store, her grandmother's couch, old bicycles, and a TV and entertainment system. The glass garage door opens onto a beautiful backyard with a cozy fire pit and tantalizing views of the ski runs on Baldy.

We settle on the couch, and Barbi gets right down to brass tacks.

For a few minutes, she asks to talk about some spiritual questions she's been thinking about. Happy to do that, of course, and in speaking with her, I can see that the sudden loss of the love of her life, despite being more than thirty-five years ago, remains devastating, still affecting her to the present day.

She had been a young, beautiful lady in her midtwenties, handpicked by a giant movie star to be his girlfriend, eventually his wife. Her life changed overnight.

Each day for Steve and Barbi was an adventure, whether riding his perfectly restored vintage Indian motorcycles or taking a flight in his classic Stearman biplane or looking in antique stores for discarded and hidden treasures.

They were planning for the future, which included retiring in the place I was visiting, sitting in one of Steve's favorite rocking chairs. Then really, without much warning, it was all gone.

I knew all about that. About sudden loss. At the age of thirty-three, our oldest son Christopher was killed in an automobile accident on a Southern California freeway—July 24, 2008. Whenever a loved one is taken away suddenly from you like that, it is life-altering and, frankly, not easy to recover from.

> To Barbi, Steve McQueen was not a movie star. He was her best friend, the love of her life, as well as her husband. A part of her is gone.

I talk with Barbi about the pain and heartache my wife, Cathe, and I still experience, then listen with compassion as she speaks about the man, her husband, who's been gone now for decades. A man she still loves. To Barbi, Steve McQueen was not a movie star. He was her best friend, the love of her life, as well as her husband.

A part of her is gone.

I share with Barbi how the hope of a future reunion with my son one day in heaven is a source of real comfort for us. I tell her how, when we believe in Jesus Christ, we can know with confidence that we will see our loved ones again who have died in faith, and that the more I've explored Steve McQueen's story, the more confident I am that he possessed that kind of faith.

I understand Barbi's disinterest in people who would want to exploit her husband's memory. She certainly saw her share of them during his dying days—shucksters and hucksters making false promises that could never be kept. This is America, of course, home of a free press, so do I need Barbi's permission to tell a story that's comprised of historical fact? No. Not really.

But I do want her blessing more than anything.

I believe this story, the story of a movie star who had it all—great wealth, fame, beautiful women, cars, homes, all the material wealth anyone could ever want—yet who yearned for and then finally found something, some One, more powerful and satisfying than anything else in his life would be an inspiration to the whole world, potentially influencing untold others to do likewise.

To show her the kinds of things I'd want to share about him, I rattle off some of his charitable deeds I'd read about, such as giving time to residents at Boys Republic, a facility for wayward youth; donations he made to an orphanage in Taiwan; sending a cancer-stricken youth and his family from the Make-A-Wish Foundation to Disneyland in a limousine and picking up the entire tab; contributing to a Catholic church in Chicago; even personally adopting a teen on the set of *The Hunter* and quite possibly saving her life. Such things, I say, show that all the things Steve had gone through as a boy—all the suffering and neglect—produced a man who, although usually hard on the outside, possessed a soft center, especially when it came to kids. He knew what it was like to walk in their shoes.

Barbi nods a few times while I talk, and when I pause she looks me in the eye and says, "Steve was fiercely private because he always had people coming at him for something or another, and he could never get a moment's rest. I think there are two things a man should go to his grave without ever having to reveal—his politics and his religion. A man needs to keep something for himself."

I was hoping for a nod to do this book, but that sure doesn't sound promising. A moment later she throws me for an even bigger loop.

"Steve never talked to me about religion. One day he came home and said, 'We're going to church.' First we went dress shopping for me, and what we bought was a bit dowdy. They had to at least come down to my knees." Noting my look of surprise, Barbi laughs, and says, "Yes, he was a bit of a chauvinist.

Moments later we're in her black Hummer H3, heading for one of Sun Valley's most fashionable restaurants. "It's Arnold Schwarzenegger's favorite place to eat when he's in town," Barbi tells me. I can see why.

"Sure, we went to church every Sunday," she continues, "but we never really spoke about it when we got home. I figured it was a private matter to him, and if he wanted to bring it up, he could. I know it made him feel good, but we never really got into a discussion about why we went. I was just trying to be a good wife."

As I try to wrap my head around this, sensing a bit of a dead end, Barbi says, "You hungry? I'll bet you haven't eaten in a few hours."

Moments later we're in her black Hummer H3, heading for one of Sun Valley's most fashionable restaurants. "It's Arnold Schwarzenegger's favorite place to eat when he's in town," Barbi tells me. I can see why. Our waitress brings us a bread basket and a dish of real butter, and I order a cup of hot apple cider, meatloaf with gravy, and mashed potatoes. Barbi has crab cakes.

As we eat and chat about lots of different things, including my love for the movies, I confess my fondness for films about organized crime. We both laugh. Barbi says she hasn't been to a theater to see a film since 1974, when she saw *The Towering Inferno* starring McQueen and Paul Newman. Besides that one, she adds, the only movies of her late husband's that she's seen are *The Blob* and part of *The Magnificent Seven* on television recently.

"I can't watch his movies," she says. "It's still too painful."

I tell her I can relate. Whenever I see a photo of my son Christopher, it triggers such a flood of memories, many of them painful, reminded of the tremendous loss, still so fresh to us and to many others who loved him. We share a real moment of understanding without words.

The food is wonderful, and for dessert she recommends the restaurant's signature cheesecake with raspberry sauce. It's over the moon, and now I'm so stuffed I'm afraid that as

It's Mexican hot chocolate with four shots of espresso, and now it's unlikely I'll sleep at all before Christmas.

soon as we plop back down on that comfortable couch, I'll fall into a food coma. But our next stop takes care of that—a coffee shop a few blocks away where I order a specialty of the house: the "Keith Richards." It's Mexican hot chocolate with four shots of espresso, and now it's unlikely I'll sleep at all before Christmas.

Driving down the town's main street, Barbi points out the Pioneer Saloon where she and Steve enjoyed many a steak and baked potato dinner. She's never been much for cooking, she says, and they ate out a lot. "The Pioneer doesn't care who you are," she said. "If there was a line and Steve McQueen showed up, he had to wait just like everybody else. That's why he liked this place."

> "When Steve died, I was just a kid," Barbi says softly, "just starting to find out what true love was. I was robbed . . ."

On Highway 93 she shows me what celebrity lives where—some of the biggest names in entertainment. Then after five miles or so, we pull up to a brown wooden emporium and RV lot that Steve wanted to buy and turn into his general store, called "Queenies." (It's also, Barbi says, where Marilyn Monroe was stranded in a blizzard while filming the 1956 movie *Bus Stop*.) Steve's plan never got off the ground, though, because city fathers threw too many roadblocks in his path. "Idaho politics are difficult for outsiders to comprehend," she says with a shrug.

We pull back out on the highway and cross onto a frontage road, stopping after a while at a sign announcing the entrance to "The Last Chance Ranch." Steve bought the five-acre property in 1978, right after he and Barbi got together.

On it are a two-story log cabin and guesthouse for which Steve personally drew up plans. But he never saw them completed because of the disease that ravaged him so quickly and the frantic quest for a cure that took them from their Gem State Shangri-la to a grubby clinic in Mexico run by a dentist with no expertise in treating cancer—not even a lab or basic x-ray equipment, where McQueen subjected himself to a daily battery of colonics, enemas, liver and vinegar flushes, Epsom salt drinks, castor oil IV drips, and other quack remedies in hopes of saving his life.

Barbi looks off into the distance and takes in a deep breath. I'm holding mine. Finally she smiles kind of wanly and says, "It's nice . . . I see what you're trying to do."

Now at the Last Chance Ranch, it all comes flooding back. "When Steve died, I was just a kid," Barbi says softly, "just starting to find out what true love was. I was robbed . . . ." I can only imagine the pain she's endured all these years. Anything I might say would be intrusive and inadequate, so I say nothing.

Finally back at Barbi's house, I take out my laptop and ask her to watch a "sizzle reel" of the proposed documentary I have in mind, to be directed by Jon Erwin (*Mom's Night Out, Woodlawn*). It's just five minutes long but ideally conveys what I want to do with this project. She watches impassively until, midway through the reel, a close-up of Steve McQueen's face appears on the screen. I flinch as she jerks her head away from the image, almost as if she'd received an electrical shock. For a moment I contemplate turning it off. Maybe I've overstepped my welcome. Maybe I'm being insensitive to her feelings. But I let it play on, and when it ends, Barbi looks off into the distance and takes in a deep breath. I'm holding mine. Finally she smiles kind of wanly and says, "It's nice . . . I see what you're trying to do."

Does that mean the project is a go? I'm not at all sure and am frankly afraid to press Barbi for a definitive answer. My visit has obviously stirred up so many memories and emotions in her, and I feel a stab of guilt for all the pain I've resurrected.

But then Barbi turns, looks me in the eye and smiles, this time not wanly at all. And she emphatically nods her head.

No words are necessary.

Thank God.

For the next half hour, we talk about my intention to travel around the country in my Ford Mustang, mapping out Steve's path to eternal salvation. Barbi knows it's likely to take me to some dark corners of his life, but she knows as well that the result will potentially help thousands of people in their own search for peace and meaning in this crazy thing we call life.

An involuntary yawn from Barbi tells me it's time to say good-bye. As she walks me to my car, I struggle to find words to express the extent of my gratitude for the time and open heart this remarkable woman has so freely shared—and the vital blessing she has bestowed on my mission. Barbara McQueen is an extraordinary human being.

"So long, preacher man. Safe travels."

We hug and I'm off.

DON'S GARAGE

Back in Orange County, my top priorities are, in order of importance, to kiss Cathe and then call my friend and long-time mechanic Don Oakes.

Don, as I've said, is an old-school classic car guy. He's a few years older than me, a real salt-of-the-earth type. He has rough hands, tousled hair, and perpetually sunburned skin and always dresses so casually that if he ever put on a suit, I don't think I would recognize him. He's usually smiling, especially when talking about cars—a fire and passion that's never wavered. It remains his fountain of youth. Whenever he gets to talking on the subject, he instantly goes from being seventy-seven years old to seventeen.

Don's garage in Riverside is about an hour's drive from our house and is strictly a functional workspace. Definitely a no-frills spot. No polished or mirrored epoxy floors, hydraulic lifts, or recessed lighting. In the past he worked on every make and model, including his amazing, perfectly restored Woodie, but now he specializes in Mustangs. Among the plethora of cool Mustangs in his stable is a tribute Shelby Mustang GT500 (also known as "Eleanor," the car Nicholas Cage drove in *Gone in 60 Seconds*) and a "Black Mamba" Mustang with all the cool after-market fixings. He's also got the Bullitt tribute car he lent to my son Jonathan on his wedding day, the one I unsuccessfully tried to buy from Don before finding my own. All told, he's got about eight Mustangs scattered about the place in various states of restoration and repair.

> He has rough hands, tousled hair, and perpetually sunburned skin and always dresses so casually that if he ever put on a suit, I don't think I would recognize him.

Mine was only partially restored when I bought it in 2015. It also had a few mechanical issues. So I asked Don to bring her up to speed for my impending road trip. He's been working on it for almost a month and a half.

One of the major problems concerned the front springs. Every time the Bullitt cruised over a bump in the road, it scraped the wheel well. The sound was almost as alarming as the high-pitched, not-very-*Bullitt*-like shriek that came from the driver (me) each time it happened. I frequently had to remind myself that McQueen wasn't cool because he drove the Mustang, but rather the Mustang was cool because McQueen drove it!

Don has also been working on the exhaust system, instrument gauges, shocks and alignment, door hinges, side reflectors, and paint job. Now he almost giddily assures me the Ford will practically sing and dance by the time he's through with it in a few days. I'm not so sure I'll be singing and dancing when I see the bill, however. (Actually, Don is only charging me cost on the restoration, but the sticker shock is still painful.)

When I first found my Bullitt, I took it to Don and said I wanted it to look like the car in the movie in every possible respect. He had a million technical questions and observations, as car gurus always do, and after each one I said the same thing: "Uh . . . can you just make it look like the movie car?"

Everything in the Bullitt is original except for the GPS system and satellite radio I'm having him install for the trip. Don gave me a sideways glance with that

Now he almost giddily assures me the Ford will practically sing and dance by the time he's through with it in a few days.

request. He's shamelessly obsessive, borderline religious when it comes to his restorations. His passion is to restore these old cars as closely as possible to their original condition, no matter what it takes. That's why he pushes for only original parts. But like I told him, if I had to rely on old-fashioned paper road maps and AM radio, I'd be ready for a rubber room before I reached the state line.

The Bullitt has never been on a long-distance journey before. Till now I mostly took it out for Saturday afternoon joyrides along the coast with Cathe riding shotgun. It's one of our favorite things to do and never fails to take us back to when we first started dating. In fact, when we get back home and I lovingly wipe the car free of any dust, Cathe jokes that I'm looking at it just the way I looked at her back then.

So while Don puts the finishing touches on the Mustang, I dive into research on Steve McQueen's life. The object of the odyssey is to see and experience the places and milestones of his life, seeing them as McQueen did, and for that I've needed to find out as much as possible about him. There are plenty of McQueen resources for me to consult—biographies, Internet articles, documentaries—and I've noticed that many of the same players show up and are quoted in them. That's fine, but I'm also going to be on the lookout for people who haven't received as much ink or interview time but are still important in decoding McQueen's story. And since I've mapped out my trip chronologically as it happened in his life, I'll be going to Indiana, Missouri, South Carolina, Washington, DC, New York City, a suburb of Philadelphia called Phoenixville, then back home to Los Angeles.

> The object of the odyssey is to see and experience the places and milestones of his life, seeing them as McQueen did, and for that I've needed to find out as much as possible about him.

One spot on the McQueen itinerary, however, is not yet set in stone in my planner—that awful clinic in Juarez where McQueen died. It will take me a while to decide whether I want to go there, or could even stand it if I did. But there's plenty of time for that, and frankly I'd just as soon not think about it right now. I'm about to set off for Beech Grove, Indiana, a suburb of Indianapolis—where Terrence Steven McQueen was born.

And I need to get there sooner rather than later, it turns out, because according to a report in *The Indianapolis Star,* the hospital in which McQueen was born is slated for demolition in November, only a month away.

Opened in 1914 with seventy-five beds and two operating rooms, St. Francis Beech Grove Hospital gradually expanded over the years, eventually servicing more than five hundred beds. But then came a steady downward spiral driven by changes in healthcare, and in 2012 the Sisters of St. Francis of Perpetual Adoration closed the facility and transferred its inpatient care services to a newer campus about seven miles away.

Catholic nuns ran the old hospital, and what I hope to find out in Beech Grove is how McQueen came to be born there in the first place, as well as whether he was then baptized in the Catholic faith.

The person best suited to provide the answers is Will Smither at the Indianapolis Public Library. It almost seems mandatory to me that if your name is Will Smither, you *should* work in a library or be involved in research somehow. Will's parents moved to Beech Grove when he was a year old. He lived there for thirty-two years. Most importantly, Will was the one who broke the story that, contrary to previously published accounts, McQueen's mother was not a teen run-away who just happened to land in Beech Grove and give birth to her son there.

One spot on the McQueen itinerary, however, is not yet set in stone in my planner —that awful clinic in Juarez where McQueen died.

This is the kind of stuff I'm looking for.

Responding quickly to an email, Will writes back that he'll be glad to meet me when I get to Beech Grove and give me the background he's uncovered about the McQueens' time there in the early 1930s. He may even be able to shed some important light on the matter of Steve's early religious upbringing.

Actually, Will's not the only one who responds quickly to my various requests. Soon I begin hearing from many others around the country willing to share information about McQueen's life and faith. Their kindness, openness, and offers of help are a revelation. Their easy cooperation allays a nagging underlying fear that's been bothering me since I started—the notion that I might spend most of my time on the road just staring at old buildings where McQueen once dwelled but whose secrets would never be tapped. What a relief to know this won't be the case. I'll be meeting and talking to people who knew McQueen personally and interacted with him, people who can fill in a lot of important blanks.

> Soon I begin hearing from many others around the country willing to share information about McQueen's life and faith.

But first I'll be meeting with Don Oakes, who says the Bullitt is ready to roll.

I love cars, but what makes them tick is way beyond my understanding. That's why I go to Don in the first place. My confidence in him is unshakable, even though I had to tell him that McQueen's Bullitt had a leather-wrapped steering wheel, not a wooden one like mine. I observed this in my umpteenth and most recent viewing of the film.

"She's tip-top," he tells me now, handing over the keys, along with the itemized bill consisting of several grease-stained pieces of paper covered with Don's indecipherable scribbles. But when I get in the Bullitt, turn over the engine, and gun it, I'm not worried about what his fixes are costing me. That awesome rumble is an internal combustion "Hallelujah Chorus" to my ears.

Don warns me I'll need to baby the Mustang by not driving over the speed limit and making sure to stop every three hundred miles or so for gas and oil breaks. Because the car gets only around ten miles per gallon, I won't need to put a sticky note on the dashboard to remind myself about that.

"Where you going, anyway?" asks Don as I put the car in gear.

"On a very important undercover mission," I say, fixing him with my best McQueen stare before hitting the gas and peeling out of there at a safe and sane twenty-five miles per hour. Well, sort of.

When I get in the Bullitt, turn over the engine, and gun it, I'm not worried about what his fixes are costing me. That awesome rumble is an internal combustion "Hallelujah Chorus" to my ears.

LAURIELAND

Teaching from the Bible and unpacking the gospel are my great passions in life. I love to study, write, and deliver messages, knowing peoples' lives are changed by God's Word. I've seen it, marveled at it, and thanked Him countless times for allowing me to play some role in it. That's why, except in case of emergency, I never miss Sundays in the pulpit. Never have, never will. It's what I've been called to do by the Lord, and shirking this obligation would be a betrayal to the thousands of people who come to church each week to hear me preach. Disappointing them would be unthinkable.

For this reason, I've divided my cross-country odyssey into separate weeklong excursions, each one beginning on a Monday morning and ending back in Southern California the following Saturday night, so I can be at church for Sunday services.

The first leg will take me to Beech Grove, Indiana, about a thirty-hour drive. Then, God willing and the Bullitt firing up, the plan is to hit Slater, Missouri, before working my way back home. Next week—the second and final leg—will be even more demanding.

For me, planning an itinerary is a lot easier than deciding what I need to take with me. That's why packing for a trip is high on the long list of things best left to Cathe. If I'd do it, I'd have to rent a U-Haul to pull behind the Bullitt, which would simply not be cool. But when Cathe packs, everything fits perfectly. She is uber-organized, which is one of our "irreconcilable differences."

I've divided my cross-country odyssey into separate weeklong excursions, each one beginning on a Monday morning and ending back in Southern California the following Saturday night, so I can be at church for Sunday services.

Here's my stab at it, for example. I have drawers full of T-shirts I love to wear until there's not enough left of them to even wash the floor with. I pitch a few of them into my suitcase, followed by long-sleeved shirts, a couple of denim jackets, and a leather one for colder weather. In addition, I pile in some underclothes, pants, baseball caps, and three pair of Converse shoes that are indispensable because they fooled Barbi McQueen into thinking I was cool.

Enter Cathe.

"Do you *really* need all of these?" she says, nodding toward my pile of prized Ts. It's not so much a question, rather a wry observation.

Ten minutes later the suitcase is back in the closet, and everything I'm taking on the trip is neatly packed into a single duffel bag.

I'm also bringing my Bible, some books on the topics I'm addressing next Sunday, and a couple of McQueen biographies. I also have a few magazines, as well as a drawing tablet and felt pens.

Okay, I'll let you in on a little secret here. Before I became a preacher, I was a graphic designer and cartoonist. No joke. One of my early dreams was to have my own newspaper cartoon strip, and I actually did get a few of my creations in print. In my early twenties I designed some album covers and posters, but my passion was drawing cartoons.

Ten minutes later the suitcase is back in the closet, and everything I'm taking on the trip is neatly packed into a single duffel bag.

I'd say I am more of an advanced doodler than an artist, but it's always been a place of escape for me. Purely self-taught, I would always have my drawing tablet and some pens with me when I was a boy. It was a private world I could disappear into while waiting up in bars late at night for my mom to finishing her drinking.

I still have a drawing of my version of Disneyland, which was my very favorite place to visit as a boy. My personal version of the world-famous amusement park is replete with funny gags and antics taking place. The name of *my* amusement park, however, is different.

Laurieland.

It's a place I visited often in the recesses of my mind because of the harsh realities of my childhood. It's not a life I would have wished on anyone, but it is *my* life, just the same.

Another necessity for this trip are my "tech toys." I'm a gadget guy and definitely need my laptop, tablet, and iPhone with me to stay on top of things and in instant touch with my family and friends.

Packing my gear and getting it stowed in the Bullitt takes several hours, but with Cathe's expert help and enjoyable company, it flies by, and when we're done I'm ready to hit the sack. My plan is to get up before the sun Monday morning and get out of Dodge ahead of rush-hour traffic. That means 5:00 a.m. at the latest.

My plan is to get up before the sun Monday morning and get out of Dodge ahead of rush-hour traffic. That means 5:00 a.m. at the latest.

I'm an early riser anyway and never have any trouble hitting the ground running, thanks to a medium 2-percent latte with an extra shot of espresso. (That's three shots total.) Try it. You won't blink till lunchtime.

I also start each day with some espresso for the soul—a daily Scripture reading, which I heartily recommend to you as well, to open your eyes and set the pace for the day.

Then a bite to eat, after which I gently wake Cathe, kiss her good-bye, and tell her I love her. She sleepily tells me she loves me too and turns over. It's now 5:15 when the rumble of the Bullitt shakes the garage and probably every other structure on our block. Thanks to me, everybody in the neighborhood today is an early riser.

As I pull out onto the street, I tune the radio to a local all-news station. I like to keep up with what's going on in the world, but I won't be able to relax and get into some tunes until I'm at cruising speed on the open highway.

After about fifteen miles on California State Route 55, I connect with the Riverside Freeway and head toward Barstow. By six o'clock the heaviest traffic is behind me, and now it's time to put the headlines behind as well and play some acceptable traveling music.

I turn the radio dial to a station called "The Bridge," which specializes in soft rock and adult contemporary hits from the 1960s and '70s. I grew up listening to that stuff, and under the circumstances it seems especially appropriate because it's also the soundtrack to Steve McQueen's reign as the most incandescent star in the Hollywood firmament.

It's now 5:15 when the rumble of the Bullitt shakes the garage and probably every other structure on our block.

And the first song that comes on couldn't be a more fitting farewell to the Golden State—the Eagles' "Train Leaves Here This Morning," written by Bernie Leadon and Gene Clark. That song evokes a lot of memories. It came out in 1972, about the time I was making plans to build our church in Riverside. The long hair and lush beard I had back then were definitely "Duck Dynasty" caliber.

I was making all of a hundred dollars per week then and was thrilled to get it. Today that ministry has expanded dramatically. Yes, I've worked hard, but what's happened to my life over the course of the last four and a half decades can only be called a miracle. It's something for which I am grateful to the Lord every waking moment.

They say if you see a turtle on a fencepost, you know he didn't get there on his own. With barely a high school education, I know I didn't accomplish these things in my own strength either.

Turning my mind back to Steve McQueen, it's easy to trace God's handiwork in his life too. What else could explain the stratospheric ascent of a man not educated beyond the ninth grade, whose alcoholic mom repeatedly cast him adrift through childhood and whose father was a mere shadow in his life?

McQueen's rise to the top from the time he started acting to his breakthrough role in *The Great Escape* took about a decade.

When his character Virgil Hilts made the stunning motorcycle jump over the barbed-wire fence with the Nazis in hot pursuit, it minted a throwaway kid into a movie star worth a king's ransom. Audiences around the globe fell in love with McQueen. He became the first American voted "Best Actor" at the 1965 Moscow International Film Festival.

> They say if you see a turtle on a fencepost, you know he didn't get there on his own. With barely a high school education, I know I didn't accomplish these things in my own strength either.

After *The Great Escape's* release on July 4, 1963, *Life* magazine anointed McQueen "the next big movie star." *Time* magazine went even further, declaring him "the next John Wayne." One veteran Hollywood writer observed, "Not since the exciting days of Bogart, Gable, Tracy and Wayne has there been such a success story as that of McQueen."

He went on from there to make some of the most memorable movies of the 1960s and '70s and remained a global superstar for the rest of his life.

But notwithstanding all his fame and wealth, a colossal vacuum lived rent-free in Steve McQueen's heart, a yawning chasm, a lack of purpose rooted in the absence of functional, involved parents. He spent his whole life avoiding his mother and searching for his father—searching for someone or something to stand in for him.

I know what that's like because I've lived with those same feelings and have done exactly the same thing. That's my bedrock kinship with Steve McQueen. Reading one of his biographies, I was stunned at the similarities in our childhoods. I, too, was emotionally abandoned by my alcoholic mother and never knew my real father, so I have no trouble closing my eyes and seeing McQueen as a misguided, unloved, unwanted youth. Sadly, I am qualified to tell the same story, based on the same experiences. If you're still wondering why a preacher would write a book about a movie star, *this is why.*

One veteran Hollywood writer observed, "Not since the exciting days of Bogart, Gable, Tracy and Wayne has there been such a success story as that of McQueen."

The other connection, of course, is that we both found the purpose we were searching for in the same place. Granted, I came to faith at seventeen, much earlier than Steve, who came to the same realization at forty-nine. But hey, better late than never.

Politicians talk a lot about "family values" and most of it is bilge designed to fit into a sound bite and win votes. I'm not running for office, but one thing I know for a fact is that children need to grow up in a stable household with a dependable, loving mother and father. *Family values.* Without them, no matter how successful you become, no matter what material goods you amass, no matter how many titles and accolades you pile up, something is missing. You can take almost all the social ills of

That's my bedrock kinship with Steve McQueen. Reading one of his biographies, I was stunned at the similarities in our childhoods.

today—from unwanted pregnancies to drug use and alcoholism, even criminal behavior—and trace it right back to a broken home. Specifically a *fatherless* home.

Those other things might dull the pain for a while, but the gaping void is always there. A great quote from actor Jim Carrey applies here: "I think everybody should get rich and famous," he said, "and do everything they ever dreamed of—so they can see it's not the answer."

> I looked over at my mother, passed out drunk on the sofa. I can still see it. That was the reality I knew. But even as young as I was, I remember consciously thinking, *This is not how it's supposed to be.* I knew. It was tragic.

My own childhood was full of empty promises and immense disappointments. Like many kids with a vivid imagination who spend too much time alone, I sought escape from the dreary realities by drawing and pulling pranks, trying to please others and make them laugh.

I remember one Christmas night when I was just a tyke, sitting on the floor in my pajamas. The lights on the artificial tree blinked on and off, and the tinsel shimmered when a breeze blew through the open window. I looked over at my mother, passed out drunk on the sofa. I can still see it. That was the reality I knew. But even as young as I was, I remember consciously thinking, *This is not how it's supposed to be.* I knew. It was tragic.

My mom often left me alone when she went out. I'd fall asleep for a while but then wake up and lay there, waiting for her to come back—hoping when she did it would be different than the last time she went out. But it never was. Mom rarely came home alone or even with the same man. I'd hear them laughing in the living room and pouring drinks. Then after a while came the yelling and smashing of things. Sometimes a neighbor would call the police, but more often than not, my mom and whoever would wear themselves out drinking, fighting, and doing other things. I'd get up when it was quiet and find mom and her company passed out on the couch or the floor. Sometimes I'd pick up the clothes they'd discarded and try to cover over their nakedness.

I'd bet Steve McQueen could match me, nightmare for nightmare.

They're indelible imprints, those memories, and when they happen, you subconsciously decide how you'll feel about what you're experiencing—and how you'll interact with people for the rest of your life.

Everything I've read about McQueen says he demonstrated resentful feelings toward his neglectful mother throughout her lifetime. And so he found it quite difficult to trust and open up to women, including the three he married.

> Everything I've read about McQueen says he demonstrated resentful feelings toward his neglectful mother throughout her lifetime. And so he found it quite difficult to trust and open up to women, including the three he married.

All of that—the flashbacks, the philosophizing, the making of shared connections—is what's playing through my mind as the clock rolls to 3:00 p.m. I'm on Interstate 40, approaching Flagstaff, Arizona. I've been on the road for almost eight hours, with only a brief pit stop in Needles, California. I'll have about three and a half hours of daylight left and will need to drive a couple of more hours in the dark before I make it to Albuquerque, New Mexico, about 325 miles away. But I'll need another tank of gas for the Bullitt and, for my own tank, another 2-percent latte with three shots of espresso.

I get both at one of those megamarts that dot the interstate system, virtual communities unto themselves offering gas, food, and just about every trinket you can think of but don't really want or need. While I'm there I pull out my laptop and catch up on emails and texts and post on social media a pic I took in Needles of my dust-covered Bullitt, with the caption "Searching for Steve McQueen."

Suddenly I'm feeling terribly lonely, a bit sorry for myself, and frankly also a bit jealous of those happy kids. Why couldn't I have been like them? Why have I had such a strange life?

Approximately four hours later, I check into a Marriott off I-40 in Albuquerque, where I head downstairs to the restaurant for a quick bite.

While waiting for my food to arrive, I text my wife and read a little Scripture. But I can't help it—I'm a big people watcher. I've read that Steve McQueen was one as well. All around me now are people enjoying a meal, like the mom, dad, and kids having so much fun together at a nearby table that I want to go sit with them. Suddenly I'm feeling terribly lonely, a bit sorry for myself, and frankly also a bit jealous of those happy kids.

Why couldn't I have been like them? Why have I had such a strange life?

It's a fruitless, frustrating, chicken-or-egg speculation. The best thing for me to do is stop and remind myself: everything that happened to me made me the person I am today. Actually, I am thankful. God does indeed work in mysterious ways. But when you don't have committed, involved parents, the yearning never really goes away. And it doesn't take much to set it off full blast.

Here, for example, is one of the ways this old emptiness can still show itself. Not many things make me angry. I can shrug off personal criticism, even insults, because in the end, only what God, my family, and my congregation think of me matters. But I cannot stand it when I see someone else who's weak or afraid or being bullied. And when it happens, I want to step up and defend them. Immediately. Forcibly. Angrily? That's because for so many years, I was the one who was weak and afraid, desperately in need of someone to stand up for me—a guardian, what a parent is supposed to be.

How many times in his life, I wonder, did the King of Cool feel that way? Plenty, I'll bet. We were members of the same unhappy club, searching for the same redemption. Ultimately, we'd each find it—a bridge over that awful chasm in the miracle of God's grace—but it was a hard way coming.

Back in my room, I climb right into bed. Fifteen straight hours of driving tomorrow will get me close to Indianapolis. But I always have trouble falling asleep in hotels. The pillows are lousy and the walls too thin.

I get up and open my computer. I have a program called "Ocean Sounds" that transmits the sounds of rhythmic, lapping waves and an occasional muted foghorn. It never fails to lull me to sleep.

Tonight "Ocean Sounds." Tomorrow, Beech Grove.

JULIAN AND CHARLENE

The landscape of America is diverse and beautiful, but after fifteen straight hours of staring at it through the Bullitt's windshield, the Homewood Suites in downtown Indianapolis is a sight for sore eyes. I greet the guy at the check-in desk like a long-lost relative—my first real human interaction since Albuquerque—then find my room, where I spiral into a deep sleep without need of a maritime lullaby.

I sleep until 7:00 a.m.—a luxury for me, as I'm usually up at five. It's Wednesday morning. My meeting with Will Smither is in a couple of hours, and Beech Grove is just fifteen minutes from my hotel, in the heart of the capital's Wholesale District.

After a shower, I go downstairs and stop for a moment in the lobby. For the first time, I take in the place. The hotel started out in the late 1880s as a shoe factory. Now it features high vaulted ceilings, exposed brick, hardwood floors, and wooden beams. I'm just a five-minute walk from Monument Circle in the center of downtown, whose 284.6-foot-tall State Soldiers' and Sailors' Monument is the Hoosier State's most recognizable landmark. The Circle has lots of restaurants, sidewalk cafes, retail shops, office buildings, and boutique hotels. It's actually kind of cool, tailor-made for pedestrian traffic. After two days in the car, it's a pleasure to stretch my legs in search of a proper coffeehouse for my morning pick-me-up. The aroma emanating from Hubbard & Cravens Coffee and Tea is even more alluring than a neon sign and wafts me inside.

> After two days in the car, it's a pleasure to stretch my legs in search of a proper coffeehouse for my morning pick-me-up.

Because I'm meeting Will Smither for an eleven o'clock lunch, a fresh blueberry muffin should tide me over. When I'm done with that, as well as my coffee and some work on the laptop, it's back to the hotel to pack up and check out. Weather report: partly cloudy, forty-seven degrees—a nice fall day to a Hoosier but downright wintry to a Californian. I should've brought a warmer jacket.

The Bullitt takes longer to warm up, too, and as I let it idle, I program the GPS for 106 Main Street in Beech Grove, site of the Ball Park Pizza and Eatery II. Will has picked this place for us to get together.

On the basis of the name alone, I heartily approve. I've never been into fancy food, preferring pizza, burritos, hamburgers, and all the other tasty, greasy, artery-clogging chow my doctor warns me to stay away from. I love the very Midwestern name for a restaurant that combines two great American ideals, baseball and pizza. Especially pizza.

According to the GPS, the drive there ought to take me just eleven minutes. That's nothing compared to what I've done in the past two days.

Beech Grove's municipal website proudly proclaims it's considered an "excluded city" in Marion County. It was a rural part of Indianapolis at the turn of the twentieth century, ostensibly named for the abundance of beech trees in the area. But mostly it's named for the Beech Grove Shops, a hundred-acre railroad repair facility constructed in the early 1900s by the Cleveland, Cincinnati, Chicago, and St. Louis railroads, also known as the "Big Four." For years the Shops were the biggest employer in town and the largest "locomotive hospital" in the world. That's not the case anymore, as it employs only a fraction of the people it did at its peak in the mid-1940s.

At the time of Steve McQueen's birth there in 1930, the population of Beech Grove was 3,552.

At the time of Steve McQueen's birth there in 1930, the population of Beech Grove was 3,552. After World War II and the start of the baby boom era, the number of inhabitants greatly expanded.

Today there are approximately fourteen thousand residents. Indianapolis completely surrounds Beech Grove, but it is separate and autonomous, with its own mayor, police and fire departments, and school system.

———

My impression driving into town is that it's a picturesque tableau of Middle America, with an abundance of lush lawns, trees, churches, schools, and homes, arranged in attractive cul-de-sacs. A good place, it seems to me, to raise a family. Will Smither seems to agree.

"I have to laugh," he says, "when I read in all the McQueen biographies and periodicals that Beech Grove is a grimy, blue-collar, industrial, hard-nosed, two-fisted drinking town. It's more like Mayberry RFD."

Will is in his midforties, I'd guess, medium build, with a touch of gray in his brown hair and a ready smile. So much for the stereotype of the dour librarian. At the very least I was expecting a tweed jacket with suede elbow patches, a bow tie, and little round glasses. Instead he's wearing a casual button-down shirt, gray jeans, and tennis shoes.

Eat your heart out, Babe Ruth. I know I'll pay for this later, when I am trying to get to sleep, having graduated from acid rock to acid reflux. But it will be worth it—I hope.

I like him even more when he hands me a menu as soon as we sit down in the Ball Park Pizza and Eatery and urges me to "swing for the fences." He doesn't need to twist my arm. I dig this place because it is so "old school" but in a good way.

I order cheese sticks for an appetizer, spaghetti and meatballs, garlic bread, and the house specialty, the "Home Run," a sixteen-inch pizza loaded with cheese, sausage, pepperoni, mushrooms, green peppers, and black olives. Whew! I purposely overextend myself so I can "sample" several items. Eat your heart out, Babe Ruth. I know I'll pay for this later, when I am trying to get to sleep, having graduated from acid rock to acid reflux. But it will be worth it—I hope.

Settling into conversation, I ask Will what sparked his interest in Steve McQueen. He says he grew up in Beech Grove and was actually surprised to hear McQueen had been born there. The city had never proclaimed the actor a native son, as most cities eagerly do with a famous citizen, making Will wonder whether it were actually true. He went to the local library and found a single McQueen biography on the shelf, which in the very first paragraph confirmed Beech Grove as the actor's birthplace.

"Some biographies state that he was born in 'Beech Grove Hospital,' but a hospital by that name has never existed in the city," Will tells me. "The hospital that did exist then was St. Francis Hospital, which is thirteen blocks from here."

McQueen's official Marion County birth certificate was recently discovered, and it named St. Francis as the hospital that delivered him. The document also names Julia Ann Crawford and William McQueen as Steve's parents. His mother, known to family and friends as "Julian," was a menial laborer, says Will, and it's likely she was a charity case when she gave birth to Steve at St. Francis.

"Alcoholic teenage runaway" is the thumbnail description of Julian that comes standard in many McQueen biographies and documentaries. Will says the alcoholic part is true but not that she was a runaway.

His research in Indianapolis directories have turned up that from 1927 to 1929, Julian—then in her late teens— lived with her parents, Lillian and Victor Crawford, at 336 S. Flemming Street. The 1930–34 telephone directories list the Crawfords (including Julian) at 1311 N. Drexel Avenue. The birth certificate also lists William McQueen at the same address.

"Alcoholic teenage runaway" is the thumbnail description of Julian that comes standard in many McQueen biographies and documentaries. Will says the alcoholic part is true but not that she was a runaway.

According to the 1930 US Federal Census, Terrence Steven McQueen, born on March 24, 1930, lived with his mother and his maternal grandparents at the Drexel Avenue address.

Therefore, contrary to previously published surmises, Steve was not born in Beech Grove by mere happenstance. The Crawfords' home in the Indianapolis suburb of Little Flower was only a fifteen-minute drive from Beech Grove and St. Francis Hospital.

Will doesn't know for sure how and when Julian met William McQueen, but he does know that at the time William was listed as a private in the US Marines and had been mustered in 1929. His best guess is that they crossed paths in one of the speakeasies that flourished in Indianapolis (and most everywhere else) as the raucous decade of the Roaring Twenties came to a close, in spite of the federal prohibition against selling booze. The "speaks" were magnets for young people who felt Prohibition was imposed on them and didn't necessarily feel the rules applied.

> The more I hear, the more similarities I feel between Steve McQueen's childhood and my own.

Julian's mother, Lillian Thomson, was born in January 1879 in Missouri, and had two brothers, Early and Claude, and a sister, Ruth. The Thomsons came to America from Scotland and had a 320-acre farm on the outskirts of Slater, Missouri, about a hundred miles east of Kansas City.

Refined, artistic, and well-read, Lillian spoke with excellent diction and was very devout in her faith, writing religious-based poetry in her spare time. At the other end of the spectrum was her gruff, profane brother Claude, who kept a homemade distillery in the barn and was an avid skirt-chaser even after he married and fathered a child. Claude followed no particular ideology or faith, but when he was sober and straight, he worked hard on the farm.

Lillian hoped to inherit a section of the land upon the death of her father, John William, in 1916, but Claude effectively blew his nose with the old man's will and claimed everything for himself.

Lillian married Victor Lee Crawford, a traveling salesman a dozen years her senior, and they moved to St. Louis, where she took a job as a secretary. She was thirty-one to his forty-three when Julia Ann was born on April 10, 1910, in Missouri.

As an only child, blonde-haired, blue-eyed Julian led the life of a little princess. Lillian made her fine dresses, sent her to private schools, and so doted on her every whim that Julian became spoiled and headstrong. Her parents were rigid Catholics who raised Julian to be the same, but by her late teens the attractive young woman was a rebellious handful and a familiar face at watering holes in and around Naptown.

The more I hear, the more similarities I feel between Steve McQueen's childhood and my own.

Steve was sent to a boys' home; I was sent to military school.

Steve was effectively raised by his grandparents; so was I.

Steve's mother Julian was a beautiful blonde woman, and so was mine.

My mother, Charlene McDaniel, was a dead ringer for Marilyn Monroe. It's one of the reasons why she was a flat-out "man magnet." Even as a little boy I remember men coming up to me, asking me to introduce them to my stunning mother.

She was from a large family of nine, raised in rural Arkansas. They went to church every Sunday morning and evening, as well as midweek Bible study. The rule was that my mother and her siblings were all expected to attend. They also had missionaries and visitors over at the house nearly every night for one of my grandmother's amazing home-cooked meals that you'd never wanted to miss: fried chicken, black-eyed peas, collard greens, and the best homemade biscuits you've ever tasted.

Yet my mom couldn't get out of that house fast enough. She bucked at the rules imposed on her by her parents (my grandparents), Charles and Stella McDaniel, rules that included never wearing pants, for example, which they thought to be not very "ladylike."

My Aunt Willie—my mother's sister—once told me a story about her. She went out one Sunday in the snow with some kids our parents didn't approve of. They didn't return until well after dark that night. My grandfather waited up for her, and when she finally walked through the door, he had a pair of scissors in his hand. Willie thought he was going to cut off all of my mother's beautiful blonde hair, but he told her to go into her bedroom, take off her slacks, and bring them to him. He stood by the fireplace, and when she returned downstairs, he took the slacks and cut them into small pieces then threw them into the fireplace. Willie said she was hiding in the dining room as this scene played out. I'm sure it was one of many tipping points that eventually pushed my mother out the door.

I, too, understand what it was like to be the unwanted, unloved son. Like he was. And I can tell you, it stays with you for the rest of your life.

She eloped with a young military man named Ken at the age of eighteen, with the help of Willie, who hid her suitcase under a crawl space at the church they attended. In running away from home, she was putting behind herself all the rules and things she'd learned in youth service and church. Too bad some of that discipline didn't rub off on her.

Charlene had seven husbands in total before her marrying days were over, with a lot of boyfriends strung along in between. Her life spiraled downward as she became a helpless alcoholic, passing out almost every night.

———

That's why the story of Julian Crawford, Steve McQueen's mother, totally resonates with me. I, too, understand what it was like to be the unwanted, unloved son. Like he was.

And I can tell you, it stays with you for the rest of your life.

I'd like to report I am so spellbound by Will Smither's tour-de-force symposium that I don't pay much attention to the repast on our table. But the fact is, it's all I can do to get on my feet and lurch to the car when it's time to go.

"Nice ride!" says Will knowingly as we approach the Bullitt for the short drive to the hospital, where the man responsible for the car's iconic status entered this world.

It's a funny thing about the Bullitt car: people either "get it" or they don't. For

As it turns out, collectors believe they have recently discovered one of the two existing original Bullitt cars in a junkyard in Mexico. For car guys, this is the equivalent of finding the Ark of the Covenant. Maybe even a bigger deal.

some, it's just a Highland green '67 Mustang with a blacked-out grill and no pony emblem. But for the initiated, it's a replica of one of the coolest movie cars ever, down to the last detail.

As it turns out, collectors believe they have recently discovered one of the two existing original Bullitt cars in a junkyard in Mexico. For car guys, this is the equivalent of finding the Ark of the Covenant. Maybe even a bigger deal. The story was major news around the world, reminding me that the mystique of McQueen continues to this very day.

Will totally gets it. Now I like him even more (though I still think he ought to at least be wearing a bow tie).

In fewer than two minutes, we're at the hospital on Seventeenth Avenue. It's been closed since 2012, but the sturdy-looking building is still fully intact and quite imposing . . . at least for a few more days, before it gets bulldozed. I wonder how Julian felt when she walked through the front door to deliver her baby. Happy or fearful?

After all, Steve McQueen was born five months after the Great Depression had devastated the United States. Emotionally and financially, Julian and William McQueen were totally unprepared and unequipped for parenthood. Julian was weeks shy of her twentieth birthday, and William had just turned twenty-three.

Domesticity wasn't in William's nature, and after his son was born, he took a permanent hike. Steve spent a good majority of his life trying to find him, and when he finally did, he didn't like the end result.

Though the county birth certificate names William and Julian as Steve's parents, Will tells me he's been unable to find any document in the Marion County (Indiana) or Saline County (Missouri) archives that indicates they were officially married. However, the 1930 US Census lists Julian as married, and in the Indianapolis city directories from those years, Julian's surname name is given as McQueen. Common law?

"Your guess is as good as mine," says Will.

Our next stop is 1311 N. Drexel Avenue in the Little Flower district, one of Indianapolis's oldest neighborhoods. It's where Lillian and Victor Crawford lived, and where Steve spent the first years of his life. The house is a straight six-mile shot up Sherman Drive, and we're there in fifteen minutes.

Built in 1930—the year Steve was born— the two-bedroom brick home with detached garage sits on a tiny lot of 5,358 square feet, only about one-eighth of an acre. Lots for sale in that neighborhood weren't moving, Will tells me, until the Phoenix Investment Co., Security Trust Co., and Rosalia Realty turned a parcel of land over to the Indianapolis diocese in 1921 for the construction of a church and school that would attract families. The result was the Little Flower Catholic Parish, the first in the world named after Carmelite nun Therese Martin of Lisieux, France, canonized in May 1924.

So taking Julian and Steve along, they moved from Indiana to Slater, Missouri, where they lived in a dilapidated former railroad car with no heat or bathroom.

It had the desired effect, as Irish and German Catholic families flocked to the area in great numbers, launching one of the biggest building booms the city had ever seen. At one point, a hundred new homes were under simultaneous construction, and more than forty separate real estate firms and home construction firms were competing for customers in Little Flower.

How does Will *know* all this stuff? He's like a walking history book.

The Little Flower Catholic Church is just two blocks from the house, and as we head there, Will tells me Victor (Steve's grandfather) was the one who'd been raised Catholic. Lillian came from a long line of Protestants and most likely converted to appease her husband. But she did so with a vengeance, and her attempts to make Julian toe the Catholic line were met with open rebellion. The Catholic Church in general held no attraction to their fun-loving daughter, and she increasingly took refuge in the bottle from her mother's harangues and admonitions.

> I can't help but wonder how he felt about what he'd been taught about a loving God as he watched Lillian spiral. His grandmother was clearly more of a mother to him than the one who'd given birth to him, before descending into raving madness. Something like that could shake a person's faith to the core.

Little Flower Church and its elementary school, which opened in September 1926, were built for a mere $130,000. There were eighty-five students when the school bell rang out for the first time, and the church saw a nightly attendance of roughly seven hundred people.

But according to Will, the Great Depression hit the Little Flower area hard. Even the church had trouble meeting its financial obligations, and parishioners held bake sales, pancake breakfasts, penny suppers, raffles, and other special events to help out.

The Crawfords no doubt did their part, until the bottom fell out of their own lives as well. Victor developed stomach cancer and was unable to work. The bills mounted, and they ending up losing their comfortable home in Little Flower.

So taking Julian and Steve along, they moved from Indiana to Slater, Missouri, where they lived in a dilapidated former railroad car with no heat or bathroom.

The car had once been used to cook meals for hired hands out in the fields at threshing time. Now it sat on blocks on Thomson Lane, right across from the family farmhouse where her ne'er-do-well brother Claude still reigned. How Lillian must've gagged whenever she looked at Claude's place.

After Victor died in June 1943, Lillian emotionally spiraled, Will says. She was often spotted walking barefoot and alone on Thomson Lane, clutching a crucifix and rosary beads, raging at the hand she'd been dealt in life. Claude had her sent to Fulton State Hospital for the insane, where she was diagnosed with schizophrenia and committed. Though a short ninety-minute drive from Slater, Lillian's family never visited her. Her grandson made *The Great Escape* in 1963. Poor Lillian finally made hers a year later, dying at the age of eighty-five and, sadly, all alone.

It's now inching up into the afternoon, and I'm taking my most gracious guide Will back to the pizza place before going on to Slater, about six and a half hours away. On the way to my car, he tells me he's sent an inquiry to Little Flower Church about whether Steve was confirmed there. If so, it was surely at his grandmother's behest, and I can't help but wonder how he felt about what he'd been taught about a loving God as he watched Lillian spiral. His grandmother was clearly more of a mother to him than the one who'd given birth to him, before descending into raving madness.

Something like that could shake a person's faith to the core.

HOG HEAVEN

As I steer the Bullitt onto westbound I-70, the classic song "The Long and Winding Road" comes on the satellite radio. The melancholy Beatles tune fits my mood perfectly as I reflect on the depressing circumstances of Steve McQueen's early life and how eerily they match my own.

"I've seen that road before," sings Paul McCartney.

Me, too.

McQueen and I both had exactly the same kind of upbringing. Our moms were alcoholics. Every place we lived had a revolving door through which all manner of strange, frightening, abusive men flitted in and out. Our dads were AWOL.

It's a dreary reverie, and I'm thankful to be jolted out of it—literally—when the car hits a pothole in the highway. The Bullitt's very basic suspension came with the car when it was built in 1967. The ones McQueen drove in the movie were modified to take the kind of abuse they got on the hilly streets of San Francisco. I must talk to Don Oakes about that when I get back to California.

My plan is to drive straight through to Slater, Missouri, where Steve McQueen came of age. I don't know much else about the place except that it's an agricultural town—hogs, a specialty—and I've heard, like too much of small-town America these days, it's withering on the vine.

Towns, like people, get old and then die. And here my mind goes back on that long and winding road . . . .

One of my heroes is Billy Graham, who turned ninety-eight a few days before I wrote these words. In a rare recent interview, he talked to Sarah Pulliam Bailey of *Christianity Today* about what that feels like.

"I can't honestly say that I like being old," Billy said, "not being able to do most of the things I used to do, for example, and being more dependent on others, and facing physical challenges that I know will only get worse. Old age can be a lonely time also—children scattered, spouse and friends gone."

> About the only good thing about being bald is that you can shampoo with a washcloth, and you're the first to know when it's raining.

For me, I've got no cause for major complaint on that score. Not yet. So far the aging process has taken its biggest toll on my hairline. I jokingly told my grandchildren recently that I was getting a hairpiece for my sixty-fourth birthday. "No, Papa!" shrieked one of them. "We like your bald head!"

That's nice, but about the only good thing about being bald is that you can shampoo with a washcloth, and you're the first to know when it's raining.

The top of my noggin tells me there's no falling precipitation when I get out of the car several hours later in the parking lot of Shirley's Bakery and Grill, just before the Slater exit. A sign says closing time is eight o'clock, which it just about is, but I'm starving. And it must show because when I step inside, Shirley Meyer, the owner, gives me a warm smile and says, "Take off your jacket, have a seat and stay a while, won't you?"

Small towns may be on life support, but small-town hospitality is clearly alive and well. So to reciprocate Shirley's, I accept her recommendation of the breaded pork tenderloin, exult over every bite, clean my plate, and then order a slice of her homemade chocolate pie. I totter out so stuffed, the Bullitt's ancient suspension actually seems to groan when I drop onto the edge of the seat and slide behind the wheel.

Under the circumstances, it seems to me that giving the King of Cool top billing would be, well, a slam dunk. But hey, I'm new in town.

Good thing the Countryside Inn is only five minutes away. Choosing it was easy. It's the only lodging to be had in the city of about eighteen hundred residents.

At the edge of town is a large billboard with two photos, only one of which I recognize. The sign proclaims:

Welcome to Slater
Hometown of Joe Kleine—NBA
Childhood home of Steve McQueen

Joe Kleine, I find out later on the computer, averaged 9.8 points per game in the best of his fifteen years in the NBA, a journeyman who shuttled between more than a half dozen teams before closing it down with the Portland Trail Blazers in 2000. Under the circumstances, it seems to me that giving the King of Cool top billing would be, well, a slam dunk. But hey, I'm new in town.

Just a couple hundred yards beyond the billboard is the Countryside Inn, and you don't see many like it anymore. It's a throwback to the 1950s when guests parked their cars right at the door of their rented rooms and considered it the height of convenience. As full and tired as I am, I am happy to have it. Plus, I can keep an eye on my Bullitt in case any car thieves are afoot in Slater, though I highly doubt it.

When I insert it in the lock and open the door, I find myself face-to-face with Detective Frank Bullitt himself.

Rooms are sixty-five dollars, but the friendly desk clerk excitedly informs me that for a mere five dollars extra I can take my pick of three specialty suites that just happen to be available tonight. One is called the Mermaid Suite; another, the Marilyn Monroe, and the third is the Steve McQueen Suite.

You'd better believe I jump at the opportunity. Who knows if I'll ever get another chance to sleep in a room named for a mermaid? Plus, my granddaughters will be delighted when I tell them.

Sorry, female progeny notwithstanding, I couldn't resist. I take the McQueen suite, of course.

The key is attached to one of those humongous oblong plastic rings that are also relics of a bygone time, and when I insert it in the lock and open the door, I find myself face-to-face with Detective Frank Bullitt himself. In the large photo of McQueen, he's got on the tweed jacket and blue turtleneck he wore in the movie. Also in the room are pictures of vintage cars, a nightstand with a black leather steering wheel, and lots of chrome.

After a few blazing laps around the room at the wheel of the nightstand, I hit the sack and am just about asleep when a thought jolts me wide awake: *Where is Joe Kleine's suite?*

Up at 6:00 a.m., I read my daily regimen of Scripture, take care of correspondence, and do some online research on Slater. Named after John Fox Slater, prominent railroad tycoon of the Chicago and Alton Railroad, the city was incorporated in January 1878. The area's fertile soil was perfect for all kinds of crops and hog farming, and the mixture of the railroad and agriculture made the town an almost instant success.

The counter is filled with baseball-cap-wearing old-timers, sipping coffee and talking to one another. If anybody owns a smart phone, it's tucked away in the pocket of his bib overalls.

By the early 1920s Slater inched toward five thousand residents, many of whom, like Claude Thomson, played as hard as they worked. To that end, there were plenty of backroom gambling dens, saloons, beer joints, and maybe a bawdy house or two in town.

Turns out old Claude threw some mean parties of his own out at the farm, some of which are still legendary in Slater. Lots of booze and live music. I wonder if they kept poor Lillian up at night, across the way in her breezy railroad car.

At eight o'clock I pull up in front of 222 Main Street, home of the *Slater Main Street News*, which has been around since 1886. I've got an appointment with Jean Black, who has lived in the area all her sixty-plus years. She's been the owner and editor of the paper for the past twenty of them, and if anybody can tell me about McQueen's life in Slater, it's she.

Right off the bat Jean kindly asks if I've had breakfast yet. I haven't, and she suggests we head down the street to the City Pharmacy. On the way I spot a discount store, a thrift/antique shop, a tiny veteran's park, a chiropractor's office (he's the mayor), a restaurant, and a few vacant properties with "For Lease" signs in the windows. There's an old fellow riding a small John Deere tractor at a snail's pace down Main Street, and no one even notices. Classic Americana. I love it.

> For years, she says, rumor was that McQueen didn't much care much for Slater, and the feeling was definitely mutual.

The City Pharmacy has been a local mainstay for as long as Jean can remember. Its old-school features include a soda fountain and those round, spinning, leather and chrome stools that made your grandparents dizzy. The counter is filled with baseball-cap-wearing old-timers, sipping coffee and talking to one another. If anybody owns a smart phone, it's tucked away in the pocket of his bib overalls.

On the way to our booth, Jean smiles and first-names folks she's known for years. We sit while the waitress pours our coffee. She calls me "honey," same as she says to all the other guys in the place. The coffee's not my preferred 2-percent latte, but it more than does the trick. Jean orders an omelet, and because I'm in the right place for it, I go hog wild—hash browns, toast, two eggs over easy, sausage, ham, and the thickest sliced bacon I've ever seen in my life.

I'm happy to report that science is on my side in regard to these culinary choices. I had just read an article about the oldest living woman, age 117, who says the secret to longevity has been her diet of two raw eggs a day. She also says she likes to eat cookies, though it's proved to be difficult now that all her teeth are gone. The secret, she revealed, is—and I'm quoting here—"lots of bacon!" She says she eats bacon with every meal.

So, bacon, ham, and eggs it is. Sounds like a good choice. I also might go back to Shirley's later and try some of her famous homemade cookies. Hope my teeth hold out.

I barely get into the reason for my visit when Jean floors me with a stunning bit of local scuttlebutt. She says it was a long time before Slater embraced Steve McQueen as a favorite son. For years, she says, rumor was that McQueen didn't much care much for Slater, and the feeling was definitely mutual.

"In a small town, if someone doesn't like you, you don't like them back," she explains. "So there were decades of, shall we say, harsh feelings toward our famous hometown boy."

"Steve didn't hate Slater," she said. "Steve didn't hate anything—except when he ran out of beer." Everyone laughed.

Maybe that's why they gave him second billing on the sign, I figure.

Those feelings didn't change until March 2007, she said, when a handful of local movers and shakers bucked public opinion to put on a festival called "Steve McQueen Days." They invited Barbara McQueen, as well as Steve's confidante and stunt fight coordinator Pat Johnson and his longtime stunt stand-in, Loren Janes, as guests of honor. Some of the old-timers snorted and said nobody would show up, including themselves, yet more than two thousand people did, some from as far away as Japan.

Barbara, Pat, and Loren accepted the invitation and came too. Jean said they blew everyone away with their friendliness. Barbara was the main speaker at the festival and made a point of setting the record straight about Steve's feelings for his boyhood home.

"Steve didn't hate Slater," she said. "Steve didn't hate anything—except when he ran out of beer." Everyone laughed.

During a public question-and-answer session, somebody asked how come Steve married all brunettes. Without missing a beat, Barbi shot back, "Sure, Steve married all brunettes. But don't forget, he had a lot of blondes in between."

"This was the Orearville School," Jean says, "the one-room schoolhouse Steve McQueen attended."

Roaring laughter again. By the time she was done, Barbi could've been elected mayor by acclamation, Jean tells me. No surprise there.

Since then, Slater has held a car show in Steve's honor every year, they've put that billboard up, and they've dedicated a highway to him. All is forgiven.

But looking back, I can't help but wish he'd received at least a little of that extra attention when he was growing up here. He and his mother, Julian, lived as Claude Thomson's houseguests, Jean says, though Julian never stuck around long. She took off for Los Angeles one time, looking for Steve's father, who'd reportedly joined the Merchant Marine. She didn't find him but found plenty of other men. I've read somewhere that McQueen said he finally stopped counting the number of husbands Julian acquired.

After breakfast—all for less than ten dollars!—Jean takes me on a tour of Main Street that starts at a vacant lot where the Kiva Theater once stood. Steve was a regular at the Saturday matinees there.

"Westerns were my favorite," he once said. "I used to bring my cap pistol and fire at the villains." Wonder if he ever imagined as a little boy, sitting in that dark little theater, that one day he would light up the screen as a gunfighter himself in the classic western *The Magnificent Seven*?

The 250-seat, single-screen theater shut down in the early '60s. Too many people were staying home and watching TV. Jean says the building was later refashioned into a bowling alley. It burned down in a 1999 fire.

A few blocks later we come to a white and green-shingled A-frame style building. "Abbott's Chapel" says the sign above the door.

"This was the Orearville School," Jean says, "the one-room schoolhouse Steve McQueen attended." Its original location was in the Town of Orearville near the Thomson farm. When Orearville ceased to exist and a new school was built, the building was then moved, literally trucked into downtown Slater and "converted" into a chapel.

Raising hogs is a hard, dirty, twenty-four-hour-a-day business.

McQueen's problems in school have been well documented. For one thing, he was dyslexic; for another, his attendance was spotty because Julian frequently dragged him along on her man-hunting expeditions, and he liked to play hooky anyway.

I like that the school was transformed into a church, which gives me a natural opening to ask Jean about Slater's faith-based community. She says the first church, Mount Zion Christian Church, was built in 1877. The first Catholic church was built in 1889. At one time, Jean says, Slater offered thirteen places of worship. She doesn't know which one McQueen might have attended or whether he went to church at all.

After we shake hands, Harold asks with the hint of a sigh, "I guess you wanna talk about Steve McQueen?" Turns out he's also well versed on that subject.

Jean and I cross the street and walk to the Slater depot, a brick structure built in 1915. This is where Claude and Steve drove the hogs in Claude's half-ton truck for shipment to the slaughterhouse. Steve imagined himself a cowboy, shepherding the animals into their holding pens.

With that piece of sightseeing completed, the downtown Slater portion of our tour is now over, but Jean has saved the best for last. "Would you like to see Claude Thomson's home, the place where Steve grew up?"

Would I!

We climb into Jean's car and take a back way to Highway 240, then turn right a half mile later on Thomson Lane. To my surprise, it's just a plain dirt road, probably no different than when Claude and Steve trucked their hogs along it.

Raising hogs is a hard, dirty, twenty-four-hour-a-day business, Jean says. The stock has to be fed, moved, watered, and otherwise tended regularly. The animals are susceptible to flea infestations and a whole range of diseases. All of a sudden I'm half-wishing I hadn't eaten all that pork for breakfast, even if it is "the other white meat."

The farmhouse is hidden behind a stand of trees. Its current owner is a farmer named Harold Eddy. Jean says he grew up on the farm next door.

Harold is in the yard as we pull in, tinkering with vintage farming equipment. He's been collecting for more than fifty years, and the property is full of antique haying and corn harvesting machines, wire-twisting machines, broom-making equipment—and more than anything else, plows. There are sulky plows, cultivator plows, lister plows, bluegrass plows, ice plows, sod plows, potato digger plows, double-wing shovel plows, left-handed plows, and an assortment of unpatented plows forged by local blacksmiths.

One birthday he gave Steve a red tricycle on which McQueen raced kids from neighboring farms on a dirt bluff, winning more than his share of the gumdrop prizes.

Jean obviously has given him a heads-up about the reason for our visit because after we shake hands, Harold asks with the hint of a sigh, "I guess you wanna talk about Steve McQueen?"

Turns out he's also well versed on that subject and starts by relating that Claude Thomson purchased the house from a Sears catalog in 1919 for about six thousand dollars. "Some of it was modified," Harold says, "and Claude put in a lot of upgrades. It was finished in 1920."

Steve and his mother moved to Slater in 1934 or 1935, and while Claude was no great shakes as a brother, he seems to have done much better by "the boy," as he usually referred to

Steve, and even developed a genuine affection for him. Steve himself once recalled his uncle as "a very good man. Very strong. Very fair."

Claude worked Steve hard. "I milked cows, worked the cornfield, cut wood for the winter. There was always plenty to do," McQueen later recalled.

His uncle didn't spare the rod. "When I'd get lazy and duck my chores," Steve said, "Claude would warm my backside with a hickory switch. I learned a simple fact: you work for what you get."

But Claude was also generous to him. One birthday he gave Steve a red tricycle on which McQueen raced kids from neighboring farms on a dirt bluff, winning more than his share of the gumdrop prizes. I assume this is where he got the bug for driving fast, something he chased until the disappointment of his 1971 racing film, *Le Mans*.

While in California, Steve ran the streets with a gang, stealing hubcaps and shooting pool.

The inside of the farmhouse is roomy, comfortable, filled with antiques. Steve's old bedroom is upstairs, and Harold leads us there. It's fairly small, but from the window there's a nice view of the property.

If it wasn't an idyllic situation for McQueen, his uncle's home at least provided a semblance of stability and love. Unfortunately, not enough to keep young Steve from being hurt and thrown off stride by his wayward mother's behavior and the local gossip it stirred up.

"There was a lot of scuttlebutt that went through the neighborhoods when she came to town," says Harold. "Sure got a lot of tongues wagging."

Steve never stopped hoping Julian would clean up her act and come home for good. He might as well have hoped to sprout wings and fly. Sometimes she dragged him off on her escapades. Months after they chased to California in search of Steve's vagrant dad, Steve ended up back on Claude's doorstep, alone, dirty, and starving. Claude's new wife Eva Mae Stewart, a former St. Louis Follies dancer many years his junior, took the teenager in and took care of him.

> A traveling carnival happened to be passing through at the time, and when it moved on to the next town, Steve went with it.

While in California, Steve ran the streets with a gang, stealing hubcaps and shooting pool. When Claude heard about it, he laid down the law: "If you get into trouble here, I'm going to send you back to your mother."

I'm sure Steve was torn. On one hand, he loved the stability of being with Claude. Though it required hard work, there was routine, well-defined rules, and three square meals a day. If Steve felt as I did toward my mom, who was so much like Julian, he would have wanted to be with her because, after all, she was his mother, and like me, he would've felt a strong, protective instinct toward her.

But despite Claude's stern warning, Harold says, Steve did get into local scrapes. After he and some friends went on a window-shooting spree with a BB gun, Claude told McQueen he was enrolling him in an all-boys school.

A traveling carnival happened to be passing through at the time, and when it moved on to the next town, Steve went with it. Years later, a widely distributed newspaper article quoted

McQueen as saying, "I hated the farm life and didn't get along with small town people. I guess they were just as glad to see me go as I was to get out of there."

No wonder it took so long for that billboard to go up.

"Did McQueen ever return to Slater?" I ask Harold.

"Once," he says. "Back in the late '50s, a few months before Old Man Thomson died."

Steve and Neile Adams (his first wife) were newlyweds at the time, living in New York. Neile signed up to perform in a six-month revue in Las Vegas, and as they traveled west, Steve made an impromptu decision to stop in Slater and reconnect with his uncle.

And as Jean and I head back down Thomson Lane, she tells me something Barbi McQueen privately told her during that appearance at Steve McQueen Days in 2007.

"How ya doing, boy?" asked the delighted Thomson as he pumped the hand of his adult-aged nephew. McQueen only answered him with a thin smile.

Claude died at eighty-three on November 28, 1957. McQueen didn't return for the funeral and never went back to Slater again. When invited to participate in the city's centennial celebration in 1978, he didn't even respond.

Well, it's time to let Harold get back to his antique farm implements, with my sincere gratitude for his time and information. And as Jean and I head back down Thomson Lane, she tells me something Barbi McQueen privately told her during that appearance at Steve McQueen Days in 2007.

Steve had just been diagnosed with terminal cancer, and as they were driving their motor home to Idaho, he told Barbi, totally out of the blue, that he wanted to see Slater one more time.

But the cancer moved swiftly. He never made it back.

THE FATHER WHO WASN'T THERE

Yesterday contained more than its share of revelations. After parting ways with Jean so she could get back to her real job, I kicked around town for a few more hours, before grabbing some take-out and heading back to the Steve McQueen Suite for an early bedtime. I could feel the road fatigue setting in, and realizing I've still got two thousand miles ahead of me, followed by way more than that the next week, I decided to let common sense overrule my need for speed. Full night's sleep tonight then refreshed for what starts all over again tomorrow.

Before pulling out on Friday, however, I swing back by the *Slater Main Street News*, wanting to thank Jean one more time for helping me tie together so many loose ends of McQueen's storyline and upbringing. Little did I expect her to serve up today, out of the blue, the *pièce de résistance*. It hadn't occurred to her, she said, until right this moment, but would I like to talk to Steve's half sister, she asks?

HUH?

I thought I was pretty well acquainted by now with all the important details of Steve McQueen's life, but I sure didn't know he had a sibling.

Terri McQueen is her name, Jean says. She was a guest at Steve McQueen Days in 2011 and is a perfectly delightful lady. She lives in Pueblo, Colorado, near her daughter Antonette. After rooting around in her desk for a minute or two, Jean comes up with a phone number in case I want to call her up on my way back to California.

> I thought I was pretty well acquainted by now with all the important details of Steve McQueen's life, but I sure didn't know he had a sibling.

I don't wait. I call her up, right here in Jean's office. And like everyone else I've encountered so far, Terri McQueen couldn't be nicer. The seventy-seven-year-old daughter of that mysterious phantom William McQueen says anytime I want to come to Pueblo, she'll be happy to show me letters, photos, and military documents, and answer any questions I have.

I do some quick calculations in my head. If I leave right now and drive straight through, I can make Pueblo by 10:00 p.m. "How about breakfast in the morning?" I ask. Terri laughs and agrees.

Minutes after offering again my undying thanks to Jean Black, I'm in the Bullitt and out of Slater like a shot, where because of my haste to make Pueblo by nightfall, I'm in need of constantly reminding myself to calm down and obey the speed limit. After a few minutes I turn on the radio to distract myself from the jumbled thoughts in my head.

Nice try. One of the first songs is "Cat's In the Cradle," the 1974 smash hit by Harry Chapin. Irony? Maybe. Providence? No doubt.

I'm sure you remember the song. Told in the first person, it's about a father too busy to spend time with his young son. Later in life, the roles reverse, and the grown-up son now has no time for his wistful dad. Its message about the swift, inexorable passage of time and the lost opportunities that can never be recovered is poignant. And hearing it now, within the context of what I've been discovering firsthand about McQueen's lonely past, instantly transports me back to my own fatherless childhood.

Clearly this odyssey is starting to wear on me mentally as much as physically. I knew our two backstories were alike in many ways, yet somehow I never quite expected the discoveries I was making to affect me quite so personally.

The man I thought was my dad wanted nothing to do with me. Whenever he was around, he was abusive, physically and otherwise. My Aunt Willie remembers coming to our house when I was still in a high chair and finding him beating the bottoms of my feet with a ruler because I wasn't eating my food.

I was still quite young when my mother left him, but I recall it as a happy day for us.

After I married Cathe and we had our son Christopher, I wondered if the years had changed my father, and so I decided to track him down and find out. He ran a dry cleaning business, and when I got the address, I took Cathe and Christopher there with me.

"This is your grandson Christopher," I said to the old man behind the counter. "I thought you'd like to meet him." He just stared at us. No words. Nothing. After a few very uncomfortable minutes, we left. On the way home I said to Cathe, "I'm not sure he even *is* my actual father. No father would react like that to his own grandson."

Turns out I was right. He wasn't my real father at all. My mom had lied about that.

I thought of Steve McQueen's alcoholic dad who was never there for him. But at least he knew his father was out there. Somewhere.

Clearly this odyssey is starting to wear on me mentally as much as physically. I knew our two backstories were alike in many ways, yet somehow I never quite expected the discoveries I was making to affect me quite so personally.

At least Colorado offers a beautiful change of scenery, and after almost seven hundred miles on I-70, Pueblo is appearing in the distance.

I'm fortunate to get a room at the Hampton Inn and Suites on a Friday night without a reservation. I call Cathe first thing to let her know where I am and why, and that I'll be home very late on Saturday or possibly even early Sunday morning. I'll be there for services, no matter how exhausted I am.

Dragging pretty good right now, I fall asleep as soon as I hit the bed. Morning comes too soon, and after my routine of Scripture and correspondence, I check out and program

I grab a seat in the waiting area and pull out my laptop to catch up on the world. Suddenly a statuesque, older woman steps forward and offers her hand. "I'm Terri McQueen," she says with a smile.

the GPS for the B Street Café in the heart of Pueblo's Historic District.

I grab a seat in the waiting area and pull out my laptop to catch up on the world. Suddenly a statuesque, older woman steps forward and offers her hand.

"I'm Terri McQueen," she says with a smile.

We're seated in a booth in back, and after explaining to Terri what I'm up to, I wonder how I've not come across any mention of her in my research about her famous half brother.

"Well, I don't go around advertising," she says, "and there are some people who would prefer I not open my mouth at all. When you go around saying you're Steve McQueen's sister, most people think you're full of it. Besides, I have nothing to prove to anybody. But if somebody asks, I'm not going to deny who I am either. I'm too old for that."

It was a McQueen biographer, Terri says, who first found out about her, via old birth records. After tracking her down in Pueblo, warning her to brace herself, then dramatically revealing that she was the half sister of Steve McQueen, Terri let the air out of him by saying, "Oh, honey, I've known that for years."

I like this woman!

Terri has a large file of documents she's accumulated over the years about Steve's dad (and hers), William McQueen. We dig in.

He was born in Nashville, Tennessee. His dad was an insurance agent, and after a year the family moved to Los Angeles,

---

Terri has a large file of documents she's accumulated over the years about Steve's dad (and hers), William McQueen. We dig in.

---

living very comfortably in the affluent Bunker Hill area. That changed, however, when Louis McQueen—William's father—died of a brain hemorrhage in 1919. Thirteen-year-old William and his mother moved to Indianapolis, her hometown.

William was a private in the US Marines from 1927 to 1929. Following his discharge from active service, he returned to Indianapolis, where he met the comely Julian Crawford. Nine months later, Steve McQueen was born.

William's military record indicates he was booted out of the Marine Reserves in July 1930 for misconduct, and after that he lammed out for the West Coast, leaving Julian and Steve behind.

> In trying to describe it, she volunteers the observation that she and Steve share the same wanderlust in their DNA.

Terri shows me copies of pages from the 1930–32 Los Angeles city directory showing that William lived on the famous Sunset Boulevard and managed a gas station. A year later, though, he was back with Julian and Steve in Slater in an outbuilding on Claude Thomson's farm, where a silo stands today, then again at her parents' house in Beech Grove, Indiana. But the reconciliation was short-lived, and in 1934, William was in San Francisco working for the Dollar Steamship Line. He joined the Merchant Marine three years later.

Terri then pulls out a handful of pictures, a birth certificate, a telegram, and a fingerprint file, proof of William Terrence McQueen's real existence. The photos, which have been tucked away for several decades, show physical similarities between father and son. They have the same head, ears, lips, nose. The same intense gaze. The two also shared almost identical builds as adults: William was listed as 5' 10¼", 160 pounds, medium build, white complexion, light brown hair, blue eyes. And indeed, they were piercing blue eyes.

I ask Terri how *she* fits into all of this. She tells me William met her mother, a twenty-five-year-old waitress named Alma Doris Moody at Joe Kelly's Restaurant in the City by the Bay. They started dating, and William ardently wooed her with poetry and moonlight canoe rides in Golden Gate Park.

As with Julian, it's uncertain whether William and Alma— who was called Doris—ever officially tied the knot, but they did live together. And on May 5, 1940, Terri Carol McQueen was born in Seattle, Washington. She shows me her King County birth certificate as proof, which lists William and Doris as her parents.

Terri's mom, she tells me, was as footloose and restless as William, and a year after she was born, Doris left her with her grandmother and moved back to San Francisco. When Terri was seven, Doris married someone else. It didn't make for a happy childhood.

In trying to describe it, she volunteers the observation that she and Steve share the same wanderlust in their DNA. "I was never a bad child—I had a lot of freedom growing up," Terri says. "I'd be out on my bicycle with my dog roaming everywhere. If I wasn't home when my mother got home from work, or if I didn't make my bed, she would always threaten with sending me to reform school. I never understood where that came from until a few years ago," referring to Steve being sent to Boys Republic in the 1940s, a reform school in Chino, California. "My mom thought, *Okay, that's what you do with kids that won't behave—you send them to reform school.* She knew Steve had been sent there, so . . . .

"She was not the nurturing mother kind at all. Both she and Steve's mother never should have had children."

Doris didn't want Terri to have any contact with her meandering father, so when William sent gifts, letters, and telegrams from whatever port of call he was in, Doris threw them away unopened.

So, like her half brother, Terri never knew her dad. It's apparent this still grieves her. "Every little girl wants to know her daddy, and I've always carried that with me," she says.

I am glad that, thin though it is, a thread of spirituality does indeed run in McQueen's family, in the voice of his half sister.

William eventually ended up back in Southern California. The 1951 Long Beach directory lists him as an "aircraft salesman." His last years were wracked by illness exacerbated by alcoholism, and William McQueen died on November 11, 1958. Official cause of death: cirrhosis of the liver.

An inventory and estimated value of assets prepared by the Los Angeles Superior Court listed William's total assets as three hundred dollars—six fifty-dollar traveler's checks stashed away in a drawer next to his bed when he passed. With no legal family members to claim him, William was declared indigent, and his body was shipped from the county morgue to All Souls Cemetery in Long Beach. The cemetery, which is sponsored by the Catholic Church, gave him a proper burial but placed his casket in an unmarked grave. It remains unmarked, though

Terri is working with the Veterans Administration to try rectifying the slight.

Terri said her mother Doris died in 2002, and sadly, was an avowed atheist. "No matter what I would tell her, she really believed there would be nothing left when she died. I'm pretty spiritual myself, and I know for a fact there is life after death," Terri says. "We are spirits living in a body, not flesh and blood. But I could never get that across to her. That's my one big thing that really bothered me—she was scared when she died."

I am glad that, thin though it is, a thread of spirituality does indeed run in McQueen's family, in the voice of his half sister.

I ask Terri whether she knows if Steve ever met her father face-to-face. She says, unbeknownst to each other, while William lived in Long Beach those last years, the son he'd abandoned lived in nearby Hollywood.

Yet the story gets sadder. When Steve's wife, Neile, was pregnant with their first child—a daughter, which they ironically named Terry—he took another stab at finding his dad, hiring detectives who scoured the seedy part of Los Angeles for a William McQueen, putting out feelers into local pool halls, bars, gin joints, and veterans' organizations.

Then, Terri says, Steve got a call one day from a woman who said she was William's girlfriend. "Come on over if you want to know about your dad," she told him. Steve and Neile went to her apartment in Echo Park, only to find out that William had died three months earlier. The woman did, however, share this one slice of haunting memory. She said William faithfully watched *Wanted: Dead or Alive* every Saturday night and would sometimes say aloud, "I wonder if that's my boy . . . ."

I ask Terri when she first discovered she had a famous half brother. She said she started stitching the pieces of the puzzle together one afternoon when she arrived home unannounced as her mother was watching that same program, *Wanted: Dead or Alive*. Prone to imbibing, Terri's mother inexplicably let her guard down, remarking how strongly Steve resembled his father.

"The thing is, my mother hated westerns and cowboy movies, yet she was paying a lot of attention to this particular show—more like mesmerized," Terri says. "After that, it wasn't too hard putting two and two together. I watched the show constantly after that day and always caught his movies at the theater."

Terri says she also caught the acting bug herself, actually moving to Hollywood in the early '60s, but was careful not to exploit the McQueen name or the relationship. "I didn't want to be seen as trying to ride his coattails," Terri says as she shows me a headshot of herself. She was a stunner. "I never wanted him to ever have that impression of me—that I came to Hollywood to use him."

Terri tells me she never met Steve but came shockingly close. After several years in Hollywood, she auditioned in front of famed *Bonnie and Clyde* director Arthur Penn for the Jane Fonda role in *The Chase*, the 1965 movie starring Marlon Brando and Robert Redford. Had she nabbed the role, Steve wouldn't have been able to avoid paying attention and taking notice of her.

Oh, and there was one other time. When *Bullitt* was being filmed in San Francisco in early 1968, she and her husband drove to the set. In the car she wrote a note to Steve and asked her then-husband to deliver it to him through an assistant. Terri recalls it wasn't a terribly long note, just telling Steve who she was, how they were related, and the name of a family friend who knew their father and could vouch for her. But Terri's husband was very insecure and jealous, and she suspects he probably just tossed the note away.

"I'd have given anything to meet him," Terri says of Steve. "He was the big brother of my dreams—dreams that I was never able to share. I'd like to believe, if that note had reached him, we would have met.

"Now we'll just have to wait to meet in another life," she says. "And when we do, that reunion is going to be very, very special."

9

HOUSE OF HORRORS

In my sixty-four years on this earth, I've never met anyone who's led a truly charmed life (though some flatter themselves, bragging that they have). We all experience difficult times and go through personal crises that test and shape us. My own early life is a testament to this. I was able to survive and persevere not because I'm special or made of sterner stuff than most but only through the saving grace of God's kindness and unconditional love.

I wonder how many times in his life Steve McQueen felt there was no such thing. Even after he surmounted his dismal childhood and adolescence to become famous and fabulously wealthy, he still felt bereft enough to mount an expensive, expansive search for the father who abandoned him in his infancy—only to discover that for several years they'd been separated by only a few miles, and now it was too late. He would never know his dad, never find out why William McQueen deserted him. The soul-rending wound it left would never heal.

It would haunt him until the end of his life.

When you understand the devastation of effectively being rejected and unwanted by your father—in Steve's case, for the most part, by his mother too—you realize a clearer understanding of the trajectory someone's life can take. You start to better understand Steve McQueen.

In what would be his last interview, he said to former Mayo Clinic professor Bru Joy, "When a kid doesn't have any love when he's small, he begins to wonder if he's good enough. My mother didn't love me, and I didn't have a father. I thought, 'Well, I must not be very good.'"

> He would never know his dad, never find out why William McQueen deserted him. The soul-rending wound it left would never heal. It would haunt him until the end of his life.

A heartbreaking statement to hear but quite telling in what must have motivated Steve throughout his life.

It's 10:00 a.m. when my breakfast meeting with Terri is over, and I'm heading home—and can't get there fast enough. The drive from Pueblo to Orange County is approximately twelve hundred miles, a sixteen-hour shot. If I don't take too many breaks, I should pull into my driveway around two o'clock tomorrow morning. I'll be able to grab a few hours of sleep and then deliver three sermons on Sunday. Only half as coherent as usual, I'm wondering if anyone will notice.

The drive from Pueblo to California offers some of the most beautiful landscape in the country, including the Rocky Mountains, several indigenous reservations in northern New Mexico, the South Rim of the Grand Canyon, and the Mojave Desert in California.

I turn on the satellite radio to a different station than I'd been listening to, and it's Sheryl Crow singing a song called "Steve McQueen." It's a great rocker to keep me awake as she sings of how she wants to be like Steve McQueen and his fast machine.

My Bullitt begins to accelerate a bit more.

Many hours and hours later, as I enter the city limits of my hometown, I don't need the radio to cue up "Ode to Joy." Being home is joy enough. I don't even bother unpacking the Bullitt—just go in, kiss Cathe hello (and good night), and instantly tumble into a bottomless sleep in our bed. The only thing missing is staying awake a minute or two longer, just to savor the blissful comfort of the sweet place called home.

Yet it seems like I've *slept* only a minute or two when Cathe wakes me at 5:20 a.m. with a cheerful, "Time to inspire the masses." I forgive her when she hands me my 2-percent latte.

My normal routine when it comes to preparing Sunday sermons is to start the Wednesday before with lots of reading in the theological library I've built up over the years. Plenty of good stuff there. On Thursday, I do a basic "brain dump" into a Word document on the computer, then on Friday start crafting the message. When things are really clicking, I'm pretty much good to go by Sunday morning, though I'm usually still tinkering right up to

I turn on the satellite radio to a different station than I'd been listening to, and it's Sheryl Crow singing a song called "Steve McQueen." It's a great rocker to keep me awake as she sings of how she wants to be like Steve McQueen and his fast machine. My Bullitt begins to accelerate a bit more.

the time I open my mouth, and sometimes I make adjustments even while I'm talking.

I'm not an entertainer, and I don't try to be one in the pulpit, but I'm amazed how some of the purveyors of God's Word are able to make it sound as dull, lifeless, and impenetrable as a recitation of the federal tax code. Those who come to our church do so to hear a message from God, and that's what I always want to give them. I always want them to know how it applies in their lives. I don't consider it my job to make the Bible "relevant." Fact is, the Bible *is* relevant. It doesn't require my spin for that. My job is simply to let "the Lion out of the cage" and let Him have His way.

Small as he was, McQueen fought back, trying to match his tormentor blow for blow. "I would have borne any punishment—anything— just for the sheer pleasure of knowing that I had given back even a little of the pain he inflicted on me," Steve recalled, adding, "God, how I wanted that."

Yet under the circumstances, I can't say the three sermons I deliver today are the most inspiring I've ever given. But at least I didn't fall asleep in the pulpit.

Back home after church, Cathe pours me a tall glass of iced tea (loaded with extra ice) and sets down a steaming pan of chicken enchiladas with green sauce and refried beans. I'm already on record as saying nobody lives a charmed life, but being married to her is the closest thing to it I can think of.

When the pan is empty, I totter to a well-worn oversized leather chair in our family room, turn on the tube, and fall fast asleep. But only for twenty minutes because there's a house in Echo Park, about an hour and a half from here, that I just have to see today. It's where Steve McQueen lived during one of his childhood excursions to California with his mother.

House of horrors, is more like it.

How Julian McQueen met her second husband, Hal Berri, is unclear, but most likely they knew each other through their work. Julian had landed a job as an estimator for a company called Smith Warren in Los Angeles. Hal held the same position with a different company called Smith Martin. He was eight years Julian's senior and married her right after divorcing his first wife in March 1937 in Monterey, California.

It was yet another in a long series of poor choices by Julian, and one with dire consequences for Steve. In interviews years later, McQueen recalled Berri as a violent alcoholic who beat both his mother and him.

> You'd think Steve's mother would've snatched him up, grabbing the first train or bus out of there. But Julian was too far gone in the bottle and self-degradation herself. She'd already lost one man and didn't want to lose another.

"He apparently beat me for the sheer sadistic pleasure it gave him—which included the joy he obviously derived from my pain," McQueen recounted to one reporter. "I was young. I even thought of bearing the beatings, vowing simply to hold on until I was old enough to run away. But I just couldn't restrain myself. It wasn't in me."

Instead, small as he was, McQueen fought back, trying to match his tormentor blow for blow. "I would have borne any punishment—anything—just for the sheer pleasure of knowing that I had given back even a little of the pain he inflicted on me," Steve recalled, adding, "God, how I wanted that."

Of course it was hopeless, boy against man, and after the inevitable beat-down, Berri would lock him in a dark room for hours without food or water.

I'm now in front of the house on Preston Avenue in Echo Park where McQueen endured that torment. It's an adobe-style, split-level residence shaded by very large trees. You'd never guess it was once a torture chamber of sorts.

But it's true. And what happened inside there changed Steve. It made him unusually wary of physical contact with adults. He was often afraid to go home. He grew withdrawn, uncommunicative, aggressive, and disruptive. He did poorly in his schoolwork and found an outlet for his uncontrollable mounting frustrations and hostility by stealing cars and thumbing his nose at law enforcement.

My mom, unconscious, lying in a pool of blood. Eddie, in one of his rages, had beaten her mercilessly, within an inch of her life.

You'd think Steve's mother would've snatched him up, grabbing the first train or bus out of there. But Julian was too far gone in the bottle and self-degradation herself. She'd already lost one man and didn't want to lose another.

Her solution was to write to Claude Thomson in Slater and ask if she could send her son back there to live. The only alternative, she said, was reform school. Claude agreed to take Steve in, and the boy returned to the farm. But as we've seen, it didn't last. Steve got into trouble and ran away with a carnival.

But that didn't last long either, and the teen runaway ended up back in Los Angeles with his mother and the stepfather from hell. Steve was later arrested for stealing hubcaps, and in court the judge warned him that one more offense would land him in jail. When he got home, Berri beat him severely, even pushing him down a flight of stairs.

This guy reminds me of one of my prize stepdads. I'll call him "Eddie." He was six-foot-plus, had sort of a raffish appearance, owned a seedy bar in Waikiki and, as the saying goes, was his own best customer.

You never knew what would trigger one of Eddie's explosive, alcohol-fueled temper tantrums. I was a bucktoothed kid, and when I ate with a fork or spoon, the silverware would audibly scrape against my protruding upper teeth. This sound annoyed Eddie to no end, and one night when it happened, he went nuts, screaming, swearing, and banging his hammy fists on the table. I started looking at him a little differently that night, my gut telling me this guy was dangerous.

Mom was a quiet eater, but she had other ways of pushing Eddie's buttons, especially when she was drinking. It wasn't at all unusual for me to get up in the morning and find the living room looking like a battle zone, broken dishes and furniture strewn all over the place. Once the front plateglass window was shattered.

What I discovered another time was much worse—my mom, unconscious, lying in a pool of blood. Eddie, in one of his rages, had beaten her mercilessly, within an inch of her life. When I ran to her, Eddie yelled at me to get back to my room. I did but instead slipped out the window, ran to a neighbor's house, and called the police.

In a rare flash of lucidity, Mom realized that staying with Eddie could be fatal for both of us, so we got out of there and hightailed it to California. Mom had found sanctuary in another man's arms.

And apparently in May 1943, Julian McQueen had one of those same flashes of rationality as my mom had and finally separated from Hal Berri. A divorce soon followed. Julian went to work as a draftsperson to support herself and her son, but Steve showed no sense of responsibility or obligation himself and continued to roam the streets, getting into trouble.

When he ended up in court again, the judge said the place for him was a school for adolescents with behavioral and emotional problems called Boys Republic, in Chino. Julian signed the remand papers. At the time McQueen considered it the ultimate abandonment by both his mother and society. That mind-set would later change dramatically.

TWO SCHOOLS OF THOUGHT

Steve McQueen and I were about the same age when our mothers sent us away. He went to Boys Republic; I went to a military school called Southern California Military Academy.

My mother enrolled me in SCMA in 1962. It was quite a year. John F. Kennedy was president. Johnny Carson was taking over from Jack Paar as host of *The Tonight Show. Lawrence of Arabia* was filling the big screen, and Sean Connery made his debut as James Bond in the first 007 spy film, *Dr. No.* Elvis was singing about his little "Good Luck Charm," and the Beach Boys went on a "Surfin' Safari." It was also the year that Marilyn Monroe died of a barbiturate overdose and was gone like a "Candle in the Wind." Most frightening of all, the Cuban Missile Crisis erupted, bringing America as close to a nuclear war as it has ever come.

SCMA was located on Signal Hill in Long Beach. At its entrance sat military armaments dating back to World War I. Cadets were issued uniforms and taught a whole new way of life. Every man was "sir," every woman "ma'am." Cadets caught using inappropriate language had their mouths washed out with soap. I still remember the taste. Those guilty of more serious infractions were spanked with a wooden "cheese paddle" that had large holes in it to increase the pain. I quickly realized the futility of disrespecting authority figures. So, willingly or not, I fell in line.

Founded in 1907 as a nonprofit institution, Boys Republic provided counseling, education, and training to teenagers referred by the California Youth Authority and, as in McQueen's case, juvenile court judges.

We stayed in barracks with a housemother keeping close watch over us. It was unnerving. So was the SCMA commandant, a longtime military man called "The General" who'd lost an arm in combat duty and kept the empty sleeve of his uniform coat pinned up at the shoulder so it wouldn't flap in the breeze. We had to be very careful how we saluted him.

The boot camp-style regimentation made me feel like I was doing a stretch in the big house. I missed my mom terribly. But I gradually came to realize I was safer there with the kind of vigilant adult supervision and clear boundaries I never got at home.

The same thing happened to Steve McQueen at Boys Republic.

Founded in 1907 as a nonprofit institution, Boys Republic provided counseling, education, and training to teenagers referred by the California Youth Authority and, as in McQueen's case, juvenile court judges.

The main campus is a 211-acre farm where, still today, students live in cottages housing about twenty-five boys each. It's a vast community unto itself where kids work at a variety of jobs and even have their own government and justice system. It's a *reform* school in the best sense of the word.

McQueen arrived there on February 6, 1945, and was assigned to a cottage with other boys ages 14–18. Each cottage was presided over by a housemother who closely supervised the boys. Daily reveille was at 5:30 a.m., followed by chores and then school.

At first Steve kept to himself and opted not to participate in group activities at his cottage. Students whose cottages ran smoothly were rewarded with monthly outings, and more than once McQueen's contrariness and bad attitude ruined things for the others. When the housemother wasn't around, they paid him back with beatings.

> But over time he adjusted to —and even thrived on—the structure and discipline, and for the rest of his life McQueen looked back on his eighteen-month stint at Boys Republic as the turning point in his life and never forgot what the school did for him.

"I got my lumps," recalled McQueen later on, "no doubt about it."

But over time he adjusted to—and even thrived on—the structure and discipline, and for the rest of his life McQueen looked back on his eighteen-month stint at Boys Republic as the turning point in his life and never forgot what the school did for him.

Max Scott started out at Boys Republic in 1965 and became executive director in 1976. I met with him on the property one day, early in my process of fact-finding but before taking off on my two cross-country road trips. He told me that McQueen faithfully visited the facility in Chino twice a year throughout adulthood until the onset of his fatal illness. "He would call and ask if he could come on a specific day," recalls Max, "but since he never stopped by my office, I rarely met him. Instead, he went straight to the cottage, to the very room he was assigned to at the school. On one occasion in late August, he and [wife] Ali MacGraw [we'll meet her later] sat on the floor of the room which was jammed with students, while the temperature hovered close to a hundred degrees."

McQueen enjoyed shooting pool with students in the Activity Center and answering questions about his stay at Boys Republic.

Invariably, says Max, "Steve would turn the attention back to the boys, asking what they were currently doing and if they were making the experience a positive one in terms of their futures.

"One time," Max remembers, "McQueen went to the shop where students made Native American-style turquoise bracelets and purchased over a thousand dollars' worth."

Every Boys Republic student who wrote a letter to McQueen received a response from him, and Max recalls McQueen frequently asking him for information about a student who'd written so he could refer to it in his personal reply. "He showed uncommon interest in and sincere concern for each individual," says Max.

While Max and I are talking, he says he knows a couple of Boys Republic alums who were there with McQueen in the mid-'40s. Would I like their phone numbers?

Would I like a full head of hair? Almost as much.

Retired businessmen Arden Miller and Robert McNamara consented to meet me on an agreed-upon date that week at Boys Republic, a forty-five-minute drive from my house. At noon we converge at the Howard Replica II 1885 Street Clock outside the Margaret Fowler Memorial Auditorium.

Each man shakes my hand heartily, and it's apparent they're happy to be back at the place that had such an impact on their lives, to share their stories and talk about the classmate who went on to movie and pop culture stardom (something none of them would have predicted back then).

We walk to the site of John Brewer Dormitory, where they and McQueen were billeted, each at different times. Built in 1912, the cottage was demolished some time ago.

Each cottage, I'm told, had a living room or common area where the boys relaxed, played games, and listened to records under the supervision of their housemother. She also planned games and activities, read aloud, mended clothes, darned socks, and served as an overall guide, philosopher, and friend, keeping a motherly eye on the young men.

At least this is what the brochure boasts.

Once a couple students who'd ticked McQueen off found their rooms ransacked, and Arden remembers Steve snickering afterward, "They'll never mess with me again."

"Yes, there were housemothers," Robert says, "but they didn't watch over us. They just made sure we were there, and often they weren't very successful at it."

(My housemother at SCMA was an old harpy I'll call "Mrs. Jones," who had the warmth of a great white shark. If she ever cracked a smile, it was while meting out punishment, the only thing that seemed to give her pleasure. She also had very bad breath. Maybe if she'd washed *her* mouth out with soap as many times as she did ours . . . .)

Robert says he came to Boys Republic in early 1946, after his stepfather, a research chemist for Shell Oil, went to Holland to help reconstruct a refinery the Nazis destroyed. Bob's mother accompanied his stepdad overseas, while they sent their son to Boys Republic. "They decided I could use a little discipline because I was a handful."

> "Steve had the aura of a loner, and no one liked him in school," Robert says. "His body language spoke volumes: *Don't mess with me.*"

Arden Miller's road to Boys Republic started behind the wheel of his father's Buick, which Arden took out for a joyride one day. A cop pulled him over and asked to see his driver's license.

"What's a driver's license?" fourteen-year-old Arden asked.

A judge sentenced him to Boys Republic until he graduated from high school. He arrived there in January 1946. By then Steve McQueen had been there almost a year.

"He wasn't big or athletic but was tough as nails," Arden recalls. "If anyone messed with him or did something he didn't like, he was going to find a way to get back at them."

Once a couple students who'd ticked McQueen off found their rooms ransacked, and Arden remembers Steve snickering afterward, "They'll never mess with me again." He also recalls when Steve took on the entire Boys Republic student court. Comprised of a judge, jury, prosecutors, and defense attorneys, the court met every Monday night to hear and adjudicate cases.

When a case involving McQueen was decided against him, he yelled out, "I'll get back at ya!"

"He made good on his promise, too," Arden says with a laugh. "He'd find a way to get back at the judge, jury, and the two attorneys involved. He'd ransack their rooms, turn over their beds, put shaving cream in their shoes. He was a real piece of work."

Robert remembers entering the Brewer dorm for the first time, dropping his belongings on the floor, then turning and looked into the piercing blue eyes of another resident regarding him with extreme wariness.

"Steve had the aura of a loner, and no one liked him in school," Robert says. "His body language spoke volumes: *Don't mess with me.* He was hardened, cut off emotionally and guarded, just like me. We never had what I would call a friendship."

In retrospect, says Robert, he and McQueen were probably too much alike to be drawn to one another. "Steve was mentally and emotionally in pain, and you can tell that through his acting." Robert should know. He did some film work of his own in the '60s and once worked in a picture with Clint Eastwood. "His independence and anger were for real, I wanna tell you. He was exactly the same way he was in Boys Republic. Same exact way."

In a display case sits a photograph of the 1946 Boys Republic baseball team. McQueen is in the top row, McNamara down in front.

"Steve wasn't a team sport player," says Robert. "He wasn't a starter, and I don't think he really cared. There's that famous scene of him in *The Great Escape* throwing the ball against the wall in solitary confinement, but that was only a cinematic feature. Steve wasn't a star player."

Robert says the baseball field and cow pasture are the only places unchanged at Boys Republic since the days he was there. "You were on somebody's short list if you were milking cows," he says, "and I was always on somebody's short list until I became a very good baseball player. Then I got a nice, cushy job taking care of the ball field. I mowed the grass, limed the field, dusted off the bases, did everything."

After a moment's silence, Robert adds, "Steve milked cows the whole time I knew him."

Though not exactly pals, McNamara and McQueen occasionally sneaked under a bridge to share smokes. One night they even tried a "Great Escape" from Boys Republic, though not together. Typically, McQueen ran away alone; McNamara went with three other boys. "I was apprehended in Long Beach, about forty miles away, while Steve was found underneath the bridge where we used to smoke," Robert says.

Their punishment was swift and painful, he recalls with a wince. "What happened to anyone who ran away was, they would get beat with a long, thick wooden paddle that had holes in the business end. I got about ten of those and my behind looked like a waffle for a couple of days."

Students were also required to attend chapel services on Sundays. I wonder what McQueen thought as he sat there. Probably what most adolescents think about squirming in a place they don't want to be. Only darker, given the circumstances.

Ah, the dreaded "cheese paddle." I knew it well—and got a taste of the "board of education" more than a few times while in military school.

Life at Boys Republic wasn't bucolic, says Arden Miller. It was, after all, a reform school. "We'd get up early in the morning to milk cows, eat breakfast, go to class all day, then milk cows again," he recalls. "No TV to watch or anything."

Students were also required to attend chapel services on Sundays. I wonder what McQueen thought as he sat there. Probably what most adolescents think about squirming in a place they don't want to be. Only darker, given the circumstances.

The chapel services I was forced to sit through at SCMA didn't make much of an impression on me either, except when we sang "You'll Never Walk Alone" from the musical *Carousel.* That always bucked me up. Whenever I felt blue, I'd sing the song to myself and feel better—though I would've appreciated it better, I think, if the song had more hope than getting to the end of a storm and finding "the sweet silver song of the lark." I felt pretty sure I'd always be walking alone, no matter what the song said. I'm sure Steve did too.

As we get ready to say good-bye, Robert says he isn't surprised McQueen came to view his stint at Boys Republic with great affection. "It was the first time he came into contact with people like himself. It was the first real home he ever had, and I can understand why he became so nostalgic about the place. It was his religion."

Then Robert tells me what happened to himself on October 18, 1978. He was out jogging when he suffered a massive heart attack. He fell flat on his face, knocking out all his teeth, and for eight minutes was clinically dead.

During that time, as paramedics fought to bring him back, McNamara recalled, "My spirit went straight down into darkness. I literally went to hell." When he was brought back, says Robert quietly, "It changed my whole life."

Robert is thrilled to hear that Steve McQueen also became a Christian. Now, he says with a big smile, "I know we're going to see each other again when I die. And this time we'll be closer friends."

11 A DEATH SENTENCE

Steve McQueen once said he felt like an old man by the time he reached seventeen. Given all the twists, turns, and upheaval in his life up until then, that's not hard to understand. Thanks to my own tumultuous upbringing, I felt way older than my years when I was that age myself. I felt like I was seventy at age seventeen.

But the similarities in our lives ended there.

McQueen enlisted in the US Marines.

I joined God's army as a born-again Christian.

Well, not right away. I was clearly part of the counter-culture revolution sweeping through America in the 1960s, which just so happened to coincide with my graduation from military school. No more housemothers, cheese paddles, and for all practical purposes, no more rules. I'd been "honor-ably discharged" back into civilian life with no intention of being told what to do or playing nice with authority. The strict conformity that had been drummed into me at SCMA went right out the window, just when I needed boundaries as never before.

Instead, I took to drinking and smoking, though I didn't enjoy either. I drank screwdrivers for the taste of the orange juice and for the effects of the vodka. But the booze made me sick to my stomach, so I switched to pot, and even briefly experimented with LSD. I'd come home late at night stoned, and my mother would be loaded. We made quite a pair.

Fast-forward a few years. The Vietnam War was raging. Protesters were hitting the streets of America, screaming at the establishment for change. The music, films, literature, hair, and dress of the day were interwoven in a happy, trippy, sometimes menacing cloak of defiance.

Southern California, where I lived, was the mecca for this hedonistic lifestyle. Kids all around me went to head shops, smoked dope, and spieled about peace, love, and joy. But there was a lot more to it than that. Most of these young people's defiance was really about sex, drugs, and rock 'n' roll. Of course, there were bound to be casualties. Brian Jones, Janis Joplin, Jimi Hendrix, Jim Morrison, Gram Parsons, and the Grateful Dead's Ron "Pigpen" McKernan immediately come to mind, all of them gone before their thirtieth birthday.

And I almost joined them on a rainy night in 1970.

I was in a car with three friends, high on marijuana, careening along the Pacific Coast Highway, headed home from Laguna Beach, California. We'd scored a kilo of weed that we

> I took to drinking and smoking, though I didn't enjoy either. I drank screwdrivers for the taste of the orange juice and for the effects of the vodka. But the booze made me sick to my stomach, so I switched to pot, and even briefly experimented with LSD.

intended to smoke ourselves, which is a pretty sad commentary in itself. My friends and I were flying along in a 1964 faded beige Volvo on a narrow part of the highway with steep cliffs on one side and the ocean hundreds of yards below on the other. Suddenly the car hit a section of wet pavement. It fishtailed, then spun. We were out of control, with lights flying by and the tires screaming. *This is it,* I thought. *This is how it ends for me.*

I offered up a desperate, feeble prayer.

"God, please get me out of this! If You do, I will serve You, or do whatever You want. Please!"

In an instant the car righted itself. We all laughed in hysterical relief, and as we continued on our way, I said another prayer, not quite so desperate this time: "Thanks, God—see You at the next crisis!"

> Suddenly the car hit a section of wet pavement. It fishtailed, then spun. We were out of control, with lights flying by and the tires screaming. *This is it,* I thought. *This is how it ends for me.*

But thankfully, it didn't take another crisis for me to give my life to the Lord. All it took was thinking back through all the years of loneliness, broken homes, the alcohol and drugs, the abysmally fruitless search for something to give my life meaning and solace and contentment. I started talking to God more. It was a little weird at first, but it was also wonderful. I finally felt some inner peace and safety. I felt like I'd finally found the family I was searching for: the family of God.

Steve McQueen's route to that harbor was much more byzantine. After his release from Boys Republic on April 1, 1946, he took a bus from California all the way to Greenwich Village in New York City to see his mother, who was living there with Victor Lukens, an artist, filmmaker, and photographer who later became an important figure in McQueen's life and career.

But Julian was still drinking heavily, and the mother-son reunion didn't go well.

> Who else would run off and join a circus, be a deckhand on a boat, go AWOL, work in a brothel, and end up on a chain gang? Only Steve McQueen.

After meeting a couple of sailors in a local bar who regaled him with swashbuckling tales of their life in the Merchant Marine, the teenaged McQueen promptly signed up as a deckhand on the SS Alpha headed for the West Indies. But the romance of the sea quickly turned sour, as all he did was swab the deck and clean the toilet. When the Alpha docked at Santo Domingo in the Dominican Republic, McQueen jumped ship.

He briefly worked as a towel boy in a brothel before making his way back stateside and working a succession of dead-end jobs. He was arrested for vagrancy and did thirty days on a southern chain gang.

Who else would run off and join a circus, be a deckhand on a boat, go AWOL, work in a brothel, and end up on a chain gang?

Only Steve McQueen.

One wonders why they haven't made a film, better yet an entire series, about his life.

Finally he returned to New York in April 1947 and asked Julian to sign a parental consent form so he could join the US Marines. Her permission was required because Steve was under the age of eighteen, and she gave it. So on April 28, 1947, he was sent to the Marine Corps Recruiting Depot at Parris Island, South Carolina.

And that's where I'm headed in the Bullitt tomorrow after my three sermons on Sunday. I'll also visit Quantico, Virginia; Washington, DC; New York City, and a place twenty miles northwest of Philadelphia—but not before making a quick run this afternoon over to Don Oakes's shop in Riverside to get the Bullitt an oil change and a once-over.

"Still on that secret mission?" he asks.

"Still can't talk about it," I reply.

While he works on the car, I flip open my laptop and start emailing folks in the east to line up meetings when I'm there. The response is quick and gratifying. Everyone is so generous and open!

> I take off at 5:15 on Monday morning, and except for overnight stops at two hotels along the twenty-four-hundred-mile route, I drive straight through to South Carolina.

I take off at 5:15 on Monday morning, and except for overnight stops at two hotels along the twenty-four-hundred-mile route, I drive straight through to South Carolina.

Bobby Joe Harris is waiting for me early Wednesday morning in front of the Marine Corps Recruit Training Station at Parris Island. He lives in Chandler, Arizona, but happened to be on an RV trip in the east when we corresponded. Bobby Joe is a decorated Vietnam vet, a former drill instructor, retired police chief—and best of all, a Marine Corps historian. By the way, no one who's served in the corps is ever a "former Marine." Once a Marine, always a Marine.

I've brought along a copy of McQueen's Marine Corps file, which was made available to the public in 2005. Thumbing through it at a table outside the station, Bobby Joe muses, "The Marines weren't as picky back then as they are today. Back then they took in a lot of troubled youth and turned them into real men, and McQueen is the perfect example of this."

Steve and the other recruits would've arrived at Parris Island exhausted from their long eight-hundred-mile journey from New York City, Bobby Joe says. But there was no respite. "Once they stepped off that train, they were immediately screamed at and told how to stand with their heels together, feet at a forty-five-degree angle, thumbs along the seams of their trousers with palms in, eyes forward, shoulders squared, chest out, and chin in. They were informed that if they eyeballed one of their drill instructors, they'd never see again. And they probably said to themselves, 'Lord, what have I gotten myself into?'"

McQueen survived boot camp and from there went to Camp Lejeune, North Carolina, and trained as a tank crewman. After five months he was promoted to private first class—an impressive feat, according to Bobby Joe. But the record also shows several citations for being Absent Without Leave (AWOL), which Bobby Joe says actually wasn't that big a deal.

"Happens more than you think. I can pretty much guess how the conversation went down: 'Hey, honey, can't you stay a little longer?' 'Yeah, it'll cost me some liberty, but you're worth it!'"

Okay, I think I get the picture. I've learned what I needed to know about McQueen and his first taste of Marine life. So after thanking Bobby Joe for interrupting his vacation on my account, I'm off to Quantico, Virginia, to meet Sergeant Cliff Anderson, who served with McQueen there.

Seven hours later, I pull into a hotel on the outskirts of Quantico and catch up on some much needed sleep. The next morning—Thursday—I'm in front of the Brown Field barracks that had housed them.

> One of McQueen's first assignments was to clean the barracks latrine—a task he actually requested so he could go in, lock the door, and take a long nap on the floor.

Cliff says he doesn't have much time, unfortunately, that he won't be able to visit as long as he'd hoped. But it doesn't take long to sum up his impressions of the man I came to talk about. He fondly recalls Steve as a "screw-up." And to confirm his point, he gives the following example. One of McQueen's first assignments was to clean the barracks latrine—a task he actually requested so he could go in, lock the door, and take a long nap on the floor.

Cliff remembers that Steve had a girlfriend in Baltimore and often reported back to base tardy with lipstick on his face. He also remembers him getting in trouble for having a ducktail haircut he refused to change. "I wish I would have taken some pictures of him back then," says Cliff, "because he was a real piece of work."

But there's one additional memory he wants to share before I leave. As we say good-bye, Cliff tells me of being on a hunting trip in Cheyenne, Wyoming, in July 1973, when he saw a newspaper item reporting that McQueen and Ali MacGraw were to be married there in a city park. Cliff contacted him, and Steve the famous actor soon became Steve the old Marine

Corps buddy while they had a drink together. "He was one of a kind," Cliff says, "someone special in my life."

Between Quantico and Camp Lejeune, McQueen's service record indicates several AWOL citations, most importantly a court-martial resulting from a dust-up with a policeman that landed Steve in jail. Add that to his other misadventures.

Tragically, his forty-one-day sentence to the brig also appears to have been a death sentence.

His punishment was assignment to the Naval Gun Factory in Washington, DC, my next stop. It's brief, too, but meaningful because Steve's job there was helping renovate ships' engine rooms—hard, dirty work that entailed removing ceilings and pipes. The latter were wrapped in asbestos. Years later, McQueen told director John Sturges, "The air was so thick with asbestos particles the men could hardly breathe."

Almost thirty years to the day, Steve McQueen was diagnosed with mesothelioma, a rare and terminal cancer caused by asbestos inhalation.

Tragically, his forty-one-day sentence to the brig also appears to have been a death sentence.

NEW YORK
STATE OF MIND

Private First Class Steve McQueen was honorably discharged on April 27, 1950. He received muster-out pay of forty dollars and a set of tools he kept for the rest of his life.

He also got something much more valuable.

"The Marines made a man out of me," McQueen later admitted. "I learned how to get along with others, and I had a platform to jump off of."

Washington, DC, to New York City is about a 225-mile jaunt north on Interstate 95. According to the GPS, it should take me about four hours, but I wonder if that's taking into account the snarling East Coast traffic and those pesky toll roads that require all my spare change. The greatest unknown is traffic on the New Jersey Turnpike leading into Manhattan.

But my timing is good so far. It's about 2:00 p.m., and if I hit the Beltway and hit the gas, I'll miss the DC traffic (which gives its LA counterpart a run for its money). Then I'll stop for a latte to fortify myself for whatever comes next—which I do at a cool little coffee place called Everyman Espresso.

Things go smoothly enough till I enter the Big Apple and spend an hour crawling through traffic to the Washington Square Hotel on Waverly Place in Greenwich Village. I check in around eight o'clock and hit the sack.

Waiting for me in the lobby early the next morning is Gene Lesser, age ninety-one. He was an aspiring playwright in the early '50s when he met Steve McQueen. Over breakfast in the hotel restaurant, he tells me they met through Steve's mother.

> "The Marines made a man out of me," McQueen later admitted. "I learned how to get along with others, and I had a platform to jump off of."

"I knew Julian through her boyfriend, Victor Lukens," says Gene. "She was a lovely looking woman who had a great sense of humor. One day we were out having a beer and she said, 'My kid's coming here and needs a place to stay. Can you put him up?'"

At the time Lesser paid nineteen dollars a month for a cold-water flat in the Village (meaning, it didn't have running hot water). He and his new roommate got along fine though Gene learned quickly that McQueen wasn't much of a talker.

"He was very careful about who he befriended and never discussed his personal life with me or anyone else," says Gene. "He was a brooder. Sometimes he shut down completely."

He says McQueen worked a succession of menial jobs in the Village, selling encyclopedias door-to-door, repairing lawn mowers, and even posing for pulp magazines such as *Crime Detective* and *Homicide Detective* to pay the rent. He bought a motorcycle, frequented the music scene, and learned to smoke weed. When he grew tired of the drudgery of regular employment, he started stealing and scamming to get by.

Then he met a part-time actress named Donna Barton. And the day after their first date, McQueen moved in with her. She was taking acting lessons at the Neighborhood Playhouse in Manhattan and suggested that Steve give acting a shot.

Further encouraged by his mother's ex-flame Victor Lukens, McQueen applied for admission to the acting program there. He was one of about three thousand hopefuls, of whom fewer than seventy-five would be accepted. But Steve's audition for director Sanford Meisner was a home run.

He bought a motorcycle, frequented the music scene, and learned to smoke weed. When he grew tired of the drudgery of regular employment, he started stealing and scamming to get by.

"He was original," Meisner recalled later, "both tough and childlike like Marilyn Monroe, as if he'd been through everything but had preserved a basic innocence. I accepted him at once."

Not everything about acting came easy. Lesser remembers when Steve came to him with the script of a Shakespeare play his class was working on and asked for help with his cues. "He didn't know what half the words in the book meant," says Gene with a laugh—quickly adding, "not that anybody else did either."

I've enjoyed hearing Gene's stories, learning how Steve first dipped his toe into acting. As I'm thanking him for his time and preparing to leave, he remembers one more. Two decades later when he worked in California as a screenwriter and play director, McQueen—then the biggest superstar in filmdom—sometimes dropped into his office on the Sunset Strip wearing a construction helmet and tool belt, telling Lesser's secretary he was a phone repairman.

"He'd lie on the leather couch in my office, and we'd talk about the old days," says Gene. "It was as if he just wanted to get away from everything and everybody."

Fame was already tightening its grip on McQueen, the same scrutiny that would plague him years later while seeking cancer treatment in Mexico, with the press hounding him every moment. He wasn't the first, nor would he be the last person to see how completely unfulfilling and empty being famous can be. Actor Kevin Costner, whose career began to soar after his star turn in the 1992 film *The Bodyguard*, was once asked, "Is it all worth it? Is the price of fame too high? Is all the money and all the glamour and all the power worth having your personal life dragged across the front pages of the tabloids like some rotting animal carcass?"

Costner's answer was firm, "No. It's not worth it to me, it's not worth it, but I don't know what to do about it."

Ironically, the script for *The Bodyguard* was floating around in the 1970s and was intended for Diana Ross in the Whitney Houston role, with McQueen in the part Costner eventually played. Costner even sported a McQueen-like haircut in the film in tribute to one of his favorite actors.

After Gene departs I walk a few blocks to 196 West Fourth Street, once the location of Louis's Tavern. Today it's a local

> Fame was already tightening its grip on McQueen, the same scrutiny that would plague him years later while seeking cancer treatment in Mexico, with the press hounding him every moment.

supermarket that features fresh produce, prepared meals, and a lunch counter offering hot dogs and sandwiches. It's been a Village mainstay for a few decades, but Louis's was a legendary Beat-era barroom frequented by the likes of Jack Kerouac, Bob Dylan, James Dean, Jason Robards, William Stryon, and a fellow named McQueen. Steve, in fact, practically lived on the house special—spaghetti and meatballs with a tomato and lettuce salad for only sixty-five cents.

I'm meeting John Gilmore there. John is a former-actor-turned-writer. In fact, he's one of America's most revered noir writers, having written books on serial killers, famous outlaws, and various Hollywood types. In his prime he was a dead ringer for Tony Curtis but now has wispy, peroxide blond hair and blue eyes he hides behind Wayfarer sunglasses. He had gone the method-acting route and befriended many famous people over the years: Marilyn Monroe, James Dean, Sal Mineo, Lenny Bruce, Jack Nicholson, Janis Joplin, Dennis Hopper.

McQueen then made it worse by flippantly remarking, upon learning Gilmore had been friends with the late James Dean, that he was glad Dean was dead because "it makes more room for me."

Steve McQueen, not so much. It was a former girlfriend of Steve's who introduced them, and the fact that she was dating Gilmore at the same time made it awkward right from the get-go. McQueen then made it worse by flippantly remarking, upon learning Gilmore had been friends with the late James Dean, that he was glad Dean was dead because "it makes more room for me."

"I sort of laughed to let him know I thought he was joking," recalls John, "when I knew he wasn't. His excitement over

James's death 'making more room for him' was a reflection of McQueen's bedrock, almost absolute self-absorption."

When they met again soon after that, McQueen picked up where he left off, denigrating Dean and sneering that he didn't like actors. Gilmore pointedly suggested he was in the wrong profession then, causing McQueen to leave in a huff.

Gilmore also tells me about the time he and Diana—who later became his wife—were having drinks at Louis's when McQueen made, shall we say, a grand entrance. "We were at this small table when all of a sudden we heard the roar of a motorcycle engine then a collision," John says. "We reflexively snatched the drinks from our table when McQueen and his bike plummeted down the steps into the barroom."

> "We were at this small table when all of a sudden we heard the roar of a motorcycle engine then a collision," John says. "We reflexively snatched the drinks from our table when McQueen and his bike plummeted down the steps into the barroom."

According to John, Steve plowed through a glass door and landed face down on the floor, at which point a couple of large gun-toting wise guys carried Steve out of the bar, depositing both him and his bike back on the sidewalk.

John was one of the people who'd seen Steve at his worst—like the night a drunk Julian McQueen was passed out on the floor at Louis's, and Steve—instead of coming to her aid, left her there.

Seeing her in that condition wasn't all that uncommon, John says. Julian often embarrassed Steve by coming on to his friends so they would buy her drinks and just as often wound up on the floor in a stupor.

John had also witnessed the scene when director Frank Corsaro upbraided Steve, then starring in *A Hatful of Rain* at the Lyceum Theatre on Broadway, after McQueen complained about not wanting to go on stage that night because of a sore throat. When McQueen continued to balk, he was replaced by another actor for the run of the play. Not long after that, the prestigious Actor's Studio also cut McQueen loose as a disruptive presence.

As Actor's Studio director Lee Strasberg told the class, "A rattlesnake cannot be aligned with the heart of the family." Though Strasberg didn't identify McQueen by name, "everybody knew who he was talking about," John says.

None of this surprises me.

McQueen was effectively parentless, and in learning to *fend* for himself, he'd also started to think *primarily* of himself. These are survivor skills that one develops when proper parameters aren't established in a child's life. We're all selfish and self-centered by nature. Steve was no exception. And he didn't have much help counteracting it.

Next up is a meeting with one of Steve's former girlfriends, dancer Janet Conway, at the Carnegie Deli on Seventh Avenue. I've heard about this old-school deli for years, where patrons have filled up on pastrami, corned beef, and matzo balls since 1937. Janet suggested this sixty-four-seat venue because it's right across the street from where she met Steve in 1956. Sadly, it's about to close its doors for good. Its aging owner told the *New York Times*, "At this stage in my life, the early morning to late nights have taken a toll, along with my sleepless nights and grueling hours."

I quickly peruse the menu, but there's really no choice other than to get the iconic four-inch thick pastrami sandwich on rye. Janet, who is still in fighting trim at age seventy-eight, orders the same.

After a few bites into our sandwiches, Janet reflects wistfully, "I met Steve at Viola Essen's dance studio, which was located on the eighth floor of Carnegie Hall," says Janet. "I was a seventeen-year-old student at the American Academy of Dramatic Arts, and Steve was a struggling actor who'd been hired by Viola to teach drama classes.

"He was intense, attractive, and kind of mumbled when speaking," she says. "His affectations were charming, and he had the most gorgeous blue eyes I had ever seen. I don't know how or when, but we became an item."

On their dates Janet often picked up the tab. "Part of my attraction for Steve was that he was dead broke," she says with a laugh. "Acting jobs were few and far between." McQueen lived in a rundown cold-water flat at the time, and Janet recalls a bus stop sign he'd stolen off the street and used as a barbell.

> "He was intense, attractive, and kind of mumbled when speaking," she says. "His affectations were charming, and he had the most gorgeous blue eyes I had ever seen. I don't know how or when, but we became an item."

About his acting, she says, "He was absolutely driven," and when McQueen landed a brief, uncredited role in the 1956 movie *Somebody Up There Likes Me,* he rehearsed relentlessly.

"He had a prop on the dresser—a switchblade—and I remember he was working hard to become comfortable with it to make the scene look real. He had talent," Janet says, "and nothing was going to stop him."

They broke up when they were leaving Carnegie Hall one night and she spotted another actor she thought was cute. Steve must have picked up on the vibe, and when she hesitated to hop on the back of his bike, he said, "Either come now or forget it."

"Then forget it," Janet told him.

And that was it.

She bumped into him a few months later when he was starring in a Broadway play. He was standing outside the stage door, invited her into his dressing room, and started to act out the entire play for her. "Steve, I didn't come here to see the play," she told him. "I just wanted to say hello and congratulations"—congratulations not so much for his work but for his upcoming marriage to dancer Neile Adams.

"I was happy for Steve," Janet says, "because it seemed as if he'd finally found the woman he'd been looking for his whole life."

It helped. For a while.

THE BLOB AND THE BIBLE

What in the world was I thinking?

Driving from California to the East Coast and back, stopping in five cities in between—and thinking I could do it all in just seven days?

Maybe if I was forty years younger.

Now it's Friday night, and I have one more stop to make before heading home. If I'm going to make it back to the West Coast for Sunday services, either the Bullitt or I had better sprout wings. I'm exhausted, and not even an espresso IV drip would put me in shape to drive all that way by Sunday.

I suppose I could stash the Bullitt in the hotel garage, hop a flight to the coast, deliver my three sermons, and fly back to New York City the next day. Or hold a Skype session with all twelve thousand members of the church. But then—*voilà!*—the perfect solution pops into my head, and I whip out my smartphone.

"Son," I say when Jonathan answers, back in California, "I have a big favor to ask . . . ."

The story of my son Jonathan is nothing short of a miracle. Today he's an associate pastor at the church I've pastored for more than forty years, Harvest Christian Fellowship. Jonathan literally grew up there. His "uncles" were fellow pastor friends of mine.

While driving to work at the Riverside church, Christopher's car collided with a truck and he was killed. We actually didn't know of it until early that afternoon when three of our pastors told Cathe and me the news no parent ever wants to hear.

Both of our boys—Christopher and Jonathan—believed in Jesus at an early age yet still went prodigal later on, drinking and even using drugs. Christopher actually spent more than nine years wandering in a spiritual wilderness; then, after a lot of prayer by his mother and me, he made a recommitment to Christ at age thirty. He fell in love with a wonderful girl named Brittany, and they gave us our first granddaughter, Stella (named after my grandmother, who in many ways was more of a mother to me than my birth mom).

Christopher was quite a talented artist and worked for a leading design firm in Newport Beach. Then he came to work at our church, heading up our design department. Jonathan took an internship in our outreach event department. I could not have been happier.

Our lives changed forever, though, on July 24, 2008, at 9:01 in the morning—the tragic story I shared with Barbi McQueen in Sun Valley. While driving to work at the Riverside church, Christopher's car collided with a truck and he was killed. We actually didn't know of it until early that afternoon when three of our pastors told Cathe and me the news no parent ever wants to hear.

It was like all the air was sucked out of the room. Time stood still. I collapsed in a heap, and for months went around in a tearful haze. Though I'd been a pastor for many years and counseled countless families who had lost loved ones, I wasn't sure how or if I would survive Christopher's death. Having grown up essentially fatherless, I'd overcompensated with my boys in an effort to give them the stable childhood I never had. And now . . . .

It was unimaginably difficult. It still is.

Jonathan and his brother were very close. He was working the day Christopher died and, like us, was unaware of it until someone who'd gotten the news told him to go home immediately. When he arrived on our street, he saw cars in front of our house and people standing around . . . then saw his dad on the ground, weeping.

At the time Jonathan was engaged in his own struggle with drugs. Just the night before, he and his brother had discussed the problem, and Christopher said, "Jonathan, what's it going to take?"

Now he knew.

Jonathan made his own recommitment to Christ, turned his back on drugs, and never looked back.

Till then he'd never been much for public speaking, but at Christopher's memorial service he spoke so profoundly and eloquently, it was obvious he was evolving in front of our eyes. Jonathan's spiritual growth in the aftermath of his brother's death was a revelation. He served as my personal assistant, we read the Bible together, and I gave him books that had positively impacted me as a young man. Today

Jonathan is a full-fledged pastor at our church and still growing in every way.

So I have no qualms about asking him to fill in for me in
the pulpit this Sunday, and his unhesitating response is pure
balm for my soul: "Dad, I would be honored. Thanks for asking. Please pray for me too."

My extra day in New York allows me to meet with actor
Michael Dante then drive to the Philadelphia suburbs without
being rushed.

Michael is eighty-five years old and in tremendous shape. A
professional baseball player turned actor, he enjoyed television
and movie success for several decades. He's also a very nice
man. I immediately recognized him from his many appearances in films and TV shows, including *Bonanza,* one of my
favorites growing up. I used to watch it with my grandparents
when I lived with them.

We're getting together at the Warwick Hotel in midtown
New York because that's where Michael first encountered
Steve McQueen when both were working on *Somebody Up There
Likes Me.* Michael, then a contract player for MGM Studios,
played "Shorty the Greek" in the film starring Paul Newman.
McQueen was an extra getting a whopping nineteen dollars
a day, and he looked on the star with envy, vowing one day to
catch up to him.

Michael says he was under the canopy of the Warwick Hotel
waiting for the limousine that would take him to the set for
his 8:00 a.m. call. It was pouring rain, he tells me, when all of
a sudden a guy on a motorcycle roared to a stop in front of
him and, in a "very hip, beatnik way," asked where the MGM

company was filming that day. Michael told him to wait there then follow the limousine.

The film set was a half hour away, and the biker—McQueen, of course—arrived there in the limo's wake, soaking wet. He and Dante were assigned to the same dressing room, where McQueen changed out of his sopping clothes into his wardrobe for the day.

In one of the scenes filmed that day, Paul Newman, playing boxer Rocky Graziano, was to stop a truck carrying fur coats and keep the driver occupied while the characters played by Dante, McQueen, and Sal Mineo looted the furs from the back of the vehicle. But the truck's brakes malfunctioned, and it plowed into some equipment, narrowly missing Newman. McQueen was busy checking out hundreds of pigeons flying around the set, and if Dante hadn't pushed him out of the truck's errant path, MGM might have needed a new extra.

> It was well known in the industry that he didn't work with actors who were taller than he was.

According to Dante, years later McQueen muffed a chance to return the favor when the cast was being assembled for *Bullitt*. Producer Phillip D'Antoni had already told Michael that he would get the role as McQueen's cop partner in the movie, and a lunch was scheduled at the Warner Brothers commissary to firm things up. Everything went fine until Michael stood up after the meal to say his good-byes and neglected to slouch. "I had forgotten about McQueen's complex regarding height," he says. "It was well known in the industry that he didn't work with actors who were taller than he was. He looked up at me and said, 'Hey, whoa, man, what did you do? Get taller?'

"I knew then that I was out of the picture."

Sure enough, the coveted role of Sergeant Delgetti went to Don Gordon.

"I liked Steve, thought he was a good guy and a terrific actor, but that one really hurt," acknowledges Michael.

Long before *Bullitt*, however, came *The Blob*.

When McQueen married Neile Adams, she was the better known and more successful of the two, earning fifty thousand dollars a year to his six thousand. When acquaintances started calling him "Mr. Adams," McQueen decided it was time to kick his career into high gear and started looking around for big projects. Nothing materialized until he was offered the lead in a science fiction movie called *The Blob*.

Made by Paramount Pictures, *The Blob* was the studio's highest grossing film of 1958, and today is a cult classic. Filmed in six weeks in a suburb of Philadelphia, the movie was actually the brainchild of an outfit called Good News Productions,

"My first impression was that McQueen was a real jerk," said Howie Fishlove. "He was annoying. He drove around on his motorcycle and kept throwing firecrackers at all of us. I thought, *What in the heck is the matter with this guy?*"

which specialized in religious films. It's owner, Irvin S. "Shorty" Yeaworth, conceived of *The Blob* as a means of connecting with secular film audiences.

The movie's climatic scene was filmed at the Colonial Theatre in Phoenixville, Pennsylvania, and that's where I'm meeting with Jack H. Harris, *The Blob's* producer, as well as Russell Doughten, associate producer, and Howie Fishlove, head grip.

Two hours after leaving New York City, I'm there. The Colonial was completely restored in 1997, and Phoenixville has totally embraced its cinematic claim to fame by hosting an annual, kitschy "BlobFest."

After reviewing artifacts from the movie in several display cases, we sit down for what I'm sure is going to be a fascinating chat. Russell recalls that he and Shorty Yeaworth met McQueen six months before he was cast in *The Blob*. Neile was working in a project for Good News Productions at the time, and McQueen was constantly underfoot, making such a pest of himself that when he expressed interest in *The Blob,* they weren't much interested in him. But he read for the lead role in the low budget ($130,000) production and got it.

> "Every day the filmmakers would go into prayer meetings. They would always finish by saying, 'And save us from Steve McQueen!'"

They almost instantly regretted it.

"My first impression was that McQueen was a real jerk," said Howie Fishlove. "He was annoying. He drove around on his motorcycle and kept throwing firecrackers at all of us. I thought, *What in the heck is the matter with this guy?*"

McQueen was demanding and temperamental throughout the shoot, and when he was arrested one day for recklessly driving his MG Sports Roadster, Jack Harris decided it was time to have a talk with him. After bailing him out, he sat down his leading man and told him to shape up. But as they talked, Harris realized something: what McQueen craved and needed, more than anything, was constant approbation—praise, acceptance, encouragement.

"He wanted approval," says Jack, who is a spry ninety-eight years old. "What he was looking for was somebody to be Daddy and say, 'You're a nice guy and I like you.'"

Harris's stroking worked up to a point, but the production staff knew they needed more than just cheerleading to keep McQueen in line. As his female costar Aneta Corsaut recalled, "Every day the filmmakers would go into prayer meetings. They would always finish by saying, 'And save us from Steve McQueen!'"

But they also prayed *for* him.

> Later, when standing at the pinnacle of success in his chosen field, Steve McQueen would find out that all the stuff this world offers isn't everything it's cracked up to be. It doesn't satisfy in the end.

"It was easy to tell Steve wasn't saved," says Russell. "He was materialistic, hedonistic, and profane, like most people. He would talk to me about the Bible; sometimes he'd argue, but he wasn't vehement. He knew he was a sinner. He wasn't trying *not* to be a sinner.

"I talked to him about materialistic things and how he was making those possessions more important to him than a relationship with Christ. I think that his time with us on *The Blob* showed him how true Christians lived, acted, and worked."

At the time, however, McQueen was only interested in movie stardom, and his singular, self-absorbed focus bothered Doughten, who says, "Frankly, I saw him entering the wilderness of the world."

When the movie was done, Doughten presented his troubled and troublesome star with a Bible, in which he'd bookmarked and underlined the verse for John 3:16 KJV: "For God so loved the world, that he gave his only begotten Son, that

Form V. S. 1

PLACE OF BIRTH | INDIANA STATE BOARD OF HEALTH
DIVISION OF VITAL STATISTICS

¹County of _264 S. Marion_

CERTIFICATE OF BIRTH

Township of _____

Town of _Beech Grove_

or

City of _____ No. _St. Francis Hosp._ St., _____ Ward)

Local No. _187_

13026

State Registered No. _264 S._

²FULL NAME OF CHILD _Terrence Stephen McQueen_
If child is not named, make supplemental report. (Please Print Child's Name)

³Sex of Child _M._ | ⁴Twins, Triplets, or others? (To be answered only in event of plural births) and ⁵Number in order of birth | ⁶Legitimate? _Yes_ | ⁷Date of Birth _March 24_ 19_30_ (Month) (Day) (Year)

⁸Full Name Father _William McQueen_ | ¹¹Full Maiden Name MOTHER _Jullian Crawford_

⁹Postoffice Address _1311 Drexel Ave_ | ¹⁵Postoffice Address _1311 Drexel Ave._

¹⁰Color or Race _W._ | ¹¹Age at last Birthday _23_ (Years) | ¹⁶Color or Race _W._ | ¹⁷Age at last Birthday _20_ (Years)

¹²Birthplace _Nashville Tenn._ | ¹⁸Birthplace _St. Louis Mo._

¹³Occupation _Gas Merchant._ | ¹⁹Occupation _Housewife_

²⁰Number of children born to this mother, including present birth _1_ | ²¹Number of children, of this mother, now living, including present birth _1_ | ²²Were precautions taken against ophthalmia neonatorum? _Yes_

CERTIFICATE OF ATTENDING PHYSICIAN OR MIDWIFE

I hereby certify that I attended the birth of this child, who was _born alive_ at _12:55_ □ M.
on the date above stated. (Born alive or Stillborn)

*When there was no attending physician or midwife, then the father, householder, etc., should make this return. A stillborn child is one that neither breathes nor shows other evidence of life after birth.

(Signature) _L. H. Stafford_
801-2 K of P Bldg
(Attending physician, midwife, householder)

Given name added from a supplemental report_____, 19____

Address _____

Filed _4-3-_ , 19_30_ _J. H. Mayer M.D._
HEALTH OFFICER

Proof of Life — Steve McQueen's original birth certificate, which finally surfaced in 2016 thanks to the dogged efforts of Diane Sharp, head of the Genealogy Collection at the Indiana State Library. The March 24, 1930, birth certificate lists his parents as William McQueen and Jullian Crawford. Courtesy of the Indiana State Library.

St. Francis Hospital in Beech Grove, Indiana, circa 1927 — This photo was taken approximately three years before Steve McQueen was born. He lived in Beech Grove for the first few years of his life with his mother and maternal grandparents. Courtesy of St. Francis Hospital.

Thomson homestead — Steve McQueen moved to Slater, Missouri, sometime in the early to mid-1930s to stay with his Uncle Claude Thomson, who ran a bustling hog farm. Claude was the first of several father figures Steve accumulated throughout his life. Courtesy of Slater Main Street News.

It's a Drag — Main Street in Slater, Missouri during the 1930s, the same decade when Steve McQueen walked these streets. It was and still is an agricultural and hog farming community, but has seen a steady decline in its population in the last half-century. Courtesy of Slater Main Street News.

William McQueen with native — a rare and vintage photo of Steve McQueen's father, William, on one of his many travels as a merchant marine. Steve searched for his father for many years, but the two men never met. Courtesy of Terri McQueen.

Abbott's Chapel — Orearville School, the one-room schoolhouse outside of Slater where Steve McQueen was first educated. It now sits just off Main Street and has been converted into a chapel. Courtesy of Marshall Terrill.

Boys Republic — Steve McQueen's delinquent behavior as a teen landed him at the Boys Republic in 1945. This team photo of the baseball team is the only physical proof of his 14-month stay at the reform school. He credited Boys Republic with turning his life around and bequeathed $200,000 to them in death. Courtesy of the Boys Republic.

Marines — Steve McQueen enlisted in the United States Marines in 1947 when he was 17. He was assigned to a tank unit and credits the organization with giving him much needed discipline and a jumping off point for acting. Courtesy of the Motion Picture Academy of Arts and Sciences.

First headshot — A girlfriend once told Steve he was "kooky" and charismatic, and should try his hand at acting. He found a sanctuary at Sanford Meisner's Playhouse. This is his first professional headshot, circa early 1950s. Courtesy of the Motion Picture Academy of Arts and Sciences.

Girl on the Run — Fame didn't come very quickly to McQueen and like many other beginners, he took whatever he could to build acting credits. McQueen served as an extra in two scenes in "Girl On the Run," a 1953 film that was unmemorable and quickly faded into the sunset. Courtesy of Astor Pictures.

The Great Escape — Steve McQueen was an expert motorcycle rider and used those skills in "The Great Escape," his breakout role. The World War II epic catapulted McQueen to international stardom in 1963 and made him the first television star to successfully transition to film. Courtesy of United Artists Films.

Cry Baby Cry — "Hatful of Rain" was Steve McQueen's first big break on Broadway, but he found the live stage difficult to conquer. Specifically, he didn't like emoting or long lines of dialogue, which he is doing in this photo with actor Harry Guardino. Sadly, McQueen washed out after three months. Courtesy of Donna Redden.

The Teacher and his Pupil — Steve McQueen was selected to the prestigious Actors Studio in New York, headed by Lee Strasberg. The famed acting coach respected McQueen's acting talents, but abhorred his self-serving behavior and asked him to leave. New York was a dead end by the late 1950s, and so McQueen headed for Hollywood. Courtesy of the Motion Picture Academy of Arts and Sciences.

Good Ol' Josh — America was first introduced to Steve McQueen as bounty hunter Josh Randall in "Wanted: Dead or Alive." The CBS television series debuted in 1958 and made McQueen a household name. Courtesy of CBS Television.

A Night on the Town — Steve with first wife Neile and his mother, Julian, for a night on the town in New York City, late 1950s. His mother was a constant source of heartbreak and they barely reconciled their differences when she passed away in 1965. Courtesy of the Motion Picture Academy of Arts and Sciences.

Party Animal — As McQueen's stardom grew, so did his appetite for drugs, alcohol and indiscriminate sex. Here he is at a party with wife Neile in the late 1960s. Courtesy of the Motion Picture Academy of Arts and Sciences.

The Kids — Steve McQueen's children, Terry Leslie and Chadwick Steven, brought him great joy. Despite his painful childhood, Steve McQueen was a kind and loving father to his children. Courtesy of Motion Picture Academy of Arts and Sciences.

A Fast Machine — Lt. Frank Bullitt and his Ford Mustang took audiences for a thrill ride in 1968's "Bullitt." The cop drama was McQueen's defining role and one of the biggest grossing films of the decade. It minted the actor into a bonafide superstar. Courtesy of Warner-7 Arts.

Epic Soldier — Director Robert Wise guided Steve McQueen to his first and only Academy Award nomination in "The Sand Pebbles." The 1966 movie epic was shot almost entirely on location in Taiwan. Courtesy of the Motion Picture Academy of Arts and Sciences.

Paris, Anyone? — Steve McQueen was the No. 1 movie star in the world and wildly popular with the public as evidenced in this 1964 trip to Paris, France, where he and his wife attended the premiere of "Love With the Proper Stranger." Courtesy of the Motion Picture Academy of Arts and Sciences.

Speed Racer – 'Le Mans' was the 1971 racing film that unraveled Steve McQueen's personal and professional life at the start of the decade. While it is hailed as a cult film today, the movie was problematic and underscored McQueen's out of control ego. Courtesy of National General Pictures.

Steve and Ali - McQueen found love and box-office success again in "The Getway." His co-star in the 1972 heist film was Ali MacGraw, whom he later married. Their union was passionate but stormy, lasting approximately five years. Courtesy of Karen Hornbaker.

Two for the Show — "The Towering Inferno" united two of the decade's brightest stars in Paul Neman (left) and Steve McQueen (right). The 1974 disaster film gave McQueen an opportunity to catch up to Newman. The foot race left McQueen emotionally drained and wanting to take a break from the industry. Courtesy of Twentieth Century-Fox and Warner Bros.

Butterfly in Bloom — Steve McQueen hit his creative stride as a safe-cracking thief in "Papillon." Many believe the 1973 worldwide smash was his finest cinematic work. Courtesy of Allied Artists.

Bearded and Guarded — After the monster success of "The Towering Inferno," Steve McQueen grew his hair long and sprouted a large beard and became nearly unrecognizable. In this mid-1970s photo, the light has clearly left his eyes. Courtesy of the Motion Picture Academy of Arts and Sciences.

Learning to Fly — In 1979, Steve McQueen moved to Santa Paula, California, known as the "Antique Airplane Capital of the World" so he could indulge in his latest passion — flying planes. He and Barbara Minty moved into an airplane hangar where they lived with a collection of planes, cars, motorcycles and antique toys. Courtesy of Barbara Minty McQueen.

Father Figure — In Santa Paula, McQueen not only found a pilot but a father figure in Sammy Mason. His influence on McQueen was profound and eventually led him to accept Jesus Christ as his Lord and Savior. Courtesy of Barbara Minty McQueen.

Malibu Barbi — Barbara Minty was a Ford Model who was almost half of Steve McQueen's age, but they had a true connection of the heart, mind and soul. They first settled in Malibu, where this photo was taken. McQueen appears to be happy and in love. Courtesy of Barbara Minty McQueen.

Here Comes the Sun — The very first picture Barbara Minty took of Steve McQueen, circa 1977. The setting was the Rocky Mountains near Denver, Colorado, and the backlight of the sun makes McQueen appear almost ethereal and vulnerable. Courtesy of Barbara Minty McQueen.

Wedding Day — The exchange of wedding vows between Steve McQueen and Barbara Minty on January 16, 1980 officially made them man and wife. Reverend Leslie Miller of the Ventura Missionary Church, married the two and received a dozen fresh farm eggs for his services. Courtesy of Barbara Minty McQueen.

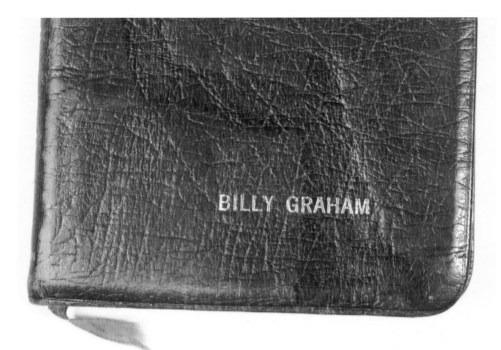

Bible Cover – The ninety-page New Testament Bible that evangelist Billy Graham gave to Steve McQueen days before his passing. It became his proudest possession in his final days and McQueen was clutching it when he passed. Courtesy of Marshall Terrill.

Inscription – Billy Graham's inscription in Steve McQueen's Bible read: 'To my friend Steve McQueen, may God bless and keep you always. Billy Graham, Philippians 1:6. November 3, 1980. Courtesy of Marshall Terrill.

A Star in the Sky — On June 12, 1986, Steve McQueen was inducted to the Hollywood Walk of Fame. But on Nov. 7, 1980, the day he died, his name was written into the Lamb's Book of Life. Courtesy of Marshall Terrill.

Last Photo — Steve McQueen having coffee, reading the newspaper and enjoying an open fire in a lit smudge pot in the backyard of his Santa Paula home. Barbara Minty McQueen said it was his favorite part of the day. She took this last photo of him in late spring 1980. Courtesy of Barbara Minty McQueen.

Christmas 2016. Jonathan, Brittni, Allie, Rylie, Cathe, Christopher, Greg, Lucy, Stella, Brittany, Robbie

Greg in his military school uniform.

Greg, age 6, hanging out with his brother Doug.

Greg and his mom (Charlene) sometime in the 1950s.

Greg and Cathe Laurie, late 1970s.

Laurie's two sons, Christopher and Jonathan. Hawaii, 2004.

Greg and Cathe Laurie, 2017.

whosoever believeth in him should not perish, but have everlasting life."

I think we can safely assume this message was lost on McQueen back then. But not forever. That's how spiritual seeds work. They're sown into people's lives at various times and places, like into a cocky twenty-something actor on the set of *The Blob,* and they begin to germinate. The gospel takes root.

This word itself, *gospel,* means "good news"—namely, that there is a God in heaven who loves every one of us. From birth we are separated from Him by sin, but God's Son Jesus died on the cross to pay for our sins so we can be free to discover what life is truly all about. Knowing this, believing this, makes everything else pale in comparison.

Later, when standing at the pinnacle of success in his chosen field, Steve McQueen would find out that all the stuff this world offers isn't everything it's cracked up to be. It doesn't satisfy in the end. But sometimes, in searching for personal peace—as he did his whole life—a guy must first discover where it's *not* before he discovers where it *is.*

CALIFORNIA DREAMIN'

The East Coast was nice, but California is home. And, boy, am I glad to be home. And warm. Winter sure comes early back east.

I met a lot of nice folks there and got a whole new perspective on Steve McQueen.

But the journey is only halfway finished. Now comes the real meat of the story: McQueen's move to California. The years of stardom. The freewheelin' 1960s and '70s. Sex, drugs, rock 'n' roll—and redemption.

Hollywood was McQueen's last hope. Steve was finished in New York after he got sacked from *A Hatful of Rain*. But he had Neile, whose unstinting belief in him was one of the chief reasons he was finally able to open up and trust someone. And when they arrived in California, she made a call to her agent, the late Hilly Elkins, begging him to help her husband.

Elkins lobbied hard to get McQueen a screen test at CBS, which resulted in a role on the series *Tales of Wells Fargo* that paid four hundred dollars for three days' work.

Then came the stardom McQueen was so desperate for, as bounty hunter Josh Randall. McQueen first appeared as Randall on a series called *Trackdown* and was so spellbinding that a spin-off series was created specifically for him called *Wanted: Dead or Alive*, which debuted on September 6, 1958.

Producer Vincent M. Fennelly chose McQueen for the lead role, he said, because Josh Randall "was a little guy. Everyone's against him except the audience. And McQueen was offbeat. He wasn't the best-looking guy in the world, but he had a nice kind of animal instinct. He could be nice but with some sort of menace underneath."

McQueen's Josh Randall preferred to bring the bad guys he tracked back alive, and it was his inherent decency that made *Wanted: Dead or Alive* so appealing. That's why I tuned in every Saturday night, sandwiched between my granddad and grandmother on the couch. There was a visceral connection between the man in the cowboy hat and me.

> "McQueen was offbeat. He wasn't the best-looking guy in the world, but he had a nice kind of animal instinct. He could be nice but with some sort of menace underneath."

To give me some insight on the star of *Wanted: Dead or Alive*, I turn to Loren Janes, who was Steve McQueen's longtime friend and favorite stunt double. We're meeting at the entrance of the CBS Studios on Radford Avenue in Studio City, the former site of Four Star Studios where Janes first met McQueen in 1958. Loren was a world-class athlete and Olympic fencer who became one of the top stuntmen in Hollywood. For a moment I am stunned because he looks just like McQueen.

For a guy who longed for showbiz success, McQueen wasn't too thrilled with it once it came. He was quite uneasy at first about working in a Hollywood "television factory." He liked the "bread" and perks of being on television, but he wanted to be a movie star, and not many of those made the leap from the boob-tube to the silver screen. Yet McQueen liked and identified with the character of Josh Randall.

"[He] seemed to be a loner," McQueen said, "a guy who made his own decisions; and he didn't have a big star on his chest. This appealed to me."

Stuntmen did not appeal to him, and on his very first day on the set of *Wanted: Dead or Alive,* McQueen fired three of them. One of them was even former Academy Award-winning actor Richard Farnsworth, who started his career performing stunts and, ironically, would not only end up in one of McQueen's last films, *Tom Horn,* but become a trusted friend.

> Stuntmen did not appeal to him, and on his very first day on the set of *Wanted: Dead or Alive*, McQueen fired three of them.

When Janes arrived at Four Star that day in 1958, he immediately reported to director Tommy Carr. As they discussed the first scene in which he would be doubling for McQueen, Janes was very much aware of the star standing nearby staring at him. Janes was dressed exactly like him, this leading man who wanted the public to believe that no one doubled him when it came time to do the stunts.

Janes performed a series of flawless stunts that even astounded the star, thus cementing a friendship that lasted up till McQueen's death twenty-two years later.

Not surprisingly, McQueen butted heads with everybody else connected with the series. "He drove them all nuts," recalls Loren with a chuckle. "Producers, writers, actors—he argued with everybody. But he had a good sense about things. Plus, he'd been around. He knew the bad part of life and the sad part. His attitude was, 'I'm here to do a job. All the nice guys in Hollywood are standing in the unemployment line.'"

That was McQueen the actor. Impossible.

But as a *person*, he was often moved by the plight of people in need and acted accordingly—and anonymously. Loren tells me that while filming *The Sand Pebbles* in Taiwan seven years later, McQueen quietly donated twenty-five thousand dollars to a local orphanage, which a Catholic priest ran and which catered mainly to young girls whose families forced them to turn to prostitution. He says it was the first of many such donations, and that he supported the orphanage for a good decade until the priest passed away in the late 1970s.

> That was McQueen the actor. Impossible.

"Steve was a very generous man," says Loren. "He would give the shirt off his back to anyone who needed it."

I find this to be a fascinating trait of McQueen's. Instead of press releases and photo ops to show a celebrity "giving back," as is so common today, he flew under the radar, never even revealing the things he did for the less fortunate.

On another movie set in a rural town, recollects Janes, "Steve noticed the town's park had no playground equipment. A week after we left, a large truck arrived at the park, bringing swings, slides, monkey bars, teeter-totters, and a small merry-go-round. No one knew who paid for it—except Steve and me."

While filming McQueen's final movie, *The Hunter*, in a rough section of Chicago, a group of young boys playing football in a nearby empty lot recognized Steve and threw him the ball. It was old and tattered, stuffed with rags and held together with wire.

"Steve handed me hundreds of dollars in cash," recalls Loren, "and I went to a sporting goods store and purchased footballs, baseball bats, mitts, and baseballs," Loren says. "Delivery men brought the bounty to a dirt lot the next afternoon. Steve and I hid in a van and watched the kids rip open the boxes, screaming in excitement. I looked over at Steve and his eyes were moist."

He did it because he was once one of them. He understood. And he never forgot where he came from.

> **"Delivery men brought the bounty to a dirt lot the next afternoon. Steve and I hid in a van and watched the kids rip open the boxes, screaming in excitement. I looked over at Steve and his eyes were moist."**

What a mercurial human being was Hollywood's most famous bounty hunter. So much of McQueen's behavior was abhorrent at the time, but then there were these intermittent glimmers of humanity, baring a heart and soul full of compassion, empathy, and charity.

Yet sadly, over the next few years the ever-striving star seemed to do everything in his power to sublimate if not sacrifice these good things to his overweening ambition and need for instant gratification.

THE AMERICAN DREAM

At the start of the 1960s, Steve McQueen stood on the precipice of the American dream, albeit a gilded, much more fantastic version of the one most people have. He was starring in a popular network television series that afforded him a nice home in the Hollywood Hills and a couple of sports cars that enabled him to pursue his passion of auto racing. He was married to a successful, supportive, and nurturing woman who put up with his wild mood swings and unpredictable temper. He was blessed with two children—Terry Leslie, born June 5, 1959, and Chadwick Steven, born December 28, 1960. As it was said of McQueen at the time, "Every man wants to be like him, and every woman wants to be with him."

Simply put, he had it all—looks, fame, security, love, and family.

So why, then, wasn't he happy and fulfilled?

Steve McQueen was not the first to deal with this conundrum. Nor would he be the last. This quest for happiness goes back as far as the recorded word. Augustine (354–430 AD) said, "Everyman, whatsoever his condition, desires to be happy." Nearly thirteen centuries later, French philosopher and mathematician Blaise Pascal wrote, "All men seek happiness. This is without exception!"

The lead singer in one of the biggest rock bands in the world said, "You ask me if I'm happy? Listen: I've bought myself a Rolls Royce. I'm part of the biggest band in the world, and I'm about to live in a luxurious mansion. Am I happy with that? No—I want more!"

The lead singer in one of the biggest rock bands in the world said, "You ask me if I'm happy? Listen: I've bought myself a Rolls Royce. I'm part of the biggest band in the world, and I'm about to live in a luxurious mansion. Am I happy with that? No—I want more!"

Jack Higgins is one of the most successful authors on earth. His thriller novels have sold more than 150 million copies in sixty different languages. When asked by a magazine writer what he knew now that he wished he'd known earlier in life, the accomplished author responded, "I wish I had known that when you get to the top, there is nothing there."

That's the way fame works. It's one thing to climb to the top of the hill; it's another thing to stay there.

What Steve McQueen was searching for, and for that matter what all of us are searching for, is something that cannot be found in material possessions, experiences, or even relationships.

Because deep down inside, we are all searching for God.

C. S. Lewis wrote, "God designed the human machine to run on Himself. He Himself is the fuel our spirits were designed to burn, or the food our spirits were designed to feed on. There is no other. That is why it is just no good asking God to make us happy in our own way without bothering about religion. God cannot give us a happiness and peace apart from Himself, because it is not there."

Up to this point in his life, Steve McQueen had so many disappointments—from a mother who was mostly a mother in name only to a father who never was. McQueen had hardened himself to survive, but deep down inside he was still like a boy looking for a father.

Bottom line, Steve was searching for God. He just didn't know it. At least not yet.

Now that *Wanted: Dead or Alive* had made him a star, McQueen acted the part to the hilt. On the set he butted into everyone's business, demanding that even the smallest aspects of the show's production be done his way. He personally liked John Robinson, the show's producer-writer, but nagged, criticized, and humiliated him to the point that at the end of the second season, Robinson went on permanent sick leave.

> Bottom line, Steve was searching for God. He just didn't know it. At least not yet.

Flush with cash from the show, McQueen bought himself a 1958 Porsche Speedster and started racing on weekends in events sponsored by the Sports Car Club of America. He won his very first race on May 30, 1959, and showed so much skill on the track that he was voted "Rookie of the Year" by the American Sports Car Association.

He loved speed and competition, and over the years would race cars and motorcycles all over the world. An inveterate tinkerer, McQueen was never happier than when rebuilding antique cars and motorcycles.

The racing itself, he once said, "keeps my equilibrium intact. It makes it difficult to believe I'm God's gift to humanity. When you're racing a motorcycle, the guy on the next bike doesn't care who you are. And if he beats you in the race, well, it means he's a better man than you are. And he's not afraid to tell you that you're lousy."

As for TV, McQueen figured it was strictly for actors who'd gone as far as they could, like Clayton "Lone Ranger" Moore. He was in a hurry to graduate to the big screen, and he got his chance when director John Sturges, impressed with Steve's looks and potential, cast him in his 1959 film *Never So Few*. Frank Sinatra, the star of the movie, lacked McQueen's fire-in-the-belly when it came to the craft of acting and didn't mind giving Steve all the rope he wanted.

McQueen was never happier than when rebuilding antique cars and motorcycles.

The result was a memorable performance. He turned the wise-cracking, scene-stealing supply sergeant into the forerunner of the roles he would later play in almost all of his movies—cool, understated, and extremely at ease with a gun in his hand or behind the wheel.

McQueen also drew raves from critics. "[McQueen] possesses that combination of smooth-rough charm that suggests star possibilities," noted the *New York Herald Tribune*, while *The Hollywood Reporter* called the picture a "catapult to stardom."

Sinatra's generosity extended far beyond MGM's back lot. Not long after the film wrapped, he invited Steve and Neile back east to spend a gala-filled week with him and his entourage. The McQueens were taken backstage to Sinatra's homecoming concert in Atlantic City and accompanied him to the glittery *Never So Few* premiere at Radio City Music Hall.

Getting to hang with Sinatra for a week opened a picture window on the A-lister's lifestyle, which included private jets, limousines, red-carpet events, screaming fans, opened doors, and plenty of respect and fawning admiration. Steve got a whiff of real stardom up close, and it must have been intoxicating.

"I want some of that," he whispered to his wife Neile. A few years later, those same courtesies would be extended to McQueen for the rest of his life.

Next came another Sturges film, the epic western *The Magnificent Seven,* whose release in 1960 stamped McQueen as the movie star he always envisioned himself to be. He was part of an ensemble cast that included Oscar winner Yul Brynner, Charles Bronson, James Coburn, Robert Vaughn, Horst Buchholz, Brad Dexter, and Eli Wallach. Topping professionals of this stature in front of the camera was a constant dogfight, and with the somewhat tacit support of Sturges, Steve used every trick in the book to do it. Brynner famously resented and raged at the upstart's tactics but was powerless to overcome them.

> Steve got a whiff of real stardom up close, and it must have been intoxicating. "I want some of that," he whispered to his wife Neile.

Having attained big screen success at last, McQueen had no more interest in or use for *Wanted: Dead or Alive.* So when CBS reluctantly pulled the plug on the show on March 29, 1961, he celebrated his release from living rooms all over America with a mighty whoop.

In 1961–62 he made *The Honeymoon Machine, Hell Is for Heroes,* and *The War Lover.* While filming *The War Lover* in England, McQueen competed in several car races with such panache that he was offered a contract to race full-time for the British Motor Corporation. He wrestled over the proposition.

"They gave me a weekend to make up my mind," McQueen told a reporter. "I spent two full days in a sweat, trying to decide whether I wanted to go into pro racing, earning my money on the track, or whether to continue being an actor. It was a very tough decision to make, because I didn't know if I was an actor who raced or a racer who acted. But I had Neile and the two children to consider, and that made the difference."

Glad to hear him say that. Considering the fact that Steve McQueen was never properly fathered himself, he chose to be a highly involved father, often taking his son and daughter and wife with him to movie sets and spending a lot of time with them. As a fatherless son myself, I can completely relate. I wanted to give my two sons the life I never had. Steve seemed to want the same thing and was deeply loved by his children.

> Considering the fact that Steve McQueen was never properly fathered himself, he chose to be a highly involved father, often taking his son and daughter and wife with him to movie sets and spending a lot of time with them.

Therefore, he ultimately stuck with acting—and was glad he did when John Sturges came around again with the script for *The Great Escape.* McQueen didn't hesitate to sign on, recognizing the film as his opportunity to achieve a new level of stardom, thanks to a barbed-wire fence, a motorbike, a steely look of determination, and the most breathtaking leap of faith ever seen in movies.

It isn't likely that McQueen recognized *The Great Escape* as a providential gift. But the only god that Steve knew at this time in his life was called Success, and he worshipped it with all his might.

A MAN AND HIS CASTLE

When Steve McQueen's character Virgil Hilts soared over that barbed-wire fence in *The Great Escape*, it was a metaphorical jump as well as a cinematic one.

The leap (actually made by stuntman Bud Ekins) took Steve from mere television celebrity to international movie star. That had never happened before, and now McQueen was about to enter his own golden era.

If the 1950s were about McQueen learning his craft, and the early '60s about his rise to stardom, the rest of the decade marked his full ascension to power and dominance. The string of back-to-back hits he assembled after *The Great Escape* would see him achieve everything he wanted, although there would be costs along the way. The actor who once grabbed any role he could get—including the lead role in *The Blob*—now had producers shamelessly pleading with him just to read their scripts.

The roles McQueen chose—a brooding musician (*Love with the Proper Stranger*), a loner card shark (*The Cincinnati Kid*), a naïve half-breed-turned-ruthless avenger (*Nevada Smith*), reluctant war hero (*The Sand Pebbles*), white-collar bank robber (*The Thomas Crown Affair*), and laconic cop (*Bullitt*)—extended his range of characters and performances to a level unsurpassed, forming an archetype still referenced and revered by actors today. McQueen consolidated his image as the leading man of the era, the quintessential action star of the twentieth century and, most importantly, became global cinema's King of Cool.

> When Steve McQueen's character Virgil Hilts soared over that barbed-wire fence in *The Great Escape*, it was a metaphorical jump as well as a cinematic one.

But a king needs a castle, and in 1963 McQueen bought his. The three-and-a-half-acre estate at 27 Oakmont Drive in exclusive Brentwood cost him a quarter of a million dollars. Today the place is worth about seven million.

He later recalled, "We had to get out of our other house because it was too small, and we started looking around, and this real estate lady, a very nice one, said she knew a house we'd love and she might be able to get it for us."

What the very nice lady didn't mention was the asking price. As the McQueens took a tour of the 5,560-square-foot, Spanish-Mediterranean-style home with five bedrooms, Olympic-size swimming pool, tennis court, and panoramic view of the Pacific Ocean, Steve decided it was probably way beyond their means. But a big Hollywood star never acknowledges such a thing to anyone, and before they left he had signed on the dotted line.

Right now the Bullitt is parked outside the front gate of this fabulous estate, just above Sunset Boulevard, which is quite fitting, considering that I'm meeting actor Edd "Kookie" Byrnes here.

Star of the popular TV show *77 Sunset Strip*, Edd is one of the few actors of that era who chose to remain in Los Angeles. The city is overcrowded, overpriced, and gets harder to navigate all the time. More than anything else, the acting business has changed since Edd made girls go, "like, Wowsville," just by running a comb through his hair and talking nonsensical hip.

A king needs a castle, and in 1963 McQueen bought his. The three-and-a-half-acre estate at 27 Oakmont Drive in exclusive Brentwood cost him a quarter of a million dollars. Today the place is worth about six million.

Back then the big studios ruled the town, as well as the actors who were under contract to them, tightly controlling their public images and especially their wallets. Byrnes says he found this out when he got into a contractual dispute with Warner Brothers after three years on *77 Sunset Strip*. Though he was the reigning TV heartthrob of that time, he was paid just five hundred dollars a week to appear in the show. Other studios came to him offering $250,000 to do a movie, but Warner Brothers wouldn't let Edd accept any of them. When he demanded a higher salary, Warner Brothers nixed that too.

His plight didn't get much sympathy, however, from fellow actors. He remembers at a party one night being confronted by entertainment legend Lucille Ball, a person he'd never met before, who read him the riot act for bucking the studio.

There was one star, though, who supported Byrnes. "Hold your ground," read a telegram Steve McQueen sent to him. Such defiant solidarity led to their becoming friends, naturally—enough that McQueen once invited him out to his new mansion after bumping into him on the street. He'd just purchased the Castle and wanted to show Edd his latest acquisition.

Most people are a bundle of contradictions. Steve McQueen was a mountain of them.

"He [Steve] confided to me, 'I have no idea how I'm ever going to pay for this place. You'd better believe I'm going to show up early every day for work," recalls Byrnes.

That was in the early '60s. And as often happens, life and work conspired after that to keep both of them busy and out of contact. Edd hadn't seen McQueen for years until one day in the mid-'70s, when Byrnes was standing outside an antique shop on the Sunset Strip, window shopping. He heard a voice behind him ask, "Do you own this shop, Edd?"

Byrnes turned and saw a bearded fellow who "looked like a hairy version of the Old Spice Man." They began to chat, and it was several minutes before it dawned on Edd that he was talking to Steve McQueen.

"He looked so unlike himself," says Edd. "By then he had reached a level of superstardom that only a few in our industry have ever occupied, and he needed a little anonymity."

Most people are a bundle of contradictions. Steve McQueen was a mountain of them: never satisfied with what he had, always wanting to impress himself more than anyone else with how far he'd come in life, never achieving the security and peace that was supposed to come with it, and determined to satisfy his every whim as a distraction from the emotional insecurity that made him a sort of Jekyll and Hyde.

And let's not sugarcoat the fact that he was less than chaste in his moral habits. By all accounts he loved his wife and children, but he was not a faithful husband who enjoyed nights in front of the family hearth.

What he did enjoy was patronizing the Whisky A Go-Go, the famous nightclub on the Sunset Strip, where I'm off to next for another rendezvous. That's the word you use when the person you're meeting is glamourous Mamie Van Doren.

Mamie in the '50s was a sex symbol second only to Marilyn Monroe. And now at eighty-five, she must have had a drink or two from the fountain of youth because to a large degree she has successfully defied the aging process.

Except for workers prepping for the evening crowd, we just about have the venerable Whisky to ourselves at midafternoon. Sad to say, unlike Mamie, the iconic nightclub has not weathered the passing years so well. The legendary venue that launched the Doors, Johnny Rivers, the Buffalo Springfield, the Byrds, and so many other classic rock acts of that era now derives most of its revenue from renting out a large billboard on its roof.

That night with McQueen was Mamie's first acid trip, and it was a bad one. She says the bizarre hallucinations haunted her for weeks afterward.

The club itself is rented out to pay-to-play bands anxious to brag about appearing at what was once the hottest spot in town when it opened its doors in January 1964.

McQueen was a regular back then in the halcyon days, and that's where Mamie first met him. One night after some dancing, McQueen suggested they get out of there and have a private party at Mamie's place.

"It was the '60s," she says with a smile and shrug.

Because Mamie had a young child at home who kept interrupting them, nothing happened that first night. A few nights later, though, McQueen took Mamie to a swinging party at the home of one of his best friends, hairstylist Jay Sebring. She says they ended up dropping acid.

McQueen chased after every worldly pleasure once he realized how fame widened his sphere of female admirers. He picked up women everywhere he went.

"You could get LSD over the counter then," says Mamie. "I had a carpenter who was always doing LSD."

That night with McQueen was Mamie's first acid trip, and it was a bad one. She says the bizarre hallucinations haunted her for weeks afterward. She never did acid with McQueen again, but they did pop amyl nitrate, also readily available back then.

Mamie says McQueen reminded her a lot of her dad, "a mechanic who rode an Indian motorcycle just like Steve and was a grease monkey at heart."

McQueen, she adds, "was a lot like all the mechanics I knew. He preferred T-shirts and jeans and always had a little grime and grease underneath his fingernails. He was just a guy in the movies and treated it like a regular job."

In their conversations he frequently alluded to problems in his marriage, but any hope for the two of them to enjoy a meaningful relationship was ended, she says, by his increasing drug use. "Steve was constantly on the edge and looking for something higher," she says. "He was on drugs a lot, and I just did not like them at all."

McQueen chased after every worldly pleasure once he realized how fame widened his sphere of female admirers. He picked up women everywhere he went, usually taking them to an office he rented in Santa Monica expressly for that purpose.

One of his best friends, Bud Ekins, told one McQueen biographer, "To Steve, the world was just a giant sexual supermarket. He constantly had women chasing him, and he couldn't say no. He just couldn't control himself. When he saw something he wanted—a woman, a motorcycle, a car—he'd go for it. Everything he did was extreme. He liked an extreme amount of sex, an extreme amount of marijuana, and an extreme amount of cocaine. Everything he did was extreme."

That approach to life would surely bring its consequences.

Steve would discover the truth of the passage from the Bible that speaks of the "Fleeting pleasures of sin " (Heb. 11:25 NLT). Forbidden things are often the most attractive, but there's a reason why they are forbidden. What we don't think about is the cold, dead feeling these pleasures ultimately lead us to.

And yet Steve could tell a reporter with a straight face, "When I'm not making a picture, I spend all of my time fixing my car. My wife doesn't have to worry about other women; she knows where to find me." He also could (and did) show genuine concern for others, such as the residents of his reform school alma mater, which he supported through scholarships and visits whenever he could manage. And unlike the other, that was no sham.

A mountain of contradictions? Mountain *range* was more like it.

MOTHERLESS CHILD

I'm at Forest Lawn Memorial Park in Glendale, California, standing next to a large cypress tree on a hill. Before me and shaded by the tree's limbs is a brass plaque that reads:

> *Julian Crawford McQueen*
> *BERRI*
> *1910 – 1965*
> *Loved By Your Son Steve*

The death of McQueen's mother at age fifty-five on October 15, 1965, came as her son's mighty star was still on the rise. McQueen had just about found a comfortable groove for himself where almost everything in his life was in balance. But real life is not like it is in the movies.

Steve and his mother had never fully come to terms with each other. After he became a TV and movie star, he installed Julian in an apartment in San Francisco's hippie haven of

North Beach, paid her bills, bought her a Volkswagen convertible, and underwrote her latest venture: a boutique store filled with antiques. The faded blonde now had an Earth Mother aura about her, but for all her new interest in herbal remedies and fad diets, Julian still liked anything with alcohol best.

> The death of McQueen's mother at age fifty-five on October 15, 1965, came as her son's mighty star was still on the rise. McQueen had just about found a comfortable groove for himself where almost everything in his life was in balance. But real life is not like it is in the movies.

Steve kept her at arm's length. The four hundred miles between Los Angeles and San Francisco was just about the right distance they needed between them. Close but not nearby.

When she visited the Castle, she would invariably get antsy and then tipsy after a day or two, quickly wearing out her welcome. But Julian was fiercely proud of what her son had become, and friends said she always saw his movies at least twice, displayed photos of him in the house, and kept a scrapbook of his cinematic accomplishments. She was also a doting grandmother, sewing clothes for Steve's children, Terry and Chad.

Steve resolutely refused to talk about her to the press. "Whatever thing I've got with my mother is a private thing I'm not about to discuss with anybody," he told one reporter. "If it means hurting her feelings to give a good story, I know which I'm going to choose."

Julian collapsed after suffering a massive cerebral hemorrhage. Steve and Neile were notified of her hospitalization as they were getting ready to fly to New Orleans for the premiere of *The Cincinnati Kid*. They went instead to Mount Zion Hospital in San Francisco to be by her side.

Whatever animosity Steve had for Julian, he put it out of mind. He kept vigil, never leaving her side. When a fan approached him in the hospital for an autograph, his chest heaved in anger, but he quickly caught himself, shook his head, and gently said, "Sorry, but the timing isn't too good."

He stayed with Julian throughout the night. She quietly slipped away at 5:00 a.m. Steve wept uncontrollably.

He stayed with Julian throughout the night. She quietly slipped away at 5:00 a.m. Steve wept uncontrollably.

I know this story well because it closely parallels mine with my own mother. She could be a delightful person when she was sober—except she was rarely sober. She drank herself into a stupor every night for most of her adult life, usually passing out before bedtime, when she came home at all. Even after suffering a horrible head-on collision while driving drunk, she found it hard to give up her hard-partying ways.

Yet as a boy, I felt a real responsibility to take care of her, even protect her. And as an adult, I continued trying to look for ways to normalize our relationship, but it was challenging. We used to let her watch our son Christopher on Monday nights when I was leading a Bible study near her house, and it became such an important event to her. She absolutely spoiled her grandson, showering him with affection and attention. Their first order of business was always a trip to the toy store. Clearly she was trying to compensate for what she never did with me. I was glad for both of them.

But it couldn't remove the sting of being forced to live without her approval. She never told me she was proud of me or even that she loved me. In her own way, I suppose, she did love me. She just never bothered to tell me. Whenever I tried to give her a hug, her back would remain rigid.

I couldn't understand it, of course—her inability to express affection or interest in me, her own son. But my Aunt Willie told me about the newspaper clippings my mother saved whenever I'd be featured or mentioned in an article. Maybe it would be a report on one of our stadium events or an interview I had given. Mom would say, "The kid's in the paper again," with great pride. But never to me.

> She never told me she was proud of me or even that she loved me. In her own way, I suppose, she did love me. She just never bothered to tell me. Whenever I tried to give her a hug, her back would remain rigid.

As the years went by, of course, I became more concerned about the condition of her soul. Near the end of her life, she was on dialysis three times a week and was miserable. At the age of seventy, she looked ninety. But whenever I brought up the subject of spiritual matters, she would immediately shut me down. Her default line was, "I don't want to talk about it!"

One day I sensed a strong leading from the Lord to go and have "the talk" with Mom. I asked my wife to pray for me, then I drove to her home.

She was alone when I got to the house and looked surprised that I was there. I didn't usually drop in on my mom, and she knew something was up.

"I want to talk to you about your soul, Mom," I said.

She quickly shot back, "I don't want to talk about it!"

My response was, "Well, today, we *are* going to talk about it."

Mom could be strong willed and usually got her way. But for better or worse, she also had a strong-willed son who was not going to be rebuffed this time. I was on a mission from God.

"Do you believe you're a Christian?" I asked. Much to my surprise, she said she believed she was. It was then I realized—for the first time, I guess—instead of thinking of my mom as an unbeliever, maybe she was more of a prodigal daughter who'd been running from God for more than sixty years.

After more dialogue, I asked her if she wanted to make a recommitment to the Lord, which to my shock and delight, she did. My mind raced with hope, thinking our relationship could actually become, even after all these years—I don't know—better, healthier.

> My pain was not about her failing me as a mother, but because I felt I had in some way failed her as a son. I felt guilty for not being there with her. I wept for what could have been between us but never was.

I even recall, less than a month later as I was leaving on a trip with my wife and some friends, I took her some DVD's of me preaching, as well as a few others, like Billy Graham, someone she greatly respected. I believe she was truly appreciative.

But while we were out of the country, my executive assistant Carol called with the unexpected news: my mother had died.

Seized by the deepest pain and sorrow, I wept for days. My pain was not about her failing me as a mother, but because I felt I had in some way failed her as a son. I felt guilty for not being there with her. I wept for what could have been between us but never was.

So when I learned the details of Julian McQueen's death, I could readily understand—at least to a certain degree—both the distance Steve kept from his mother, as well as his vigil he kept at her bedside. I also understand his deep sorrow.

No doubt he, too, wept for what might have been but never was.

David Foster is with me at the cemetery. He was Steve's publicist in the *Wanted: Dead or Alive* days and later coproduced *The Getaway*, the 1972 smash film pairing McQueen and Ali McGraw. David was also one of a handful of people at the brief graveside service for Julian.

"We kinda grew up in this business together," he says of McQueen and himself. "He had this rebel image, and we just connected. We were the same age, and our wives were the same age. We had kids who were the same age. My kids would go to his kids' birthday parties and vice versa."

But that didn't mean his friendship with McQueen was smooth sailing.

"He was a difficult personality to get along with," says David. "A psychologist would have a field day with him. One day he would be your best friend, the next day your enemy. Let's just say he was moody.

"Quite truthfully, he would fire me three times a year, I would fire him three times a year, then our wives would say,

> "Steve took great care of his mother, but every time he mentioned her, it was with great hostility and anger. It was, 'That drunk! She messed up my life! She never gave a crap about me'— then, 'Here's another check for her.'"

'You guys are jerks,' and then they'd get us back together. This went on throughout our relationship. It was definitely a love/hate thing."

Multiply that a few zillion times, says David, and you'd begin to get an idea of the complicated, ambivalent, and explosive dynamic between McQueen and his mother.

"Steve took great care of his mother, but every time he mentioned her, it was with great hostility and anger. It was, 'That drunk! She messed up my life! She never gave a crap about me'—then, 'Here's another check for her.'"

Yet Steve was so broken up over Julian's death that his wife had to make all the funeral arrangements. What Steve did, David recalls, was issue a blanket order to Julian's friends: "No interviews about my mother's death. No interviews. No reporter's going to be allowed to know anything."

Comprising the sparse contingent at Julian's graveside service were Steve, Neile, their two children, Foster and his wife Jackie, and Steve's agent Stan Kamen.

No clergyman spoke. Steve managed a brief eulogy that Foster recalls as heart-wrenching. "Julian liked shade," McQueen said. "She would have liked this spot . . . shady, with no sun." Then he folded his hands and prayed.

"Steve might have been a bastard, literally, but he cried at the funeral," Foster says. "He was a lost soul."

A lost soul, indeed.

Losing a parent is a major passage of life for anyone. It's a reminder that we are all transient figures on the human stage. For Steve to lose his mother so soon only added to that pain. For though he'd in effect been an orphan all his life, now

McQueen, at thirty-five, was truly one. And the knowledge that there would never be a true reconciliation or at least a clearing of the air with his parents opened up another fissure in his psyche he would try to fill by whatever means possible.

The question of why he could insult and dismiss Julian while she was alive yet weep uncontrollably at her grave is not difficult to understand. When she was alive, Julian could still hurt Steve, so he put on an "I don't care about her" suit of protective armor. But he did care, and that's why he wept.

> In time that whole attitude and lifestyle began to disgust me. And in time it would have a similar effect on the man who was the King of Cool.

Don't forget, he had the words "Loved by her your son, Steve" inscribed on the brass plaque on her grave.

Julian contributed to Steve's complexity as a young man—not only by her neglect of him but also in her indiscriminate choice of men that further hardened him. He was forced to survive. And the way he chose to do it was by attempting to dominate men and by treating women as conquests, which, of course, was very wrong.

But ultimately Steve McQueen was responsible for his own choices. He made a long string of poor ones yet in time would make the best choice of his life.

I felt the same way about my mother, Charlene, that perhaps Steve felt about Julian.

My wife once pointed out that Mom may have actually been a major contributor to my coming to faith. In effect, she showed me all that this world had to offer. At various times (and with various husbands), we lived both in borderline poverty and great luxury. She was of the swinging Rat Pack generation of Sinatra, Dean Martin, and Sammy Davis Jr.—a drink in one hand, a cigarette in the other. Men were kings; women were "broads."

In time that whole attitude and lifestyle began to disgust me. And in time it would have a similar effect on the man who was the King of Cool.

THE CANYON

The day after visiting the grave of Julian McQueen, I'm parked in front of a house in Benedict Canyon where her famous son almost met his death almost 47 years ago.

The address is 10050 Cielo Drive. On August 9, 1969, five people were killed here—Sharon Tate, Jay Sebring, Abigail Folger, Wojciech Frykowski and Steve Parent. They were bludgeoned, stabbed and throttled by members of Charles Manson's whacked-out "Family" in a grisly massacre that chilled the world.

Poor Sharon Tate was the last to die. According to the court testimony of her murderer, Susan Atkins, Sharon begged, "Please don't kill me. I don't want to die. I want to live. I want to have my baby!"

But Atkins did kill her in an act of pure evil.

One of the killers wrote "Helter Skelter" on the refrigerator in blood, along with references to Beatles songs. Their vileness slammed the door on the era of free love and flower power once and for all.

Steve McQueen was close to two of the victims.

"Jay Sebring was my best friend," he said in a 1980 death-bed interview. "Sharon Tate was a girlfriend of mine."

"I was sure taken care of," McQueen added. "My name never got drawn into that mess."

He was blessed, indeed, because McQueen himself was sup-posed to be at 10050 Cielo Drive the night of that horrible mass murder.

If Steve McQueen was the "King of Cool," Jay Sebring, whom Steve met in the early '60s, was the "Architect of Cool." Before Sebring began styling men's hair, they went to barber-shops redolent of moldering copies of *Field & Stream* and chose what haircut they wanted from several diagrams posted on the wall. ("Flattop with Fenders" was as exotic as it got.)

> "Please don't kill me.
> I don't want to die."

After his discharge from the Navy, Thomas John Kummer headed to Los Angeles and changed his name to Jay Sebring, after the famous Florida town and car race. Then he changed barber-ing into men's hair care and styling, creating fashionable new looks for the Age of Aquarius and launching a multi-million dollar industry in hair products and toiletries.

With financial help from his father, 25-year-old Sebring opened his first salon in Los Angeles in 1959. The red ankh (ancient Egyptian symbol of life) on the front door proclaimed it was not your old man's barbershop. If that didn't convince you, Sebring's prices did. You could get a barbershop haircut for $1.50. Sebring's coiffures started at $25.

Sebring gave public cutting and styling demonstrations that drew the attention and then the patronage of the biggest names in Hollywood, and before long numbered among his clientele were Steve McQueen, Paul Newman, Kirk Douglas, Frank Sinatra, Henry Fonda, Robert Wagner, Glen Campbell, Bruce Lee, James Garner and Andy Williams.

When they and other stars wouldn't let anyone else near their heads, the movie and TV studios had no choice but to hire Sebring at a cool $2,500 per day, plus expenses.

No one benefited more from Sebring's innovative techniques than McQueen. He gave Steve his trademark hairstyle—short, sharp and molded beautifully to the shape of his Roman head. It was Sebring who lightened McQueen's hair for *Love With the Proper Stranger*, transformed him into a sex symbol in *The Thomas Crown Affair*, and made Lieutenant Frank Bullitt, a cop in an era when police were called "pigs," look totally cool.

> It was Sebring who made Lt. Frank Bullitt, a cop in an era when police were called "pigs," look totally cool.

Larry Geller was a hairstylist with Sebring from the beginning. We're meeting at the site of Sebring's salon on Melrose and Fairfax in West Hollywood, just a few miles where Jay and the others were tragically murdered by the Manson Family.

Decades later it's still a salon, now only catering to a strictly female clientele. Geller says he had just graduated from beauty school when he first saw the stained-glass window decorated with the ankh.

"My first thought was that it was a beauty salon, but it was wood paneled inside," says Larry. "Jay was on a ladder hanging a potted plant. He said his shop was something new, and called it 'hair architecture for men.' I started the next day."

Sebring's methods and approach to everything were unheard of till then. Male patrons first had their hair shampooed (by aspiring starlets) before it was cut. Sebring was one of the first stylists to use a blow-dryer, which he imported from Europe and also sold to his clients for home use. Sebring's styling technique, says Larry, was based on the size and angles of the customer's head, not what style looked good at the moment.

> "Steve and Jay were very much alike and close, close friends. They were both military veterans and self-made men."

Within six months, Geller says, the salon employed 17 "stylists" and two manicurists. If customers wanted their shoes shined, there was someone for that, too.

Once he started making money hand-over-fist, Sebring bought the swanky 1930s Bavarian-style mansion once owned by MGM producer Paul Bern and his wife, actress Jean Harlow, a fleet of sports cars, closets full of tailored suits, and took karate lessons from Bruce Lee. He had his pick of female companions, and was engaged to starlet Sharon Tate for a time. She wanted to marry right away; he wanted to wait. Director Roman Polanski swooped in and married her instead. Despite that, there were no hard feelings, and Sebring remained friends with both.

As for McQueen and Sebring, says Geller, "Steve and Jay were very much alike and close, close friends. They were both military veterans and self-made men. Jay, like Steve, was very straightforward and honest, never shy about letting you know his true feelings."

Larry shudders recalling what Sebring said to him just a week after Geller started working at the salon.

"We worked together, ate together, talked a good many hours alone together, and all of a sudden Jay says to me, 'When I go, the whole world is going to know about it.' I said, 'What? What are you talking about? How do you know this?' He said, 'I don't know, I just know it.'"

Sadly, he would be proven right.

The night before the murders, Sebring went to The Castle to give McQueen his weekly trim. McQueen was at the apex of his career. The year before he had received an Academy Award nomination for Best Actor for *The Sand Pebbles* (he lost to Paul Scofield), then showed he could play against type and still rake in box-office dollars in *The Thomas Crown Affair*, and made the rare transition from movie star to pop-culture icon in 1968's *Bullitt.*

There is no question that God spared the life of Steve McQueen on that night.

Roman Polanski was in London working on a script, and had asked Sebring to keep an eye on Sharon Tate while he was gone. Tate was eight-and-a-half months pregnant. Would Steve like to go out to dinner with him the following night, asked Sebring as he cut McQueen's hair, and afterwards accompany him to Tate's estate on Cielo Drive? McQueen agreed.

But it didn't happen. The next evening McQueen's plans changed at the last minute when he hooked up for an impromptu tryst with a woman. He never made it to Tate's house, and it saved his life.

There is no question that God spared the life of Steve McQueen on that night.

But why him and not the others?

Who can say? As it is with your and mine, life is filled with so many twists, turns and, yes, unexpected tragedies like what happened to the occupants of 10050 Cielo Drive on August 9, 1969.

This is hardly a new question.

More than 2,000 years ago the disciples of Jesus asked Him about an incident in which Roman Governor Pontius Pilate had a group of men from Galilee murdered. Jesus responded, "Do you think those murdered Galileans were worse sinners than all other Galileans? Not at all. Unless you turn to God, you, too, will die."

> This event did not happen to the victims that night because they were worse than anyone else. We are all sinners.

Such horrible things happen because of the disease of sin that has permeated our planet since Adam and Eve, and because of evil people like Charles Manson and members of the so-called Manson Family, who did his evil bidding.

This event did not happen to the victims that night because they were worse than anyone else. We are all sinners.

The fact is that inexplicably bad things happen to good people—although the Bible makes, it clear, there are no truly good people—as well as bad people.

Jesus Himself would soon stand before the very Pontius Pilate referenced above and be whipped, beaten, nailed to a cross and murdered in cold blood.

Jesus's point was that tragedies happen and innocent people suffer. Christ Himself was innocent of any crime, yet was murdered.

The main point Jesus was making was, "Unless you turn to God, you, too, will die."

In other words, everyone dies. Some die old, some young; some from illness and others from old age; some from accidents and others from tragedy.

The statistics on death are impressively immutable—100 percent of us will die. None of us knows how long our life on earth will last. So Jesus tells us to "Turn to God" while we can.

Heartbreakingly for Jay Sebring, Abigail Folger, Wojciech Frykowski, Steve Parent, Sharon Tate and her unborn child, August 9, 1969 was their last night on earth.

But for Steve McQueen there would be another chance to make right choices.

Steve gave the eulogy at Sebring's funeral a few days later. In the waistband of his suit pants was a handgun. Like just about everyone else in Hollywood, the ghastly murders convinced McQueen that deranged hippies were out to get him, and in addition to going around packing heat, he turned The Castle into an armed camp with weapons stashed all over the place and had a state-of-the-art security system installed.

It turned out that McQueen had cause to be spooked. When Charles Manson and his crazy band of long-haired misfits were arrested months later and put on trial, it was revealed that McQueen was on their celebrity kill list. So were Frank Sinatra, Elizabeth Taylor and Richard Burton and Tom Jones.

So much for peace and love. The flower children and their visions of utopia were never real to begin with, just a drug-induced fantasy. The Manson Family served as the wake-up call.

> Steve gave the eulogy at Sebring's funeral a few days later. In the waistband of his suit pants was a handgun.

McQueen's paranoia was probably justifiable under the circumstances; but it surely didn't help that at the same time his use of illicit drugs escalated, and once again he was spinning out of control.

Once again, God intervened in Steve McQueen's life.

Steve's life would come to an end sooner then he expected as well.

But not yet.

From his first childhood bike to his fastest car, Steve was always on the move, both from and to something. At this point in his life and career, he was at the absolute pinnacle of success and global fame. It may not have been apparent yet to even him, but Steve was systematically discovering where the answers weren't.

Once again, God intervened in Steve McQueen's life.

He was never given a stable family with a loving mother and strong father. He was left at a very early age to his own devices to navigate life.

Unbeknownst to himself, Steve McQueen was going through a process of elimination.

So did I, but at an earlier age than Steve.

I knew the answers were not in the alcoholic haze of my mother and her myriad of husbands and boyfriends and the "swinging" life they lived.

Nor were they found in the drugs and counter-culture I immersed myself in as a teenager.

So where, then, were the answers to life's greatest questions?

Mine would come on the campus of my high school.

Steve's would come in the cockpit of an antique airplane.

THE MONSTER WITHIN

As someone who grew up in less than ideal circumstances myself, I have empathy for anyone who survives a brutal childhood and am more inclined than most to try understanding questionable behavior. Up to a point.

There is a rational explanation for Steve's behavior at this time and for all of it to greater or lesser degrees. It's because of a disease that first came from our parents and has spread through every son of Adam and every daughter of Eve.

That disease is called sin.

Sin darkens our heart and eats us up from the inside. Some seem to control it better than others, but ultimately sin controls us. And the focus of sin in our lives is to make us completely selfish people. We don't care how our actions affect others, so naturally, we just think of ourselves.

Part of the problem, as I see it, was that Steve fought so hard and for so long to reach the summit of the mountain, his determination to stay there made him even more ruthless.

The adoration of the public certainly inflated his ego way out of proportion, creating a false sense of worth and entitlement. Fans went crazy to get his autograph or just eyeball him on the street. Flashbulbs popped whenever he ventured out in public. Calling McQueen a big Hollywood star at this point fails to adequately gauge the extent of his fame. Fundamentally, he was one of the most popular, most recognizable faces on the planet.

There is a rational explanation for Steve's behavior at this time and for all of it to greater or lesser degrees. It's because of a disease that first came from our parents and has spread through every son of Adam and every daughter of Eve. That disease is called sin.

To put in today's celebrity culture, Steve McQueen was basically Brad Pitt, George Clooney and Johnny Depp all rolled into one.

That kind of fame would be difficult for anyone to deal with. For someone like McQueen, it meant he increasingly turned to the things that gave him pleasure—friends, cars, bikes, family, drugs, women, and power. By then he'd essentially created a monster that needed to be constantly fed and appeased.

In the first book of the Bible, God gave a warning to the proud and selfish Cain about his monstrous human nature. When the Lord accepted the offering of his brother Abel, but not his, Cain threw a fit. And God said to him, "Why this tantrum? Why the sulking? If you do well, won't you be accepted? And if you don't do well, sin is lying in wait for you, ready to pounce; it's out to get you, you've got to master it" (Gen. 4:6–7 MSG).

God was telling Cain that sin and the selfishness it brings is like a crouching beast, waiting to strike. You either master it, or it will master you. And at this point in his life, it appears that the monster got the better of Steve McQueen.

This process began in mid-1970 when he decided to produce and star in a movie called *Le Mans*. It seems as though he could not make any sound decision regarding this particular film, and his selfishness was at full wattage.

Le Mans had no coherent story, and McQueen himself floundered trying to explain what he was going for. "The emphasis here is on film as a visual—I guess opposed to verbal," he said. "We are also interested in reality." When pressed for something more tangible, he shrugged and said, "The script is in my head."

Confusion followed.

Don Nunley served as the property master on this racing picture. He and I are meeting at Cupid's Hot Dogs on Lindley Avenue in Northridge. Serving the Los Angeles area since 1946, Cupid's signature chili dogs are legendary and actually have a connection to *Le Mans*.

"*Le Mans* was filmed entirely on location in France," Don says, "and it was originally supposed to be a simple, straightforward movie shot in six to eight weeks. It turned into a five-month nightmare of epic proportions, and we were all stressed."

One day, in an effort to lighten the tension, Don says the studio had a crate of Cupid's chili dogs shipped

---

To put in today's celebrity culture, Steve McQueen was basically Brad Pitt, George Clooney and Johnny Depp all rolled into one.

Don calls the making of *Le Mans* "a bumpy ride for all of us and the strangest picture I worked on in three decades of filmmaking. It was not a fun experience." Thanks mostly to McQueen.

---

from Los Angeles to the film set. "After attending a bloodless bullfight in a nearby town on a Sunday afternoon, we returned to Solar Village [the film's headquarters] and chowed down," Don says. "It was an entertaining diversion while it lasted."

Don calls the making of *Le Mans* "a bumpy ride for all of us and the strangest picture I worked on in three decades of filmmaking. It was not a fun experience."

Thanks mostly to McQueen.

Le Mans was supposed to be his cinematic dream come true, but from the start it was a disaster. There were conflicts with original director John Sturges, personal excesses, budget woes, a war with the studio, a shutdown on the set, weeks of delays, and an accident that left one driver without a leg.

When McQueen disliked something in the script, says Don, he literally started ripping out pages.

Le Mans coincided with McQueen's midlife crisis. During its production, his fifteen-year marriage to Neile ended, he broke up with his longtime agent and producing partners, his production company collapsed, and McQueen lost a personal fortune. At the end of the snake-bitten picture, McQueen was presented with a seven-figure bill by the Internal Revenue Service for back taxes.

Today at seventy-eight, Don remembers well how he started in the business in 1959 and first encountered McQueen on the set of *Wanted: Dead or Alive* when he was an assistant propmaster at Four Star Studios. He recalls McQueen as "young, feisty, and often prickly," and says, "He liked to have his own way and had no qualms about bucking the system whenever he felt something was out of order or was not in sync with what he thought his character, Josh Randall, would do in a particular situation."

When McQueen disliked something in the script, says Don, he literally started ripping out pages.

"When he disagreed with a director's suggestions, he emasculated the poor soul right in front of the crew. He would tell the other actors to ignore the director and play a scene the way he thought it should be done."

But believe it or not, Don tells me, the McQueen who played Josh Randall was a choirboy compared to the one on the set of *Le Mans*.

The idea was to film the actual 24 Hours of Le Mans race from the viewpoint of McQueen's character, driver Michael Delaney. But on the very first day of shooting, McQueen refused to put on his driving suit and walk through the pit area as a way of getting back at the studio for not allowing him to actually drive in the race. They wanted to use a stunt double. Steve wouldn't have it.

After several days and more than seventy thousand hours of racing footage, nobody knew yet what the film's story line was. McQueen hired six writers to patch one together, but because he was unable to communicate his vision of the film to anyone, it was hopeless.

McQueen's petulance signaled the start of a long and frustrating shoot. "On account of Steve's refusal to cooperate," Don says, "we had to recreate 90 percent of the paddock area shots later, which cost Cinema Center [the studio] a bundle. They were not happy."

After several days and more than seventy thousand hours of racing footage, nobody knew yet what the film's story line was.

McQueen hired six writers to patch one together, but because he was unable to communicate his vision of the film to anyone, it was hopeless.

Even as the faint outlines of a story finally began to emerge, several of the racing scenes resulted in accidents, further complicating matters. Six cars crashed at a cost of forty-five thousand dollars per automobile. McQueen himself had a close call or two behind the wheel. The most serious of them was off the set when he drove his Swedish costar to her hotel and crashed his Peugeot on a winding road. They both went through the windshield but were miraculously unhurt. The actress was knocked unconscious but was revived at the scene.

McQueen fought with everyone, including director John Sturges, who had practically given the actor his start in movies. Finally studio executives flew in from California to survey the carnage. They shut production down for two weeks and ordered McQueen to "pick a script, shoot the picture, and be done with it."

Says Don, "We were all adults and understood this came with the territory called superstardom, but Steve's behavior bordered on manic—as if he had to prove his manhood to everyone. When he wasn't working, he was usually running around on his motorbike, often shirtless, giving rides to young women in the countryside or on the track. He was never secretive, either, about disappearing with them into his trailer for an hour or two."

McQueen and Neile were now separated, but she brought their children to France during the filming in hopes of reconciliation. It didn't work.

Five weeks into filming, Don says, there hadn't been much forward progress. Expenses were mounting thanks to the foreign location, race car maintenance, the salaries of professional drivers, and an international crew whose members did not always understand each other, not to mention uncooperative weather. And an uncontrollable star.

McQueen fought with everyone, including director John Sturges, who had practically given the actor his start in movies. Finally studio executives flew in from California to survey the carnage. They shut production down for two weeks and ordered McQueen to "pick a script, shoot the picture, and be done with it."

Sturges eventually left, causing a permanent rift in his friendship with McQueen. His replacement was TV director Lee Katzin, who was berated, humiliated, and scorned by McQueen throughout the remainder of the shoot.

The way I see it, Steve was not mastering the monster within; it was mastering him.

Then in an even more tragic turn a few weeks before production wrapped, racer David Piper lost control of his car and crashed as the cameras rolled. Years later, Piper recounted to a reporter, "I suddenly found myself sitting in only half a car, surrounded by smoke and dust, and I thought, *Good Lord, that's my shoe over there—and my foot is still in it!*" The wound in his right leg became infected, and the limb eventually was amputated.

The shoot that had started in June staggered into November, and on the seventh day of that month, director Lee Katzin finally called it a wrap.

"There was no traditional wrap party," says Don, "no grand farewells by the cast and crew. We all just wearily shuffled off the set and looked forward to happier days and better projects."

The cost of *Le Mans* went beyond dollars and cents. Friendships were irretrievably broken, reputations besmirched. A steady and loving marriage ended. And the finger of blame for all of it was pointed directly at Steve McQueen and his hubris.

The way I see it, Steve was not mastering the monster within; it was mastering him.

20

THE FALL

At the height of his popularity Steve McQueen said, "I believe in me. God will be number one as long as I'm number one."

Wow.

Sounds like the legend of the *Titanic* builders who famously proclaimed, "God Himself couldn't sink it." We know how the rest of that story turned out, and now we look at Steve's. He, too, was taking on water fast.

God survived *Le Mans*, of course, but McQueen's life and career went into freefall.

The actor had taken every advantage possible in his professional life, and now Hollywood was paying him back in spades. After years of sticking it to producers, directors, and studios, he was finding out the truth of the biblical law of "reaping what you sow," for which McQueen was long overdue.

Le Mans took away his box-office heat, serving as a vivid reminder that McQueen wasn't omnipotent and all-powerful. In one fell swoop he lost his wife, his agent, his production company, and a good deal of his personal fortune. Cut loose were old friends, business associates, and virtually everything and everyone connected to his past glory. It was out with the old and in with the new.

So he retrenched, dissolving his three companies and ridding himself of all the lawyers, accountants, managers, and public relations folks he supported. The tailored suits and expensive ties he wore to the office were mothballed in favor of a simpler wardrobe of blue jeans, casual button-down shirts, turquoise belt buckles, and denim jackets. He later recalled, "I had put up a suite of offices, a lot of secretaries, accountants, lots of people on the payroll. I was producing my own movies. Just terrific. But I wasn't making any money, I was working sixteen hours a day, and I was the president of three corporations. And I was not very happy."

> After years of sticking it to producers, directors, and studios, he was finding out the truth of the biblical law of "reaping what you sow," for which McQueen was long overdue.

Not as rich, either, especially when he got that $2-million bill from the Internal Revenue Service for back taxes. It couldn't have come at a worse time. He had worked tirelessly for years to achieve financial security. Now he could well end up flat broke again.

It was a long fall from the top, and McQueen hit every step on the way down.

"When I met Steve, he seemed a little lost and confused as to what he wanted in life," says Barbara Leigh. She was McQueen's costar in *Junior Bonner,* his first movie after *Le Mans.* "He spoke of his marriage to Neile and how it was nearing the end. He spoke of her with respect, which I found admirable. I think he needed to spread his wings and wanted to be free to take the next step in his life. The romantic part of his marriage was over, and he wanted excitement. Sadly, Steve and Neile still loved each other deeply, but Steve, from what I knew and read, couldn't be faithful to her."

"*Wouldn't* be faithful" would be more like it. Steve had made a series of bad choices, and now he was facing the consequences, learning that when you make your choices, your choices make *you*.

Barbara has graciously joined my wife and me for lunch at the California Pizza Kitchen in Westwood Village. I figured I had enough alone time on this journey, and because we were close to home, Cathe hopped in the Bullitt and came with me. And since she's a good sport, she didn't mind if I pretended to be Steve McQueen behind the wheel.

> It was a long fall from the top, and McQueen hit every step on the way down.

Years before, Barbara says this establishment was a family-owned Italian diner called Mario's—a quaint place with checkered tablecloths, jug wine, candles with dripping wax, and food "that was just out of this world." She and McQueen often dined here after they began seeing each other off the movie set. It's a place, she says, with both good and not-so-good memories.

Barbara recalls one dinner when Steve twice rudely rebuffed fans who'd requested his autograph. "It embarrassed me that he wouldn't just sign a piece of paper for people who appreciated him and acknowledged him as a movie star," says Barbara. "He was a little mean-spirited about it." McQueen defended his behavior by maintaining that by interrupting his dinner the fans showed no regard for his privacy. "It wasn't how I would have handled the matter," she continued, "but then again, he was a superstar and I wasn't."

Barbara was a top international model when she auditioned for the part of McQueen's love interest, Charmagne, in early June 1971—the same month and year when Neile filed for divorce. Barbara read through part of the script for director Sam Peckinpah with McQueen himself but left with the feeling she wouldn't get the role. As she reached her car, McQueen came running up. "I don't think the part's going to work out," he said, "but I'd like to take you to dinner."

They went to a nice restaurant on Sunset Boulevard near the Pacific Coast Highway and over dinner discovered they had several things in common. Both had been deserted by their fathers and had unstable mothers. Barbara was a product of the foster care system, Steve a product of the Boys Republic.

Their relationship quickly progressed, and when McQueen left for Prescott, Arizona, to start filming *Junior Bonner*, Barbara agreed to come for a visit. Three days before the cameras rolled, McQueen called to offer her the role of Charmagne because actress Tiffany Bolling had unexpectedly bowed out.

"I was at a loss for words," recalls Barbara, "absolutely dumbfounded. Just like that, out of the clear blue. That was the single greatest thing to happen in my acting career, starring in a Steve McQueen movie directed by the great Sam

Peckinpah. But that's Hollywood for you—overnight, anything can happen."

They ended up in a relationship and lived together, rehearsing lines over breakfast. Things seemed fine until Elvis Presley called her up one day and invited her to Las Vegas.

Free-spirited Barbara, you see, had also been dating Elvis—oh, and also MGM president Jim Aubrey—the whole time things were heating up with McQueen. When she told Presley she couldn't get away, the singer said he would come to Prescott instead to see her. That's when Barbara got around to telling him she was staying with McQueen.

After that, she recalls, "Whenever Elvis inquired about Steve, it was, 'How's that motorcycle hick?' And with Steve it was, 'How's that guitar hick?' Both came from humble beginnings, but it was funny they called each other hicks."

Working with McQueen on the movie, says Barbara, "was a trip. Steve's approach to acting was different than most, and that's what separated him from other movie stars. He was a reactor instead of an actor. He didn't initiate action or dialogue; he reacted with his facial expressions and body language.

"Most actors fight for lines," Barbara says. "Steve fought for the shot. Where he placed himself was more important to him than what he had to say. He didn't appear to be acting at all, but that was his gift."

> "Whenever Elvis inquired about Steve, it was, 'How's that motorcycle hick?' And with Steve it was, 'How's that guitar hick?' Both came from humble beginnings, but it was funny they called each other hicks."

Living with him off the set, however, wasn't always so fascinating. McQueen was often irritatingly rude, boorish, and profane. And when *Junior Bonner* wrapped, so did Barbara's relationship with its star. At least she *thought* so, until McQueen began demanding to see her again back in California. When they did get together, he told her he wanted her exclusively—no more Elvis, no more James Aubrey. Barbara agreed.

A child who was never allowed to live, and a man who had dodged death and didn't know what his life was really about.

Then she discovered she was pregnant. At first she thought the father was Aubrey, until he told her he'd had a vasectomy years ago.

Turned out it was McQueen's.

But she never told him. "In hindsight, it was a rotten thing to do," says Barbara. "He had every right to know I was carrying his child. I'll regret forever my choice not to tell him. I should have given him the opportunity to have a voice in my decision."

That decision was to abort her pregnancy.

Right before she entered Cedars-Sinai Medical Center on November 6, 1971, McQueen called to offer his support. Later he visited her at the hospital, bringing food, a kind word, and showing the tender side of his personality. This, of course, is one of the most tragic outcomes of the selfish, reckless lifestyle he had lived with such abandon up to this point: a child who was never allowed to live, and a man who had dodged death and didn't know what his life was really about.

Barbara reflects wistfully: "Through the years I've often wondered what my child would have been like and the differences he or she might have made in my life. It's a decision

I've thought about many times during the last four decades." She also relays to us the hope that perhaps in the afterlife her unborn child and Steve have met. I say it's entirely possible because I believe when children die they go straight to heaven.

Here's why. The Bible tells of a day when people were bringing their little children and infants to Jesus so He could touch them. His disciples tried to shoo them away, but Jesus rebuked them: "Let the little children come to Me, and do not forbid them; for of such is the kingdom of heaven" (Matt. 19:14 NKJV). That's the heart of Christ for little children. So could Steve have already met his son or daughter on the other side? Absolutely.

God's heart of grace and redemption toward us is something that should never cease to amaze us. He is so loving and forgiving that He extends His hand to us throughout our lives and gives second chances. In Steve's case, he was well beyond a mere second chance. He was pushing the envelope for sure in his rough and tumble life. But salvation was coming and in a way he probably never expected.

Barbara hadn't seen Steve in many years, but in late 1976 they met for dinner in his private suite at the Beverly Hills Hotel while he was filming *An Enemy of the People*. She was shocked by his appearance. "Steve was one of the sexiest men alive when I knew him on *Junior Bonner*. Now I was looking at a man who was

"Steve could be terribly charming, and for a split second I considered the idea of going back with him," Barbara says, "but I knew it wouldn't work out in the long run. There was no going back in time for either of us. I kissed his cheek gently and bid him farewell. It was the last time I ever saw him alive."

older, heavier, with shaggy, long hair and a big, bushy beard. He reminded me of Heidi's grandfather."

McQueen was married to Ali MacGraw at the time, and he acknowledged to Barbara during dinner that things weren't going too well on the domestic front. Before the evening was over, he'd asked Barbara to spend the night with him.

"Steve could be terribly charming, and for a split second I considered the idea of going back with him," Barbara says, "but I knew it wouldn't work out in the long run. There was no going back in time for either of us. I kissed his cheek gently and bid him farewell. It was the last time I ever saw him alive."

Yet even as the trajectory of Steve's life was trailing downward, what he didn't know was that God was getting him ready for the greatest adventure of his life. We're talking greater than the chase scenes in *Bullitt*. More exhilarating than the motorcycle jump in *The Great Escape*. More liberating than the prison escape scenes in *Papillion*.

When you hit bottom like Steve did, the only way left is up. Way up.

A JAMAICAN
SEED

Junior Bonner was Steve McQueen's third box-office clunker in a row. And in a town where you're only as hot as your latest film, he was in danger of fading to the back of the pack. But the forty-one-year-old superstar was never one to take anything lying down and actually worked his hardest and best when his back was against the wall.

Over the next few years, McQueen not only recovered his box-office crown but achieved new heights, becoming the highest-paid movie star once again and standing head and shoulders above the rest of Hollywood.

The great comeback started with the 1972 movie *The Getaway*. Based on the gritty crime novel by Jim Thompson, the film was about a husband-wife bank robbing team looking for one last score. The role of Doc McCoy was perfect for McQueen, and today it is still considered one of his best performances. It helped that he probably strongly identified with the character who starts the movie in prison brooding about the injustice of life.

The title of the film refers not only to the McCoys' last caper but also to the transition McQueen's character makes over the course of the film—from hard-bitten criminal to a more sympathetic, multidimensional human being who's coming to terms with himself. In a very real way, *The Getaway* was almost biographical for McQueen. It gave him an opportunity to act out all his frustrations and contradictions.

It was also a seminal event in his personal life. McQueen's costar was Ali MacGraw, who fell in love with him the first time she laid eyes on him at the Beverly Hills mansion where MacGraw lived with her husband, movie producer Robert Evans, and their young son, Joshua. She would later say she fell in love not so much with him but with her "invention of Steve McQueen," comparing it to "a drug high."

> Over the next few years, McQueen not only recovered his box-office crown but achieved new heights, becoming the highest-paid movie star once again and standing head and shoulders above the rest of Hollywood.

McQueen was intoxicated by her as well. And a month after filming on *The Getaway* started in Texas, he and Neile were officially divorced. It's quite possible he might have felt he was cleared to embark on another relationship.

When McQueen was smitten, his macho exhibitionism would go into overdrive. And when MacGraw arrived in San Antonio, he fetched her at the airport and tried to impress her with his driving skill by doing doughnuts on the busy freeway. Another time the pair almost drowned when McQueen drove a rented station wagon into a natural spring on purpose. Actor Ben Johnson, shaking his head at McQueen's juvenile behavior, ran to the submerged vehicle and rescued them.

But all his bluster and antics, instead of pushing her away from him, somehow drew her even closer. And in the summer of '72 she divorced Robert Evans and married McQueen almost a year later.

All the tabloid attention paid to the McQueen-MacGraw romance boosted *The Getaway* at the box office when it opened in late 1972. It ended up the seventh-largest grossing movie of that year, taking in $36 million. With a percentage of receipts on the back end of the picture and other financial incentives built into his contract, Steve made almost $6 million. And just like that, he was back in the Hollywood catbird seat as one of the most bankable star in pictures.

His next film, *Papillon*, made in 1973, resulted in another major breakthrough for McQueen, though not professionally or romantically.

It was, at long last, a spiritual breakthrough of sorts.

The man who played a key role in that was legendary stuntman Stan Barrett, Hal Needham's protégé, who doubled for Paul Newman and Burt Reynolds and was one of the highest paid Hollywood stuntmen at the time. Stan was a former Golden Gloves champion, motorcross racer, held black belts in two styles of karate, an Air Force veteran, and more importantly to Steve, a solid Christian man. Stan was one of the most sought

When McQueen was smitten, his macho exhibitionism would go into overdrive. And when MacGraw arrived in San Antonio, he fetched her at the airport and tried to impress her with his driving skill by doing doughnuts on the busy freeway.

after stuntmen in Hollywood and his salary reflected that fact. He was called to double McQueen on *Papillon* but in order to meet his established fee, he was put on two contracts—one as an actor and the other as the stunt double for Steve, which didn't seem to be a problem until later in the production.

His next film, *Papillon*, made in 1973, resulted in another major breakthrough for McQueen, though not professionally or romantically.

I've had the pleasure of knowing Stan myself for many years, having first met him in Franklin Graham's office in North Carolina. He's a fascinating guy to talk to and a real man's man. Stan is rugged and cool and has lots of great stories about his amazing Hollywood career.

Now we're meeting at his favorite hamburger joint in Marina Del Rey, a forty-five-minute drive from Orange County, to talk about his memories of Steve McQueen.

How somebody who's broken his back a couple of times, had a dozen operations on his body and enough stitches to quilt a blanket can still look so hale and healthy at seventy-three is beyond me.

His accomplishments are legendary beyond filmdom. Stan would go on to race NASCAR with several top-ten finishes after becoming the first human to break the on-land sound barrier when he drove a missile-shaped Budweiser rocket 739 miles per hour on December 17, 1979, (the same day, as it happens, that McQueen was diagnosed with mesothelioma).

Stan says his momentous conversation with McQueen about his spiritual condition happened when the production company tried to change the terms of his contract a month after he reported to the set of *Papillon* in Jamaica. By then the film company was experiencing budgetary problems and tried to cut corners. When it became apparent the company wouldn't live up to its obligations, this was unacceptable to Stan. Then he told them to get his ticket ready to fly back to the States because he was going home.

> "We made a deal and they broke it. I think the fact that I was a principled guy, acting on what I said I was going to do, and had credentials, made an impression on Steve. A guy like Steve McQueen, you had to earn his respect."

"We made a deal and they broke it. I think the fact that I was a principled guy, acting on what I said I was going to do, and had credentials, made an impression on Steve. A guy like Steve McQueen, you had to earn his respect."

When McQueen found out about Barrett's decision to leave Jamaica, he went to Stan and said, "Hey, Stan, what's up here, buddy? I hear you're going home?" Stan told him about the company's maneuver to cut his salary, and Steve offered to make up the difference if he stayed. Stan refused.

As they continued to talk, Steve touched on the breaking news that a mutual friend of theirs, off-road motorcycle racing legend and stuntman J.N. Roberts, had openly declared his faith in Jesus Christ. McQueen was discomfited by the public revelation, Stan says, and expressed his opinion that Roberts was "way out there."

"I tried to explain the transformation in Roberts's life," says Stan. "I said to Steve, 'This is a new, remarkable and dramatic experience in J.N.'s life, and he's pretty excited about it.'"

McQueen became a bit defensive at that point, telling Stan that he, too, was religious and had gone to church but saw no need to make a big show of it. This left Stan a big opening for his follow-up question:

"But are you a Christian? There's a difference between believing and having a personal relationship with Jesus Christ. The demons believe and they tremble . . . two different things, Steve." Pressing his advantage, he added, "Just because you go into a barn doesn't mean you're a cow or a horse, any more than going to church makes you a Christian."

With that the floodgates opened, and for a half hour McQueen and Barrett went at it. "It was a very intense conversation," Stan recalls, "and I hit him pretty hard. I didn't let him off the hook either. Usually people don't like to be questioned like that, but Steve was open to it or tolerated it because of who I was. I could talk to Steve that way because he respected my credentials. Paul Newman had helped cement those, since he and Steve were friends, as was Bruce Lee."

This is just Stan's way, then as now. "I was quiet but bold. I didn't push my theology on anyone, but, boy, I was ready when the opportunity presented itself. I wouldn't have asked Steve, 'What's your relationship with God?' unless *God* hadn't arranged that first."

Stan wound up the discussion by offering to give McQueen a couple of books that would open his eyes to what it means to truly follow the teachings of Christ—*Mere Christianity* by C. S. Lewis and *Basic Christianity* by John Stott. He left the books with McQueen before departing Jamaica.

A year later, the two men saw each other again on the set of *The Towering Inferno* when Stan was visiting Paul Newman. He was originally going to double both Newman and McQueen on the epic disaster film but was unable to as he had a shattered knee cap removed.

Stan asked Steve if he read the two books, and McQueen confirmed he had indeed.

"I asked him, 'Are you sure, Steve, if you were killed or died tomorrow where you would go? You're always pushing the envelope, doing more than your share of a lot of dangerous stuff with race cars and motorcycles. No one gets out of here alive. Have you ever thought about it? This is not a rehearsal. Are you confident where you'll spend eternity?"

McQueen was a hard nut to crack, for sure. Because of his bizarre upbringing, he'd developed a hard shell around himself for both protection and preservation.

McQueen hemmed and hawed, and Stan told him it was simply a matter of making a knowing decision for Christ.

"Looking back," says Stan, "I am sure it was very unusual for anyone to have that deep of a conversation with Steve. I believe in my heart the only reason I went to Jamaica was that God put me in that position on that film far from home to challenge him. God's timing is perfect. I know he was struggling at the time and obviously this had been a long and pressing theme in Steve's life."

McQueen was a hard nut to crack, for sure. Because of his bizarre upbringing, he'd developed a hard shell around himself for both protection and preservation. He was certainly a very proud man. And that pride was keeping him from admitting he needed help of any kind, including that he needed God in his life.

> As a kid, I had a chip on my shoulder and a permanent smirk on my face. I remember a teacher once saying to me in class, "Laurie, wipe that smirk off your face!" Problem was, that was my normal expression.

In the book Steve read, C. S. Lewis writes, "As long as you are proud you cannot know God. A proud man is always looking down on things and people; and, of course, as long as you are looking down you cannot see something that is above you."

I know because having come from a similar background I, too, had that shell, as well as that pride—a cynical view of people based on disappointment repeated over and over again.

As a kid, I had a chip on my shoulder and a permanent smirk on my face. I remember a teacher once saying to me in class, "Laurie, wipe that smirk off your face!" Problem was, that was my normal expression.

Late in my teen years, I decided to transfer from Corona Del Mar High to Harbor High, a wealthy suburb of Newport Beach, California. I was looking for a new identity in an attempt to fit in. I had been hanging around with the coolest kids on campus but had tired quickly of smoking, drinking, and weekend parties. They reminded me too much of my mother's crowd. That wasn't for me.

But at this time the whole drug scene was exploding. The maxim of the day was, "Never trust anyone over thirty." And the older I got, the more this concept resonated with me from personal experience because I had been continually disappointed by the adult world I'd been exposed to. Harbor, I was told, was a much more relaxed atmosphere with not much hassle from the powers-that-be, and so I transferred there. I started growing my hair out and went from preppie to hippie practically overnight.

> I was smoking weed every single day and using LSD on the weekends. I actually believed I would find some kind of answers in drugs.

I was known to many of my fellow students because, among other things, I was the cartoonist for the school paper and reveled in mocking the authorities. A lot of the kids liked the way I thumbed my nose at "The Man." (Ironically, one of the projects assigned to our art class that year was to go down to a local restaurant and paint a giant mural on an inside wall—a mural of the King of Cool himself, Steve McQueen.) I was smoking weed every single day and using LSD on the weekends. I actually believed I would find some kind of answers in drugs.

After I transferred over to Harbor, my other druggie friends warned me to watch out for the "Jesus freaks," as there were quite a lot of them on campus. I laughed off such a concern, retorting, "Trust me, the last thing Greg Laurie will ever do is become a Jesus freak!"

Famous last words.

I thought these Christians were collectively nuts. I could not, for the life of me, understand why they would openly carry a Bible and talk about God like He was their next-door neighbor. But I must say, I was definitely intrigued.

Unlike Steve, I didn't have a courageous man like Stan Barrett to speak directly to me. But being a people watcher, I observed the Christians carefully, thinking this was some cleverly devised act they were putting on. Or *was* it? At certain times of day or the middle of the night—times when I was thinking more clearly—I knew there was a good chance my course of life was likely leading me down a dead-end street. Was it possible these Christians were on to something? I always quickly dismissed the thought, but a seed was planted, just as it was planted by Stan Barrett in the heart of Steve McQueen.

> Things were about to change for me. And in time, things would also change for Terrence Steven McQueen.

Recently, I was honored to be included in a ceremony at Harbor for their Hall of Fame. In my little acceptance speech, I told them I was more qualified for the "Hall of Shame"—that is, until I started listening more carefully to the message the Jesus freaks actually believed.

Things were about to change for me. And in time, things would also change for Terrence Steven McQueen.

THE TOWERING BABEL

I've always maintained that only when you get to the end of yourself do you get to the beginning of God. In other words, it's hard to have your heart filled with the Holy Spirit when you're already so full of yourself.

Steve McQueen wasn't there quite yet. He was still going through the sorting process we all undertake at some time in our lives. Only he had much more to sort through than most.

He was married to one of the most glamourous women in the universe—Ali MacGraw—and his status as a global superstar had been firmly reestablished with the success of *Papillon*. The prison-drama grossed more than $100 million worldwide in 1973 dollars, roughly the equivalent of a half billion dollars today.

The career slide that started with *The Reivers* (an adaptation of a William Faulkner novel) and accelerated to the cellar with *Le Mans* and *Junior Bonner* had now been reversed, and

McQueen was on top of the cinematic world again. His next movie would elevate him to the stratosphere.

McQueen was advanced $1 million for 1974's *The Towering Inferno*, a star-loaded film about a runaway blaze in the world's tallest skyscraper. Steve also got 7.5 percent of the picture's gross profits. In the USA alone it brought in $116 million and almost triple that amount in total worldwide receipts. Do the math. All that for a film in which he didn't have his first scene till forty-three minutes into the picture!

The Towering Inferno was called a "disaster film," a genre that was much in vogue in the '70s, but its groundbreaking special effects and McQueen's bravura performance as the heroic fire chief who swoops in and saves the day made it a huge critical and financial success. It was hugely satisfying to McQueen on a personal level, too, because his billing was before Paul Newman's (star of *Somebody Up There Likes Me*, the 1956 movie in which McQueen was an uncredited extra). McQueen's one-sided rivalry toward Newman had simmered over the decades and had resulted in a missed opportunity for McQueen in the 1969 revisionist western *Butch Cassidy and the Sundance Kid*. McQueen was offered the role of Sundance opposite Newman's Cassidy, but he turned it down because of his demand for top billing over Newman, who had been a star for much longer. The role eventually went to Robert Redford instead, making him a huge star.

> *The Towering Inferno* was called a "disaster film," a genre that was much in vogue in the '70s, but its groundbreaking special effects and McQueen's bravura performance as the heroic fire chief who swoops in and saves the day made it a huge critical and financial success.

The movie went on to become one of the top grossing films of the 1960s, and today is considered a classic.

In *The Towering Inferno* Steve had finally achieved his goal of first billing over Newman.

How could he top that?

He didn't even try. In a move that confounded all of Hollywood, McQueen more or less disappeared for the next five years.

His decision is as mystifying to me today as it was to everyone back then. Like the tower of Babel, McQueen had built a career that reached into the heavens—I suppose in an effort to make himself so Godlike that he would have no need (he thought) of the real deal. "Babel," by the way, means confusion, and the word fits because now Steve was more confused than ever.

One of the few people close to McQueen during his sabbatical from the spotlight was Flo Esposito, a barmaid at the Old Place in Agoura Hills, California. Thanks to Flo's kindness, I'm sitting with her in a booth at this establishment as she reminisces about the McQueen she and other regulars knew and loved.

> In *The Towering Inferno* Steve had finally achieved his goal of first billing over Newman. How could he top that?

"Steve was looking for a family, and here at the Old Place we definitely were a family," Flo says. "When you take on a family, there's baggage that comes attached. There's a honeymoon period for a while. But when that door closes and it gets dark at night, the honeymoon might not be there anymore, but Steve was the kind of guy who wanted to take a chance on a family."

McQueen started frequenting the Old Place in the early '70s, becoming friendly with owner Tom Runyon and his wife, Barbara, who opened the rustic roadhouse on Mulholland Highway in 1969. The ambiance is a tip of the hat to the Old West, with a hardwood bar, rugged booths, and swinging doors. The kitchen is known for its steak and clams and a beef stew that'd make Dinty Moore find another line of work.

McQueen started frequenting the Old Place in the early '70s, becoming friendly with owner Tom Runyon and his wife, Barbara, who opened the rustic roadhouse on Mulholland Highway in 1969.

Back then the Old Place catered to an eclectic mix of bikers, renegades, actors, beach bums, cowboys, and local characters who weren't impressed by anybody's pedigree, résumé, or reputation—which according to Flo was exactly what appealed to McQueen about it. "He could walk in here and nobody would gasp, 'Ohhh, Steve McQueen!' That's not the kind of place this is. Movie stars and famous musicians could walk through that door and not be bothered."

McQueen definitely didn't want to be bothered, toward which end he made himself as unrecognizable as possible by growing a shaggy beard, letting his trademark blond locks grow long, wearing grungy clothes, and packing on a few extra pounds. For him it was literally a matter of life and death.

"A movie star has a very strange situation going," McQueen once said. "To have your identification and your obscurity is the ultimate. But if you have heat on you all the time . . . people constantly wanting me to live up to the stuff they see on the screen all the time . . . I'll die."

When he found the Old Place, Flo says, he found a sanctuary of sorts. "Hollywood was rush, rush, rush, and he'd have to be somewhere all the time. Here, you could come and go as you please. You could come in raggedy clothes. Women didn't have to fix their hair or wear makeup. You could be yourself. Steve felt that peace. We all felt that peace."

And come they did, with celebrities such as Bob Dylan, Nick Nolte, Bill Bixby, director Sam Peckinpah, and Jason Robards. The Old Place was also a favorite of Ronald and Nancy Reagan when they owned a nearby ranch, having been introduced to the restaurant by Steve McQueen himself.

Steve's new appearance fooled plenty of customers when he served their drinks from behind *the log*. "It was his way of having fun," recalls Flo. "A couple of people would walk up to him and ask, 'Are you . . . ?' and he'd shake his head, no, and walk to the other side of the bar and ask patrons if they needed a refill or a drink. He'd never say who he was. Most Hollywood types like to wear their popularity on their sleeves but not Steve. He'd downplay it."

McQueen found another father figure in owner Tom Runyon, an Armed Forces pilot during World War II who rose to the rank of major. He was also a part-time actor and contributor of fiction to *Argosy* magazine. Steve gave him a role as a heavy in *The Getaway*, and he nailed it!

"A movie star has a very strange situation going," McQueen once said. "To have your identification and your obscurity is the ultimate. But if you have heat on you all the time . . . people constantly wanting me to live up to the stuff they see on the screen all the time . . . I'll die."

"Runyon was the most generous, crazy, loving man I had ever met," Flo says. "When he loved you, he loved you hard. And he loved Steve. Steve felt that love of a father figure."

McQueen's abandonment as a boy by his biological father and the indifference and outright hostility of his mother's ne'er-do-well string of boyfriends opened a gaping hole in his heart, one that I understand all too well. I had that same empty space in my own life. Extensive studies have been done on children who come from broken and especially fatherless homes, and there is no question—it leaves them marked for life.

Steve had fatherlike figures in his Uncle Claude and to some degree in some of his film directors, including John Sturges, Henry Hathaway, and Norman Jewison. McQueen, said Jewison, "was a loner, and he was troubled, and he was looking for a father."

Steve's new appearance fooled plenty of customers when he served their drinks from behind *the log*. "It was his way of having fun."

Perhaps that was part of his reason for hanging out and bartending at the Old Place. Flo believes it was therapeutic for the man who craved a break from the pressures of celebrity. "When you work in such proximity to someone, you come to know who they are and where their heart is, and Steve had a big one," Flo says as small tears make their way down her face. "There was kindness in his heart from the beginning. You can't be a good and bad person at the same time unless you're crazy. Steve wasn't crazy. He was intelligent; he was sane; he was focused."

Every Christmas, she recalls, Steve bought dozens of wreaths from the Boys Republic and gave them away to friends. One morning Flo was awakened at 6:30 by a light tapping on her own door. When she opened it, there was Steve hanging a holiday wreath. One Mother's Day she received an early morning telephone call from him, wishing her a happy Mother's Day.

"He loved kids and animals so much," she says. "He had a real heart for the underdog. He wasn't a big talker, but his kindness came in the form of his actions."

I can't help but agree, just in having observed him from a distance. He certainly showed love for his children and his wives—at least when he was with them. Coming from such a radically dysfunctional home, it was virtually impossible for him to show emotion. He kept his feelings bottled up, but there's no doubt, as Flo says, that he felt genuine love for others. He also felt deep empathy and compassion for the underdogs of life because all the statistical cards had been stacked against him, too, yet he'd succeeded on a level few have known.

"When you work in such proximity to someone, you come to know who they are and where their heart is, and Steve had a big one," Flo says as small tears make their way down her face.

Part of his drive came from his circumstances and upbringing, from his desire to prove himself. It's doubtful he would have become the star he did without his hardscrabble beginnings. Like a phoenix rising from the ashes, Steve got knocked down but always got back up. Yet it didn't heal his emotional wounds and eliminate his desperate need for love and approval.

This is a world I know well.

I, too, wanted to achieve something significant with my life, going back to my earliest days. Coming from somewhere

I didn't actually understand, I had an incredible amount of confidence that one day I would make my mark in the world. My mother didn't encourage this ambition, of course, and no father was in my life to affirm me, no one to tell me how to be a man. So just like McQueen, I endlessly searched for some father figure to fill that gap, while never letting myself doubt that I could still overcome it.

> "He loved kids and animals so much," she says. "He had a real heart for the underdog. He wasn't a big talker, but his kindness came in the form of his actions."

I was knocked down many times, but I was never knocked out and kept coming back for more. When the real world became too harsh, I would create imaginary worlds with my artwork, retreating into them, dreaming of becoming a professional cartoonist. Needing to fight so hard and cope so feverishly is not an existence I would wish on anyone, and surmounting it requires virtually a whole different kind of DNA and drive than those who come from stable and loving homes. The more fortunate ones find a way through it, but too many from broken and alcoholic homes give up, spiraling into destructive cycles that first land them in the gutter and then on a coroner's slab.

If not for the grace of God . . . .

Flo doesn't recall faith being a big topic of conversation when McQueen was around. But she says he and everyone in their circle openly wore their hearts on their sleeves and showed affection and mutual regard by attending one another's parties, watching out for one another's kids, and just enjoying one another's company.

The Old Place became even more of a refuge for McQueen as his marriage to Ali MacGraw unraveled. They'd been happy for a while, but the relationship was volatile, and there were knock-down, drag-out fights as their disparate personalities grated on them. "There were certain kinds of independent lady behaviors that I showed that really threatened him on a profound level," MacGraw would say. "Not on the level that the press likes to call 'Steve McQueen wouldn't let Ali MacGraw work.' That's a total distortion. It was a much more profound thing. It was a deep, deep sense of being abandoned like a child."

Flo says it boiled down to the simple fact that McQueen wanted out of Hollywood and MacGraw wanted back in after briefly joining him on sabbatical.

"The Hollywood thing took over his life, and he couldn't overcome it until he sat down. Steve wanted to stay home," Flo says. "He wanted that slowness, that normality. He wanted to sit at the kitchen table and be still."

> The more fortunate ones find a way through it, but too many from broken and alcoholic homes give up, spiraling into destructive cycles that first land them in the gutter and then on a coroner's slab.

I understand this. And so do you. When we're quiet, when we're listening, when we're ready, that's when God talks to us the loudest. Steve was finally slowing down and beginning to think deeply about the meaning and purpose of his life. He'd had his fill of fame and fortune.

He just wanted to be left alone.

McQueen's third wife and widow, Barbara, told me that his ultimate hope was to move to Idaho and live a much simpler life. She thinks he would have transitioned nicely into a character actor, preferring it to the burden of being a movie star. This had already been realized to a certain degree in his amazing performance in *Papillion*.

From my view, I think the Lord was beginning to whisper to Steve. The Bible speaks of the "still, small voice of God."

Steve was finally beginning to listen.

Good things were about to happen to him. He would finally find the ultimate father figure he'd been searching for, as well as the peace that had eluded him from the beginning.

> Steve was finally slowing down and beginning to think deeply about the meaning and purpose of his life. He'd had his fill of fame and fortune. He just wanted to be left alone.

NOTHING NEW
UNDER THE SUN

If Steve McQueen thought going into self-imposed exile from the silver screen would make people forget about him and leave him alone, he was badly mistaken. What occurred next was exactly the opposite of that. The studios and the public's interest in him actually became even more insatiable, if that's possible.

Hollywood was like an alternate universe where "no" meant "yes," "up" meant "down," and "let's do lunch" meant "I hope I'll never see you again." The more McQueen said no to studios and producers, the more they kept coming at him with scripts and offers. The films he turned down during this period became huge blockbusters with others in the starring roles. The list includes *First Blood, One Flew Over the Cuckoo's Nest, The Gauntlet, A Bridge Too Far, Silent Movie, Close Encounters of the Third Kind, Dirty Harry, The Bodyguard, Superman,* as well as sequels to *The Towering Inferno* and *Gone with the Wind.* In November 1975, McQueen refused the lead role in Francis Ford Coppola's *Apocalypse Now.*

When the offers kept coming, McQueen ripped the mailbox from its post and tossed it into the ocean. He arranged for his mail to be delivered to the local gas station and usually sent his son Chad to pick it up there. In a further effort to get the studios to leave him alone, McQueen demanded fifty thousand dollars just to look at a movie script. When his agent told him no one would pay it, Steve said, "Good—then I won't have to read anymore lousy scripts."

> The more McQueen said no to studios and producers, the more they kept coming at him with scripts and offers.

He even went so far as to personally bequeath his crown as King of Hollywood to Burt Reynolds. Reynolds was getting fitted one day for a film wardrobe at Western Costume Company in Hollywood when McQueen walked in. At the time, *The Towering Inferno* was smashing all box office records.

"It's all yours, kid," McQueen told Reynolds, who was coming into his own as a film star after transitioning from the small screen the way McQueen had. Reynolds had no idea what he was referring to and asked him what he meant.

"Number one, kid," said McQueen. "It's yours. I'm stepping down."

In many ways, Steve reminds me of the biblical king Solomon. Though surely Steve was not the wisest man in the world, as Solomon was said to be, they nevertheless had quite a bit in common.

The son of King David, Solomon as a young man found himself placed on the throne as king of Israel. His reign started off well, but then he began to squander his opportunities in pursuit of pure hedonism. With unlimited wealth to indulge his every whim, Solomon went after it all. There were epic drinking binges and interminable parties. He had a thousand women at his beck and call, of whom seven hundred were wives and the rest concubines. Compared to him, Hugh Hefner is a celibate monk.

Solomon eventually decided to embark on a research project. He would try every experience and every pleasure this world had to offer. No stone would remain unturned. In pursuit of that goal he ignored affairs of state and neglected his family.

Solomon later wrote,

> **When the offers kept coming, McQueen ripped the mailbox from its post and tossed it into the ocean.**

> With the help of a bottle of wine and all the wisdom I could muster, I tried my level best to penetrate the absurdity of life. I wanted to get a handle on anything useful we mortals might do during the years we spend on this earth . . . . Everything I wanted I took—I never said no to myself. I gave in to every impulse, held back nothing. I sucked the marrow of pleasure out of every task—my reward to myself for a hard day's work! Then I took a good look at everything I'd done, looked at all the sweat and hard work. But when I looked, I saw nothing but smoke. Smoke and spitting into the wind. There was nothing to any of it. Nothing. (Eccles. 2:3, 10–11 MSG)

Isn't it amazing how things have changed so little over the thousands of years that have passed? People chase after the same empty things, generation after generation, ignoring what Solomon learned: "There is nothing new under the sun" (Eccles. 1:9 NKJV).

It boils down to, as journalist Malcolm Muggeridge once wrote, that, "All new news is old news happening to new people."

Steve McQueen was at the very pinnacle of his hard-won success. He was again the biggest movie star on the planet.

In many ways, Steve reminds me of the biblical king Solomon. Though surely Steve was not the wisest man in the world, as Solomon was said to be, they nevertheless had quite a bit in common.

He had the fame, the women, the booze, and the drugs. And like Solomon he found out, "There was nothing to any of it. Nothing."

His self-destructive demons seemed to be off and roaring louder than ever at this point in his life. His second marriage was crumbling, he'd been in exile for two and a half years, and now the studio lawyers came at him with a contract he'd signed in 1971, guaranteeing them two more films. Later, at the end of his life, McQueen expressed the belief this movie deal triggered the cancer that was killing him.

Backed into a legal corner, McQueen had little choice but to do it. But instead of the action film the studios and public wanted, he chose to make a big-screen adaptation of Henrik Ibsen's *An Enemy of the People*, a turn-of-the-century play about a doctor who stands up to municipal corruption in a Scandinavian resort town. It was and still is widely believed that

McQueen made that choice out of spite to stick it to the studio forcing him to come out of retirement.

The film's thirty-three-day shoot occurred while McQueen's Trancas Beach home was being remodeled, so he moved into a suite at the Beverly Hills Hotel, ostensibly to be free of distractions that might impair his concentration on the movie. All he really did was substitute another distraction in the form of an endless parade of starlets, models, and professional party dolls.

Ali MacGraw purposely looked the other way, a decision she came to regret.

"It was a place I never went," she later said, referring to McQueen's hotel suite, "which was stupid. I should have gone in, opened the door, and kicked the crap out of whomever was in bed with him. He would have enjoyed it!"

Shunning most public appearances, industry parties, and private get-togethers, McQueen ventured out in public only when it was something he felt was important. Sometime in 1975 he attended a birthday party in Canoga Park for the son of his karate instructor, Pat Johnson. That's where Mel Novak met McQueen.

"Of course Steve was a big star, but you wouldn't have known it," says Mel. "He was a friendly, gracious person who gave my daughters a big, warm hug. We talked about life in general but not much about the movie industry. After meeting successful actors who are so full of themselves, it was impressive and refreshing to see he was just a good old boy."

Isn't it amazing how things have changed so little over the thousands of years that have passed?

Mel Novak is an actor, martial artist, ordained minister, and an evangelist who preaches on skid row and in prisons—a villain on the screen and a hero in the streets. I first met him a few years ago at Fred Jordan Missions on LA's Skid Row. Fred Jordan was my uncle, and the mission is now run by his wife, my Aunt Willie Jordan. Mel regularly conducts chapel services there, and I'm meeting him at the mission today.

> All he really did was substitute another distraction in the form of an endless parade of starlets, models, and professional party dolls.

At one of our first meetings, Mel gave me a flyer about his ministry that included a picture of him with Steve McQueen. It definitely grabbed my attention. Mel has appeared in more than forty movies and always does his own fighting and stunts, even at age seventy-four. He dueled Yul Brynner in *The Ultimate Warrior,* duked it out with Chuck Norris in *Eye for an Eye,* shot and killed Bruce Lee in *Game of Death,* and verbally jousted with Steve McQueen in *Tom Horn.*

In real life he's still a brawler but more of "street fighter," reaching out to those who are knocked down in life and have lost hope.

"God's forgiveness is bigger than anyone's sin," is the theme of Mel's message, and it has brought many to faith in Christ over the years.

Mel tells me now how his friendship with Steve McQueen evolved into something much deeper.

"The second time I met Steve was at a karate match," he recalls. "He was married to Ali MacGraw. I shared my walk with Jesus Christ with him, and he didn't mock me like some do.

As I reflected over that conversation over the next few weeks, I realized there were wounds underneath. His childhood sometimes haunted him, and he had carried around this baggage for years."

Mel knows a thing or two about childhood baggage. When he was young, he injured his leg so badly that doctors advised amputation. But in a sweet answer to fervent prayer, God saved the leg. Years later, the Lord healed Mel's throat after ten operations failed to do the job. Mel calls himself a "walking and talking miracle" and is determined for as long as he has legs and a voice to use them for the glory of God.

"You've gotta keep going, and this is what I do," he says. Mel averages close to twenty services a month at which "I get down to the nitty-gritty, and people express their pain and hurts to me."

That's what happened with Steve McQueen.

Their friendship really blossomed in 1976 when Mel went trap shooting with directors Steven Spielberg and John Milius and studio head Ken Hyman in Sylmar, California. "I saw this guy walking down Little Tujunga Canyon Road, who had this huge, full beard and really long hair," Mel says. "It was only after I saw his steel-blue eyes that I realized it was Steve."

McQueen had never shot trap before, but Mel offered him his shotgun and invited him to give it a try. "Steve popped one

> "I shared my walk with Jesus Christ with him, and he didn't mock me like some do. As I reflected over that conversation over the next few weeks, I realized there were wounds underneath. His childhood sometimes haunted him, and he had carried around this baggage for years."

after another, and we were all impressed," recalls Mel. "He said Francis Ford Coppola wanted him to play the role that Robert Duvall eventually landed in *Apocalypse Now.* The offer was $1 million for two weeks' work in the Philippines, but Steve said he passed because he didn't want to leave the country at the time."

When McQueen finally decided on his own to return to work, he requested Mel's services on the set of *Tom Horn* after firing a couple of actors who couldn't handle the dialogue.

"Steve told producer Fred Weintraub to call me because he knew I didn't drink or do drugs," says Mel. "Fred called me at three o'clock in the afternoon and offered me the job. I asked, 'When do I have to be on the plane?' He said, 'Your plane leaves at six o'clock.' So I get there, and I didn't get the script until the next morning. Then when I arrived on the set, they told me they wanted me to play a *different* part than what I was told on the phone. So I said, 'Lord, help me here.'"

As usual, Mel didn't require much help. He nailed his scene after a brief rehearsal, and McQueen was so delighted with his work he offered Mel a part in his next movie, *The Hunter.* But Mel had already accepted a part in a big-budget film in Europe in which he would get equal billing with three big stars. When he called McQueen to tell him, Steve told him to go ahead with the film in Europe and not worry about it. They'd work together again, he said, "down the road."

> When he called McQueen to tell him, Steve told him to go ahead with the film in Europe and not worry about it. They'd work together again, he said, "down the road." Neither knew at the time, of course, that McQueen was running out of road.

Neither knew at the time, of course, that McQueen was running out of road. A week after *The Hunter* wrapped, Steve was diagnosed with cancer. As soon as Mel found out, he began writing letters to McQueen. The letters were filled with Scripture. Then came numerous telephone conversations about God and healing. Mel knew plenty about both. In addition to the healing of his leg and throat as a child, he had prayed for God's healing touch of the prostate cancer.

> "I was a good encourager, and I'd uplift and edify Steve. When I would write him letters, he'd call me back and tell me, 'That really encouraged me.'"

God answered Mel's prayer.

"When you get healed from cancer," he says, "people call you, and they know you'll be faithful to pray for them, as I did for Steve. They know that prayer can invade the impossible. Sometimes they get miracles; sometimes they don't. But they know I will never give up. That's why I'm even alive. I battle all the time."

Mel was one of the first people to know about McQueen's condition and one of the first to pray for him.

"When I knew he was really, really sick, I'd write letters and call him every two to three days and encourage him," Mel says. "There's a lot of healing passages in the Bible, like Luke 1:37 which says, 'Nothing's impossible for God.' I was a good encourager, and I'd uplift and edify Steve. When I would write him letters, he'd call me back and tell me, 'That really encouraged me.'"

The last time Mel spoke to him, Steve's coughing fits had become so intense and prolonged Mel would need to momentarily put the phone down because it was so painful to hear. "It was this deep, horrible cough I'd first started hearing on *Tom Horn,* and it just got worse over time. It was haunting. It gave me the chills. Oh dear, that cough was just brutal."

Mel's prayerful outreach to McQueen by mail and phone continued until Steve stopped responding. Then Mel read that McQueen had gone to Mexico for cancer treatment, and figured the end was near.

It was. But this end was gloriously preceded by a new beginning.

THE VISITOR

A few days after meeting Mel Novak at Fred Jordan Missions, I'm surprised to get an email from Barbi McQueen. When we said good-bye in Idaho, I made an open-ended offer for her to come visit Cathe and me in Orange County, see firsthand what our ministry was like, share a few meals, and generally get to know each other better.

Now that the holidays are over and her guests have all gone home, Barbi says she wouldn't mind at all starting the new year in the California sunshine. And while she's at it, and if I'm interested, she would be happy to show me what her and Steve's life in Santa Paula was like.

I'm doubly thrilled. Barbi and I may appear to be polar opposites in some things, but we also have a lot in common, including a love of '60s music and a crazy sense of humor. We're also the same age, so there are a lot of familiar cultural touchstones Barbi, Cathe, and I share.

Barbi arrives on a Saturday in mid-January. Cathe and I pick her up at John Wayne Airport, and the two of them hit it off immediately. Cathe is instantly charmed by Barbi's openness, and Barbi just as quickly responds to Cathe's natural warmth and beauty. This is a very good start.

We head for El Cholo, our favorite Mexican restaurant in nearby Corona Del Mar. Hanging on the wall is a photo of a man I was blessed to befriend toward the end of his amazing life. Louis Zamperini ran in the 1936 Olympics in Berlin and ran so fast in his races that Hitler himself made a point of shaking his hand.

> Cathe is instantly charmed by Barbi's openness, and Barbi just as quickly responds to Cathe's natural warmth and beauty. This is a very good start.

Louis enlisted in the military when World War II broke out, and while flying a search and rescue plane called "The Green Hornet," a mechanical failure forced Louis down. After forty-seven days adrift at sea, a Japanese ship spotted and picked him up. He spent the remainder of the war as a prisoner. His truly inspiring story is told in the best-selling book *Unbroken* by Laura Hillenbrand and also in a film by the same name.

Louis said one of the things that kept him going in that hellhole of a POW camp where he was singled out for harrowing torture because of his Olympic fame was thinking about his favorite item on the El Cholo menu—the hallowed #1 plate, consisting of a rolled taco, cheese enchilada, and beans and rice. In honor of this great man, I order the same.

Over dinner Barbi, Cathe, and I chat away like old friends about whatever comes to mind. I make a point of not bringing up Steve. (That will wait for another time.) For now we just enjoy a great meal and one another's company.

Afterward we get Barbi settled at her hotel and tell her we'll pick her up in the morning for church. She says she can't wait to see me in my "element."

And after church is over, she seems satisfied. I'm happy about this, to be sure.

By afternoon, the three of us are driving up the coast to a great seafood place. Barbi has a fondness for Dungeness crab. We grab a table on the patio with an expansive ocean view. It's the perfect day to be outside. Gazing out at the blue Pacific, Barbi reflects somewhat wistfully, "The only thing I miss about California is the ocean. And Steve, of course."

It's the first time his name has come up.

Barbi came along in McQueen's life when he was broken. The heartache brought on by the failure of his marriage to Ali MacGraw, as well as the professional failure of *An Enemy of the People* (Warner Brothers refused to distribute the movie) pushed Steve to his lowest point and left his heart hanging by a thread.

Then he saw a picture of international model Barbara Minty in a Club Med advertisement and was so taken by her beauty that he contacted her agent and said she was perfect for the part of an Indian princess in *Tom Horn*, a movie he was contemplating making.

A meeting was set up. As Barbi recalls it, when she walked into the room at the Beverly Wilshire Hotel, she got her first

Afterward we get Barbi settled at her hotel and tell her we'll pick her up in the morning for church. She says she can't wait to see me in my "element." And after church is over, she seems satisfied. I'm happy about this, to be sure.

look at the bearded, long-haired McQueen. "To me he looked more like a San Pedro beach bum than an international movie star."

But as they talked during the next two hours, Barbi found the actor's gentle demeanor so appealing that after he left she announced to her agent that one day she would marry Steve McQueen. Of course her agent was astounded but, after watching them interact with each other, not totally surprised.

> "To me he looked more like a San Pedro beach bum than an international movie star."

"It clicked for me right away," she tells Cathe and me. "And I think it did for him too. He was exactly what I'd been searching for . . . the love of my life."

But, she adds, "My relationship with Steve wasn't exactly flowers and chocolates in the beginning. Even though he made quite an impression in our first meeting, I was starting to have second thoughts."

> "I might as well have worn a sign around my neck that read, 'Fresh off the farm,'" she laughs.

Those second thoughts started the day after that meeting with McQueen and her agent, when she was lying on a lounge at the hotel pool and Steve appeared, sat next to her, and "started yapping away."

In midsentence he sprang up and left. A few minutes later he returned with a couple of glasses of iced beer and said to Barbi, "Come with me for a second."

She followed him into the men's sauna, where he gave the attendant on duty a hefty tip and instructed him not to let anybody else inside.

"We sat down in the sauna, and Steve began asking me some very personal questions, wanting to know about me," Barbi recalls. "Perhaps my appeal was that I was a little naïve. I was not part of the regular Hollywood scene, and he sensed I wasn't looking for a Rolex or Porsche. Whatever I said must have passed the test because he asked me out to dinner that night. We set a time for seven o'clock."

Still jet-lagged from her flight, Barbi was sound asleep in her room when seven o'clock rolled around, and fifteen minutes later he called to ask if she was still coming to his suite.

"Yeah, I guess so," she groggily replied—and promptly fell asleep again as soon as the receiver hit the cradle. Steve called back at 7:30, then again at 8:00, and finally Barbi got up and dressed. She wore no makeup and put her hair into a simple ponytail. "I might as well have worn a sign around my neck that read, 'Fresh off the farm,'" she laughs.

> He was coming to the end of one life and stood on the verge of another. He just didn't know what or who he was searching for. Not yet.

She wasn't laughing when McQueen answered her knock on the door of suite 220. "Right behind him were two of the tallest, most beautiful blonde-haired women I had ever seen in my life," Barbi recalls. "They were typical Hollywood chicks with tight designer jeans, gold chains, and heavy makeup. They didn't look like they were there for choir practice."

Barbi told McQueen she would see him another time, but he quickly ushered her inside and said the women were just leaving. They went, and Barbi and McQueen ended up having a lovely dinner in the suite—sand dab fish with little grapes.

So, obviously, Steve was still caught in his selfish, hedonistic world. Barbi had definitely caught his eye, but he was still playing the field, looking for something and someone that was, for lack of a better word, "good." He had his share of sleazy, easy girls who wanted him as a conquest, and he was more than a willing accomplice. But things were changing for McQueen. He was coming to the end of one life and stood on the verge of another. He just didn't know what or who he was searching for. Not yet.

_____

She takes out her iPhone to show Cathe and me the very first picture she ever took of Steve.

_____

When Barbi returned to Idaho, McQueen called her frequently. After she completed a modeling job in New York City, they got together in Denver. She was loading her luggage into Steve's car when he noticed her 35-millimeter camera. She carried it with her everywhere, always loaded with film.

McQueen was notoriously camera shy. Except for maybe a dozen paparazzi shots and a few publicity stills for his movies, he hadn't willingly let anybody photograph him for the last five years of his life.

"I like to take pictures," Barbi told him, "and wherever I go, the camera goes. I don't sell anything, and I won't do anything with them. It'll just be between you and me."

McQueen halted, seemingly suspicious for a moment, then said, "Okay. That's fine."

And that's how Barbi ended up photographically documenting their whole three-and-a-half-year relationship.

She takes out her iPhone to show Cathe and me the very first picture she ever took of Steve. The setting sun backlights him, lending an almost ethereal quality to the photo. The long-haired, thickly bearded McQueen isn't smiling, but his expression isn't stern either, and there is something so vulnerable and so *questing* in those famous blue eyes that it's almost as if Barbi's lens had peeked into the man's very soul.

It's the face of a weary wanderer looking for home.

He was getting very close.

BROAD BEACH MEMOIRS

Around ten o'clock the next morning, Barbi, Cathe, and I are in the Bullitt headed for Trancas Beach, north of Malibu off the Pacific Coast Highway. Rush-hour traffic has subsided by this time, and the seventy-five-mile-drive north is effortless and relaxing.

The two women have truly bonded already. In Cathe's presence, Barbi is open, unguarded, and engaging as she talked about her husband.

"I was twenty-six when Steve died, and he was fifty," she says. "When I approached my own fiftieth birthday, I really sank into a deep depression. Friends threw a party for me to celebrate the occasion, but I left early, went home, locked the doors, closed the windows, and went right to bed."

The next day, Barbi says, it was as if a veil had been lifted. She could finally look back at her three-and-a-half years with Steve without the deep anxiety she'd been feeling.

Barbi, Cathe, and I have planned a nice lunch at Neptune's Net, a Malibu landmark on Pacific Coast Highway. Barbi and

Steve came here often in the '70s. The original restaurant was established in 1956, and the fryer and grill haven't changed in more than fifty years. Same goes for the fare—live, fresh, and fried seafood, plus hamburgers and tacos.

"I was twenty-six when Steve died, and he was fifty," she says.

Barbi orders a cup of clam chowder and Dungeness crab. Cathe orders halibut.

I'm tempted by the Dungeness crab. After all, it's their specialty and I love it, but I've always felt it was too much work with too little payoff. So I go for a medley of street tacos.

The area has changed plenty since the McQueens lived here. It's now crowded with restaurants and boutique office buildings. Old beach hideaways have been replaced by ornate modern-style homes, and traffic is bustling.

"The town at the time was very quaint and intimate," Barbi says. "It had two gas stations, the Trancas Supermarket, and a country and western bar. That was it."

Their immediate neighbors were Arthur E. Bartlett, owner of the Century 21 real estate empire; garment district millionaire and recording studio owner Howard Grinel; and the irrepressible Keith Moon, legendary drummer for the Who. Finding out that Moon was Steve McQueen's next-door neighbor makes me chuckle involuntarily, and I remark, "That must have been interesting."

"It most definitely was, Greg," Barbi laughs.

Moon had earned the nickname "Moon the Loon" for his wild behavior, usually fueled by alcohol and drugs. He was famous for trashing hotel rooms, hanging from chandeliers, destroying plumbing fixtures with firecrackers, and driving expensive automobiles into swimming pools.

Next to Moon, McQueen was St. Francis of Assisi.

"Steve told me he once found Moon passed out on the beach after an all-night drinking binge," says Barbi. Instead of a swimming suit, "he was dressed in a full Nazi uniform. There was no time to ask questions because he was about to be swept to sea, so Steve pulled him to safety and deposited him on his doorstep for someone else to deal with."

Moon had a giant stained-glass window in a bathroom of his house that faced the window of the McQueens' bedroom. Barbi says the light in Moon's bathroom was on all the time, frequently disturbing Steve's sleep. He called Moon repeatedly to ask him to turn off the light, but nothing ever happened. Finally Steve took matters into his own hands.

"He grabbed a shotgun from under the bed, walked out to the patio, and blasted Moon's stained-glass window," Barbi recalls with a smile. "The blast reverberated throughout the neighborhood. Then Steve marched calmly back into the house, put the shotgun away, walked to the kitchen, and cracked open an ice-cold Old Milwaukee."

Another day in the life of Steve McQueen.

"He grabbed a shotgun from under the bed, walked out to the patio, and blasted Moon's stained-glass window," Barbi recalls with a smile. "The blast reverberated throughout the neighborhood. Then Steve marched calmly back into the house, put the shotgun away, walked to the kitchen, and cracked open an ice-cold Old Milwaukee." Another day in the life of Steve McQueen.

After lunch we drive ten minutes to a magnificent three-story wood and glass structure with a panoramic view of the Pacific. It's the residence on Broad Beach Road where Barbi and Steve started their life together. They lived there for close to a year and a half.

Barbi says their days at Trancas Beach were very tranquil. They'd play on the beach and take drives up and down the coast in search of antiques, as well as longer jaunts in one of Steve's beat-up pickup trucks to Utah, Montana, and Ketchum—the central Idaho town where Barbi maintained her five-acre ranch. They also attended motorcycle and swap meets and visited friends. Steve's buddies were stuntmen, mechanics, racers, pilots, karate instructors, and others active in physical pursuits.

Steve also drilled her on weaponry. He was very proficient with firearms of all kinds—pistols, handguns, rifles, and shotguns. He knew how to field strip a weapon and expected her to learn how.

Occasionally a celebrity dropped by, Barbi says—Elliot Gould, Sam Peckinpah, Lee Majors, James Garner (whom she spontaneously addressed as "Mr. Rockford"). Barbi recalls the time Peter Fonda, his former wife Becky, and their daughter Bridget came over for breakfast. Bridget was just a youngster then and a ball of energy. She practically bounced off the walls.

"I've never been much of a cook, but I managed to make breakfast for the Fondas," Barbi says. "And they actually ate it. Most likely Steve ordered everybody to either eat their eggs or wear them."

Once Steve sat Barbi down in the house and tried to teach her about motorcycles. She dutifully watched him take one apart in their living room and methodically explain each part's function, why it was engineered the way it was, and how it contributed to helping the motorcycle run. After a few minutes, she confesses her eyes glazed over, and it was all she could do to nod her head once in a while and say, "Yes, honey."

Steve also drilled her on weaponry. He was very proficient with firearms of all kinds—pistols, handguns, rifles, and shotguns. He knew how to field strip a weapon and expected her to learn how. He also devised an escape plan in case an intruder ever broke into the house.

"The plan called for me to roll out of bed, drop to the floor, take a .45 apart, put the bullets back in, and have the weapon ready to fire," Barbi says. "Of course, it would have been much easier and safer just to keep the safety on, but Steve wanted me to be ready for a combat situation."

Disco was the rage then, and "Steve wore this flowery silk shirt, white pants, and a gold chain around his neck," she recalls with a laugh. "And he danced like Austin Powers.

This is understandable considering that not only was McQueen an internationally known celebrity, but he was a regular target for kooks and attention-seeking radicals. He had been on the hit list of Charles Manson, like I said, and in 1977 received a death threat from an unstable man, which was noted in his FBI file.

Steve and Barbi mostly enjoyed simple things—nature, quiet rides in one of his beloved old trucks, and rummaging through old antique shops. "When Steve and I traveled, we stayed off the interstate, preferring back roads and little-known routes to get to our destination, taking our own sweet time,"

Barbi says. "Often we'd pull out a road map and flip a coin to see what route to take. Time was not a concern, but our journey itself was—kind of like our relationship and how we lived our lives at the time."

Sometimes, Barbi acknowledges, the almost-quarter-century difference in their ages was almost painfully obvious, like the time Steve took her dancing at the Daisy, a members-only nightclub on Rodeo Drive. Disco was the rage then, and "Steve wore this flowery silk shirt, white pants, and a gold chain around his neck," she recalls with a laugh. "And he danced like Austin Powers. He did the Twist, the Shag, the Watusi, and the Clam, while everyone else disco danced. I thought I was going to die of embarrassment."

> "He did things like that—in the snap of a finger," Barbi says. "Learning how to fly became Steve's latest passion, and like everything else he did, he jumped into it with both feet."

Another time, the Rolling Stones made a West Coast swing on their *Some Girls* tour in July 1978, and McQueen scored tickets and a backstage pass. Barbi was thrilled, thinking she might witness some good old-fashioned rock 'n' roll debauchery. Instead, she says, "we arrived backstage and mostly wandered around. Finally Steve bumped into bass player Bill Wyman, and they shared a beer and had a heartfelt conversation about kids. Here was this rugged, tough-guy actor and one of rock 'n' roll's greatest self-professed ladies' men, and they just talked about how much fatherhood meant to them. It was very dignified and proper—not at all what I expected."

That same year McQueen plunked down $75,000 for his own five-acre parcel in Ketchum, adjoining Barbi's. He planned to build a log cabin and call it the Last Chance. Several months later he purchased a four-hundred-acre property in East Fork, about a half hour from Ketchum, on which he intended to build a cabin, guesthouse, and a private runway for his planes.

Steve grew interested in planes and flying after *Tom Horn* wrapped in early March 1979. Back at Trancas Beach, Barbi says, Steve would get up in the morning, read the newspaper, and "start poring over the classified ads in his cheap dime-store reading glasses, looking for the latest bargains. He was reading *Airplane Trader* magazine one day and something caught his eye—a bright yellow PT Stearman bi-plane."

The Stearman was built in the 1940s for the US Navy and had been a basic trainer for about fifty thousand pilots in World War II. The one pictured in the ad had a newly overhauled 220-horsepower Continental engine. It was in mint condition and had a $35,000 price tag. Steve picked up the phone, called the owner, and bought it within minutes.

"He did things like that—in the snap of a finger," Barbi says. "Learning how to fly became Steve's latest passion, and like everything else he did, he jumped into it with both feet."

Santa Paula, a small town about an hour north of Malibu, was called the "Antique Plane Capital of the World," and that's where McQueen went in search of someone to teach him how to fly his new baby. After asking around, he was told a fellow named Sammy Mason would be the best man for the job.

He was, in more ways than one.

LEARNING TO FLY

Malibu was an emotional trip down memory lane for Barbi, and when we drop her back at the hotel, I'm not sure she will be up to going to Santa Paula the next day. The last time she was there was in 2007 for a tribute to Steve, and it wasn't easy for her. She's noncommittal about tomorrow, and we decide to see how she feels in the morning.

When we pull up the next day, Barbi is waiting for us in the lobby. She climbs in the car and says, "I was just about wrecked, but I'm determined to see this through. There's something telling me I need to go. Besides, there're some old friends I want to see."

She means Pete Mason.

Pete is the son of Sammy Mason, the man who taught Steve McQueen how to fly an airplane and then piloted him to a much higher level. Sammy passed away in December 2001, but his name is still legendary in aviation circles.

The GPS indicates today's drive is 110 miles—about two hours if we don't hit any heavy traffic. Driving a rented SUV, I've decided to give the Bullitt a break today, as a 1967 fastback

Mustang is not the most comfortable car on a long drive for *one* person, much less three. The backseat is basically nonexistent, and so is the legroom. Barbi asks me to turn on the satellite radio to the '60s on 6 station. I'm happy to comply. Much to our delight, "A Hard Day's Night" by the Beatles is playing. I have all their records and have memorized most of their lyrics. In my opinion they are far and away the greatest rock band of all time.

Pete is the son of Sammy Mason, the man who taught Steve McQueen how to fly an airplane.

Barbi's increasing anxiety is palpable as we take the turnoff from Interstate 5 onto California Highway 26, which will take us into Santa Paula. Ten miles before we get there, we enter the Fillmore city limits and Barbi sighs, groaning as if in pain. Cathe puts her hand on Barbi's shoulder and says gently, "It's going to okay, Barbi. God is with us."

When Steve and Barbi lived here, it was a rural town of about twenty thousand wonderful, homespun people who weren't impressed by power, money, or Hollywood luminaries— just the way Steve liked it.

I know well the angst Barbi is experiencing. I know the reverie. It happened when our son Christopher was killed in the automobile accident in 2008. And it still happens on the 91 Freeway in Corona. Many times as I've driven by or even near that spot, I don't just sigh but break into anguished tears. Now it's just a dull ache.

A few minutes later we are in Santa Paula, an agricultural town reminiscent of mainstream America but with a Mexican flavor. When Steve and Barbi lived here, it was a rural town of about twenty thousand wonderful, homespun people who weren't impressed by power, money, or Hollywood luminaries—just the way Steve liked it. Santa Paula reminded him of his hometown of Slater, Missouri, and he fell in love with the place and its people. "This is as close to home as I can find," he told Barbi. "I want to die here."

When they first moved to Santa Paula, beginning in mid-1979, Barbi and Steve lived in the three-thousand-square-foot airplane hangar that housed his Stearman. When I ask Barbi what it was like to live in what was in essence just a large garage, she gets a dreamy look on her face and says, "It was the coolest thing ever. I'd do it again in a heartbeat."

Eventually they purchased a four-bedroom home on fifteen acres a few miles from the airport, but while it underwent extensive renovation, they contentedly occupied the hangar with the plane and all the antiques McQueen had collected and crammed into it. They slept on a mattress and box spring on the floor, and in the morning, Barbi says, "Steve would make coffee and bring it to me, open the hangar door, and we'd watch the world from our floor-mounted bed."

> They slept on a mattress and box spring on the floor, and in the morning, Barbi says, "Steve would make coffee and bring it to me, open the hangar door, and we'd watch the world from our floor-mounted bed."

Driving through the town's Main Street, Barbi sits up a little straighter. She starts pointing out some of the places she and Steve frequented—an antique store where they found lots of bargains, a used bookstore where they purchased most of their reading material, and a Chinese food place they frequented at least once a week, coming in through the back door.

"The food was horrible, and whatever I ate there was orange," Barbi says. "It didn't matter. It was better than my cooking, which the first time Steve ever tasted it, said, 'We're going out for dinner!'

"And I never made dinner again."

Before we head to the hangar, Barbi asks me to turn down a side street called South Mountain Road to take a peek at their former house. It's a beautiful Victorian structure built in 1896.

"Everything that looked new was tossed out in favor of antiques that would have been true to the period when the house was built," Barbi says. "That included old-fashioned toilets with high wall-mounted tanks and chain pulls, antique marble wash basins, brass fittings, period ceiling fans, period multiglobe chandeliers, filigree light fixtures, wooden crank telephones, and an old-fashioned stove and oven."

The man standing in front of the hangar as we pull up is Pete Mason. Barbi rushes out to hug him and then introduces Cathe and me.

Barbi says she did put her foot down, however, when it came to the washer and dryer. "There's no way you'd find me hand washing laundry or using a clothesline," she quips.

It took two minutes at most to get from the house to the airport. The man standing in front of the hangar as we pull up is Pete Mason. Barbi rushes out to hug him and then introduces Cathe and me. The current owner of the hangar is there, too, and opens the massive, weathered, electric green door so Barbi can have a look inside. The interior is filled with every imaginable thing from a large model plane suspended from the ceiling to old movie posters, oil cans, trophies, piles of magazines, metal signs, and much more. Those guys from *American Pickers* would have a field day here.

When Steve died, Barbi hired a moving van and packed up as much of his stuff as it would safely carry—antique slot machines, cash registers, knives, Kewpie dolls, bicycles, vintage gasoline pumps, and, of course, lots of motorcycles. The rest stayed behind, and thirty-seven years later, and some of it is still here.

After the Cook's tour, we sit down at a table outside the hangar with Pete—who, it turns out, was the one who *actually* taught Steve how to fly because at that time his dad wasn't accepting new students.

When the McQueens moved to Santa Paula, Sammy Mason was a living legend in aviation. He'd been flying for forty-plus years, having been both a stunt pilot as well as a test pilot for Lockheed. When he met Steve, he

> When Steve died, Barbi hired a moving van and packed up as much of his stuff as it would safely carry—antique slot machines, cash registers, knives, Kewpie dolls, bicycles, vintage gasoline pumps, and, of course, lots of motorcycles.

was in his sixties, semiretired, and didn't have the time or inclination to teach Flying 101. When McQueen phoned to inquire about lessons, he didn't say who he was, and Sammy later said he figured McQueen "was either the attendant at the service station where I filled up my car or the butcher." He then concluded it was the latter, "because he could afford to fly."

Sammy told him to try his son Pete, an excellent flight instructor in his own right, but McQueen wouldn't take no for an answer and kept calling back. When he finally disclosed his identity, it meant nothing to Sammy, who went to Pete and asked who the heck was Steve McQueen? Turned out *The Great Escape* was one of Sammy's favorite movies, but that didn't cut anything with him, and he continued to rebuff McQueen's entreaties. But he did agree to at least come check out the Stearman.

Sammy told him to try his son Pete, an excellent flight instructor in his own right, but McQueen wouldn't take no for an answer and kept calling back. When he finally disclosed his identity, it meant nothing to Sammy, who went to Pete and asked who the heck was Steve McQueen?

Nobody was more charming and persuasive than Steve McQueen when he wanted something, and by the time Sammy left the hangar, he had agreed to take Steve under his wing—but only after McQueen got his introductory flying lessons from Pete.

McQueen was a natural in the cockpit. Racing cars and motorcycles had given him razor-sharp hand-eye coordination, and he was a quick study. He spent hours in the air with both Masons, and on May 1, 1979, flew his first solo flight and became a licensed pilot. It was one of his proudest moments. And as only Steve McQueen would, he went all in.

"Steve loved wearing the old-fashioned goggles, jumpsuits, and leather bomber jackets," says Barbi. "He could hardly wait to get in his plane and taxi down the runway and fly around the sky, free as a bird."

But the vintage Stearman wasn't the only thing McQueen was learning about from his hours in the air because Sammy turned out to be much more than a flight instructor. The time they spent together made him another surrogate father, for one, but also a role model that Steve desperately needed in his life.

Sammy was totally unflappable and comfortable in his own skin. He had a natural inner core that exuded confidence without braggadocio and drew the respect and admiration of everyone who knew him. Steve, too, was in awe of him. And as they became closer over the months, he started asking questions of his new mentor. What he wanted most to know was what gave Sammy the kind of serenity and peace that Steve had vainly searched for his entire life?

The answer, Sammy told him, was that he was a Christian.

Over time, they began to talk about God. Mason didn't preach or even try to persuade. He just answered Steve's questions to the best of his ability and told how faith in the Lord had impacted his own life.

"Sammy and me would fly, and he'd tell me about the Lord," McQueen later told a friend. "Flying and the Lord . . . I learned about the Bible. I'd listen and fly. It made sense. It made me feel good."

The impenetrable armor Steve had developed over a lifetime was finally beginning to crack. He'd personally seen the emptiness of the life he lived. He'd had his

> He spent hours in the air with both Masons, and on May 1, 1979, flew his first solo flight and became a licensed pilot. It was one of his proudest moments. And as only Steve McQueen would, he went all in.

> "Sammy and me would fly, and he'd tell me about the Lord," McQueen later told a friend. "Flying and the Lord . . . I learned about the Bible. I'd listen and fly. It made sense. It made me feel good."

nose rubbed in it, in fact. He knew where the answers *weren't,* and now he was talking to someone who seemed to know where they *were.* Others had shared this gospel message before with Steve, from producer Russell Doughten to stuntman Stan Barrett to actor Mel Novak. Those were seeds that had been planted in McQueen's heart. But having conquered every world he'd ever entered as an adult—from acting to driving—learning to fly was one of the last things on his bucket list. And God arranged for both the seeker and the one with the message to connect at just the right time.

> Santa Paula and Steve's new down-to-earth neighbors had finally provided him with the home, the no-strings-attached camaraderie, and the emotional security for which he'd yearned so long.

There could not have been a better person to embrace Steve than Sammy, and eventually Steve and Barbi ended up alongside Sammy and his wife, Wanda, in the balcony of the Ventura Missionary Church for Sunday services.

Santa Paula and Steve's new down-to-earth neighbors had finally provided him with the home, the no-strings-attached camaraderie, and the emotional security for which he'd yearned so long. Now it was up to *him.* Would he accept God's call? Or would he continue his aimless search?

HELLO, PREACHER MAN!

Returning from Santa Paula, the mood in the car is more mellow than melancholy. Seeing the hangar again and talking to Pete Mason seems to have been actually cathartic for Barbi and put her in an expansive mood. So I plunge right in and ask how Steve told her he wanted them to start attending services at Ventura Missionary Church.

"One day he walked into the hangar and out of the blue said, 'We're going to church on Sunday,' and that was it," she says. "He never explained why he wanted to go, never explained why he wanted me to go with him. I just figured it was the wifely thing to do. So I did." She put on one of those "dowdy" (Barbi's word) knee-length dresses he'd recently bought for her, and she went.

A few faithful people who wanted to serve God started the Ventura Missionary Church in July 1960 in a dance studio. Three years later they had a proper church erected on the corner of Telegraph and Day Roads and in 1971, called Reverend

Leonard DeWitt to be senior pastor of the seventy-five-member congregation. Under his leadership Ventura Missionary Church had such a massive growth spurt that a bigger facility was built in 1975.

Once Steve made the decision to attend services there, Barbi says, it was important to him that his presence not be a distraction to other worshippers. "He thought the focus should be on the Lord and not Steve McQueen," she says.

"One day he walked into the hangar and out of the blue said, 'We're going to church on Sunday,' and that was it," she says. "He never explained why he wanted to go, never explained why he wanted me to go with him. I just figured it was the wifely thing to do. So I did."

But of course, unless he intended to wear a bag over his head, people would recognize the movie star in their midst. (At this point he'd cut his hair short again for *The Hunter.*) He didn't, and they did, but it never became a problem, Barbi explains. "Several members recognized him, but he wasn't perturbed or upset, happily shaking hands with many of them. He said later on that the people seemed genuine and that he felt very comfortable in that setting."

The McQueens sat in the balcony of the church with Sammy and Wanda Mason almost every Sunday, and over time their little group expanded as Steve brought along his son Chad whenever he visited, as well as friends from the airport and anyone else he could convince to come with him. Church became part of the weekly routine, and Steve McQueen began to change before peoples' eyes.

The change came with at least one unintended consequence, as related by Steve's ranch foreman, Grady Ragsdale, in his 1983 book *Steve McQueen: The Final Chapter:* "Steve liked to roll his old desk chair out in front of the hangar doors and, leaning back with beer in hand, watch the planes take off and land. He had finished one can and was starting another when he remarked, 'This beer tastes awful.' He made a face, then added jokingly, 'They told me if I started going to church I'd lose my taste for it. I guess they were right.'"

The McQueens had attended services for about three months, Barbi says, when Steve finally introduced himself to Pastor DeWitt. McQueen invited him out to lunch, just the two of them. He never told Barbi what happened, but she says upon Steve's return home, it was immediately apparent his session with DeWitt had had a profound effect on her husband. "He was a little more quiet and reserved than usual," she says. "He seemed different."

> The McQueens sat in the balcony of the church with Sammy and Wanda Mason almost every Sunday … Church became part of the weekly routine, and Steve McQueen began to change before peoples' eyes.

My mind is racing with all manner of possibilities. Did Steve open himself up and profess his faith to Pastor DeWitt at that lunch? Or did they just talk about matters of faith in general? Did Steve test DeWitt like he did everyone else he'd talk to about God? What was their relationship like? I desperately wanted to know.

But all of a sudden Barbi seems a little different herself, pensive and more guarded. So instead of pressing her about that mysterious lunch, I simply ask if Leonard DeWitt is still alive. She says she hasn't seen him since he officiated at a private memorial service for Steve two days after he passed away in November 1980. If he's still around, Barbi guesses he'd be about eighty years old. Unless retired ministers go into the Witness Protection Program, she adds, perking back up, it probably wouldn't be too hard to track him down.

McQueen invited him out to lunch, just the two of them. He never told Barbi what happened, but she says upon Steve's return home, it was immediately apparent his session with DeWitt had had a profound effect on her husband.

Barbi is going back to Idaho in the morning, scheduled to catch an early morning Town Car to the airport. At the hotel door we say our good-byes to this warm, engaging, generous free spirit who's become very special in our lives. Cathe and Barbi hug like lifelong friends, and when it's my turn, I thank her for everything and wish her Godspeed.

As she's about to enter the hotel, Barbi stops, turns around with a big smile on her face, and calls out, "Tell Leonard DeWitt I said hello, Preacher Man!"

Then she's gone.

———

There is no question that God arranged for my path to cross with Barbi McQueen and so many others. It all started with my fixation on finding a Bullitt car then intensified when I saw a documentary about McQueen and tried to put my finger on something I'd heard somewhere about him becoming a Christian. The people I've met since then are not actors repeating lines. They are friends and family who knew Steve better than anyone. And as this story unfolds before my eyes, I wonder why it's never been told publicly. Whenever I share a brief version of it, people are amazed by it.

I think back to that offhand talk with Mel Gibson in the green room before I interviewed him on stage at one of our recent SoCal Harvest events about his new film *Hacksaw Ridge*. I'm privileged to have gotten to know Mel a bit and find out firsthand what an amazing guy he is. Among other things, he possesses a great sense of humor.

Mel never met Steve McQueen but is a big fan.

"He [McQueen] developed a new kind of hero that wasn't your typical two-dimensional hero," Mel said. "He was kind of antiheroic. He was the bad boy you could dig.

"And he understood the camera. He understood the level of which he had to operate in front of the camera. He understood what sort of intensity he needed to bring at what minute. Sometimes it wasn't much. It was hardly on the Richter scale. It was effortless. It was small. It was subtle. He could switch it on. This is what you need to be an actor.

"He was so cool, man. What was his legacy? Well, there has never been another one. He is singular. He was very good. He was the best at what he did. He was the best Steve McQueen there was. Nobody else could do that."

> "He [McQueen] developed a new kind of hero that wasn't your typical two-dimensional hero," Mel said. "He was kind of antiheroic. He was the bad boy you could dig."

Mel actually reminds me of Steve, starting with their blue eyes. When Mel hit the big time with *The Road Warrior*, a *New York Times* film critic compared him to McQueen.

In the course of our chat that night, I told Mel about Steve's conversion to Christianity. And like so many others, he said he'd heard it happened after McQueen found out he had cancer. He was stunned when I said Steve came to Jesus *before* his cancer diagnosis. It happened when he was at the very top of his game, and it was his faith that enabled him to face the horrible news.

Mel Gibson is also a man of faith. He directed the wildly successful and powerful movie about the last hours of Jesus called *The Passion of the Christ*. He knows like few others what it's like to breathe the rarified air of international superstardom.

"Many people have very hard lives. You have to look at that and say, 'Where is the justice in that?,'" Mel said. "For me there has to be a place where that evens out somehow. It is about the journey we make here. I think ultimately it is about our eternal life. That is my belief. That is what really keeps you going. Otherwise, let's all just step off of the building like lemmings because this is a drag sometimes. If you look at the big picture, it is not a drag. It is an adventure."

I asked Mel if he would consider endorsing this book, and he agreed without blinking an eye. For that I am very grateful.

I am equally grateful to have met and befriended Barbi McQueen.

SOMEBODY UP THERE LIKES ME

I was prepared to go full-on Sam Spade in my search for Pastor DeWitt and so was almost disappointed when all it took was a single phone call to Ventura Missionary Church.

He was no longer pastor there, I learned, but was serving at Ventura Baptist Church just a few miles away as head of the "Jubilee Ministry" for senior members of the congregation. The classes for adult singles and couples provide Bible study, more traditional music, and a variety of activities for worship and fellowship, including monthly luncheons and dinners, guest speakers and singers, and special excursions.

I got the number for Ventura Baptist Church and had my secretary Carol call. Turns out that Pastor DeWitt and I had actually met several years earlier at one of our Harvest Crusades in Ventura. Small world!

Speaking with him was like talking to an old friend. His voice exuded warmth, and within moments we were on a first-name basis. Then to business. I wanted to find out what happened

STEVE McQUEEN: THE SALVATION OF AN AMERICAN ICON

at that lunch Barbi told me about. Did Steve McQueen really make the decision to become a Christian?

Leonard says he'll meet me at noon tomorrow at McQueen's old airplane hangar in Santa Paula. After I thank him with all the dignity I can muster—dignity he surely deserves—and hang up the phone, I skip around the office whooping like a six-year-old who's just found out he's getting exactly what he wants for Christmas.

Turns out that Pastor DeWitt and I had actually met several years earlier at one of our Harvest Crusades in Ventura. Small world!

This may well turn out to be the most important encounter in my quest to learn about Steve's journey to God. I need to do a lot of thinking and preparing—and I need to fly solo this time. Cathe understands. She always does.

In the morning I take off early and arrive in Santa Paula with enough time before my meeting with Leonard DeWitt to stroll the historic district where Steve and Barbi shopped for antiques and ate meals without being fawned over. No wonder Steve liked it here. This is where he finally went from being Superstar Steve McQueen to Solid Citizen Steve McQueen, an approachable, companionable, and contributing member of the community.

At noon on the head, Leonard walks up to the hangar, and we shake hands and take a seat on two random chairs over toward a corner. Leonard knows this space well as he spent time with Steve there before. He told me when it was Steve's hanger it was filled with perfectly restored motorcycles and many antiques.

"Steve had always been one of my favorite actors," Leonard begins. "I didn't know much about him personally but liked the way he portrayed the characters in his films. His characters always seemed to have a decency and authenticity, and you could tell he was always pulling for the underdog."

Leonard says he chuckled when he heard Steve was taking flying lessons from Sammy Mason. "I laughed because I knew Steve had met his match. Sammy was a guy who really lived the Word. Didn't preach it but lived it. I knew that it would catch Steve's attention."

Leonard had no idea McQueen was attending services at Ventura Missionary Church until one of his children asked, "Did you know Steve McQueen was in church this morning?" Of course he was

At noon on the head Leonard walks up to the hangar and we shake hands and take a seat on two random chairs over toward the corner.

intrigued by the news, but Leonard decided to do nothing and let McQueen approach him in his own good time. Thankfully, other congregants also gave Steve his space, says Leonard. "Steve asked to be treated the same as the rest of the congregation. People respected that and did not ask for autographs. Steve was coming to the house of God to seek the Lord and worship. Everyone wanted him to have the privacy he needed."

Approximately three months after Steve started attending church, McQueen and DeWitt finally met. Steve made the first move, introducing himself to the pastor after services and inviting him to lunch.

They went to the Santa Paula Airport diner, says Leonard, and for two hours McQueen peppered him with questions about Christianity.

"What kind of questions?" I wonder.

"Steve wanted to know if all of his sins could be forgiven, if the Bible could be trusted, and what did it look like to be a Christian," answers Leonard.

It's pure speculation on my part, but Steve was probably trying to wrap his mind around the notion of "Steve McQueen—Christian." After all, he had been Steve McQueen—movie star, race car driver, motorcycle legend, sex symbol, fashion icon, and, of course, King of Cool.

> "Steve wanted to know if all of his sins could be forgiven, if the Bible could be trusted, and what did it look like to be a Christian."

After the horrible treatment he had received from a string of uncaring and abusive stepfathers, one could easily see how Steve might recoil from the idea of God as a "Father." I surely resonate with this personally due to my own fatherless childhood. When I heard there is a God who loves me, it was a huge revelation. Because of the absence of an earthly father figure, I was pretty much a blank slate and therefore completely open to the idea of a heavenly Father who actually loves and cares for me.

Actually, no negative baggage was attached the term *Father* for me. Perhaps Steve felt the same way.

Leonard says he answered each of McQueen's questions as best he could and recalls it as an intense conversation more than an interrogation. He says he never felt Steve was trying to trip him up or challenge him.

"Finally," says Leonard, "Steve sat back, smiled, and said, 'Well, that about covers it for me.'"

Ah, that familiar McQueen smile. We know it well from *The Great Escape* when the Germans marched him back to his solitary cell with his baseball glove and ball to bounce against the wall. A hint of menace was in that smile. "You won't keep me here for very long!" it said.

But there would have been no menace in Steve's smile this time. This one was a smile of pure joy in the knowledge something wonderful had happened to him.

Then DeWitt says he had only one question for him, but before he could ask it, Steve said, "You want to know if I'm a born-again Christian, right?"

Leonard nodded and said, "Steve, that's all that's really important for me."

McQueen quietly revealed that during a service a few Sundays back when the pastor invited everyone to pray with him to receive Christ, he had prayed and it had happened.

"Yes," said Steve, "I'm a born-again Christian."

My heart leapt.

Contrary to what some have written and said over the years about McQueen's profession of faith, it was not occasioned by the death sentence he received from the doctors. Steve's meeting with Leonard DeWitt occurred fully six months before McQueen was diagnosed with cancer. His decision to accept Christ was entirely of his own free will and totally unfettered by the specter of his final judgment day.

> "Finally," says Leonard, "Steve sat back, smiled and said, 'Well, that about covers it for me.'"

After that lunch Leonard arranged for McQueen to have weekly Bible study sessions with him and an associate pastor, Reverend Leslie Miller. "I had given him a very comprehensive book on Christianity. I think it was *More Than a Carpenter* by Josh McDowell," Leonard says. "It was the kind of book you'd give a beginner and that would take him step by step how to grow. His interest in spiritual things was genuine. You could tell that he was thirsty and that he was following through like he said he would."

> "Yes," said Steve, "I'm a born-again Christian."

Leonard says McQueen possessed a good sense of humor and genuinely cared about people. Santa Paula, he says, was a "place of healing for Steve."

He got a kick out of Barbi McQueen, too, and recalls the time Steve asked if he wanted to see his ranch. "You'll have to drive because Barbi has my truck," Steve said. But when they walked to Leonard's car, the keys were locked inside.

> Leonard says McQueen possessed a good sense of humor and genuinely cared about people. Santa Paula, he says, was a "place of healing for Steve."

"Wait here," said Steve. He went inside and returned a moment later with a wire coat hanger.

"We tried and tried and tried but couldn't get the car to unlock," Leonard says. "Then Barbi pulled up in his old pickup and asked, 'What are you guys doing?' Steve said, 'The Reverend locked the keys in his car and we're trying to get this thing unlocked.'"

Barbi grabbed the wire hanger from Steve, recalls Leonard, and unlocked the car "on the first try. We kind of wondered about her background after that."

In December 1979 Leonard received a phone call from Steve asking if they could meet. He knew by the tone of McQueen's voice "something major was going on."

When they connected later that day, McQueen told Leonard he had just been diagnosed with cancer. "He said, 'Leonard, now that I know Christ, I really want to live. I believe God could use me, but if He doesn't hear me it's okay because I know where I'm going.' It was so transparent, so genuine, so honest.

"Many of us prayed for the Lord to heal Steve," says Leonard, his voice cracking, "but it was not God's plan."

McQueen had finally placed his faith in the Lord but, as sick as he was, he still wasn't done looking for answers and covering all bets—including some off-the-wall ones.

> "He said, 'Leonard, now that I know Christ, I really want to live. I believe God could use me, but if He doesn't hear me it's okay, because I know where I'm going.'"

A TEST OF FAITH

Being a Christian isn't for the faint or weak of heart. Many people are under the impression that all of life's ills or problems go away once we commit our lives to Jesus Christ. I've been around long enough to know it's the exact opposite in many cases. Jesus knew all about this when He said, "In this world, you will have tribulation."

For centuries, Christians have had it rough. We've been mocked, spit upon, stoned, and crucified for our beliefs, and we're reaching that tipping point yet again in today's increasingly secular society. "In God We Trust," one of the founding principles of this country, is deemed offensive, even incompatible with our ideals. We adhere to a strident and false political correctness that seeks to bar religion and faith from our public discourse.

When Steve McQueen learned he had cancer, I'm sure he was perplexed and had questions for the Lord. *Why now?* Why, when he was finally at the happiest point ever? Why, when he had just made the most important and best decision of his entire life? Steve was quite new in the Christian faith.

He was just getting his bearings and now came the worst news imaginable.

McQueen's prognosis was grim, but he did as he always did when his back was against the wall. He fought back, living life to the fullest. On January 16, 1980, just one month after his cancer diagnosis, Steve and Barbara Minty were wed in the living room of their ranch home in Santa Paula.

Sammy and Wanda Mason were the witnesses at this ten-minute ceremony, after which McQueen called a friend on the phone and said, "This is the greatest thing to happen to me."

A month later, Steve went back to Cedars-Sinai Hospital for additional tests. They disclosed that his cancer was out of control. It had spread to the lining of his stomach, and tumors as big as golf balls were growing at the base of his neck and on his chest and abdomen. Surgery and chemotherapy would be futile, the doctors said. He had a mere 5-percent chance of living through the end of the year.

> Steve was quite new in the Christian faith. He was just getting his bearings and now came the worst news imaginable.

He was, in other words, the definition of a dead man walking.

Faithful to his character and the attitude that had made him what he was, McQueen stubbornly refused to give in. "I can't believe it's over. I *won't* believe it," he said. "There is so much I want to do . . . so much I have to do!"

He made a mental list of friends, associates, and people he cared about and contacted every name on it. Some he told about his condition; others he just said he was calling to offer his best wishes. The ones he had wronged, he apologized to—including his first wife, Neile, for the many indiscretions he committed during their marriage. It was an incredibly brave act.

It was also the right thing to do.

The Bible talks about restitution. It states that as much as possible we should seek to right the wrongs we've done to others in life.

The Gospels tell the story of Zacchaeus, a tax collector abhorred by his fellow Hebrews because he not only collected exorbitantly high taxes for the occupying force of Rome but also sliced off a little extra for himself.

One day Jesus came to town and invited himself to Zacchaeus's house for lunch. This created quite a stir among the townspeople because Zacchaeus was such a notorious sinner.

But Jesus specializes in turning notorious sinners into notorious Christians, and that's what happened with Zacchaeus, who following their lunch said, "Master, I give away half my income to the poor—and if I'm caught cheating, I pay four times the damages" (Luke 19:8 MSG).

Zacchaeus had spent a lifetime taking advantage of others; now, his heart touched by God, he would make restitution.

In his own way, Steve was doing the same. He was a very private person, but he recognized the impact he had on the lives of those around him. It was closure

> He made a mental list of friends, associates, and people he cared about and contacted every name on it. Some he told about his condition; others he just said he was calling to offer his best wishes. The ones he had wronged, he apologized to—including his first wife, Neile, for the many indiscretions he committed during their marriage. It was an incredibly brave act. It was also the right thing to do.

in a sense but also a poetic and valorous thing to do in the face of his prognosis. With so little time left, he was thinking about others, and one by one he said his farewells.

He knew he was going to die. He intended to fight with every ounce of his being, but he was a pragmatic man and knew the odds were against him. And now as a newly-minted Christian, McQueen knew he was set for the afterlife with a reservation guaranteed by Jesus Christ Himself. But he wanted to be ready, to be prepared.

> He knew he was going to die. He intended to fight with every ounce of his being, but he was a pragmatic man and knew the odds were against him.

Because, after all, heaven is a prepared place for prepared people.

On March 11, 1980, McQueen's condition became public knowledge when the *National Enquirer* ran a cover story with a screaming headline: "Steve McQueen's Heroic Battle Against Cancer." Some of the information in the story was wrong—it said McQueen had been diagnosed with lung cancer, for example, when it was actually mesothelioma—but it did correctly report there was little hope for the actor.

The *Enquirer* story was the first of a slew of tabloid eruptions that turned the time left to Steve into a horrible circus. At first he called what they reported "garbage" and tried to back it up by making some staged public appearances. But he lacked the stamina necessary to keep up the charade, and finally he sat down with Barbi to talk about what to do.

"When Steve was told his cancer was inoperable," Barbi says. "He gave me a choice."

They would continue their lives together as newlyweds, enjoying what little time life afforded him, or Steve could fight this cancer with everything he had.

"I was a young bride and wanted a life with my new husband, so for me there really was no choice. I said, 'Let's fight this thing.' Looking back, it may not have been the best idea because his quality of life really suffered in the end and it was a painful ordeal, but I was so in love with this man, I wanted to do everything humanly possible to help him get well."

Modern medical science had written Steve off—which left only alternative treatments, mostly propounded by shills and hucksters hoping to make a big financial score off the misery and desperation of others.

The first alternative practitioner McQueen saw told him that several weeks of intravenous feedings, megadoses of minerals, vitamins, and antioxidants, and a special cleansing diet would save his life. Hoping to avoid the paparazzi, Steve rented a fully equipped RV and parked it outside the doctor's San Fernando Valley office. The painful treatments required McQueen to lie flat on his back six hours a day, five days a week, for seven weeks. I can only imagine what went through his mind during those long ordeals. Barbi herself gave him the injections ordered by the doctor, who said he was legally prevented from doing so himself.

"The whole thing was *way* illegal," Barbi said, "but Steve was desperate to find a cure, and that led us down a desperate path."

Tragically, the treatment did nothing to alleviate his condition. Then Steve heard about Dr. William D. Kelley, who claimed that most cancers could be eradicated through strict dietary measures.

But as the saying goes, "Once burned, twice shy." This time McQueen hired a detective to conduct a background check on Kelley before putting himself in his hands. It turned out that Kelly's only medical degree was one from the Baylor College of Dentistry, and that he claimed to have gotten into the alternative medicine business at the direct behest of Jesus—who, Kelley said, had sat him on His knee and personally given him his marching orders when Kelley was three years old.

Of course, this is completely absurd on its face. More than once as I have uncovered and written this story, I've wished I could step back in time and offer some sound biblical counsel to Steve, the new believer, to help him discern between legitimate and illegitimate people claiming to be believers.

In 1964, the thirty-seven-year-old Kelley said he was diagnosed with malignancies on his liver and pancreas and given only weeks to live but survived and thrived after his mother threw all the junk food out of their house and fed him only fresh fruits, veggies, nuts, grains, and seeds. This led to experimentations with such supposed detoxifying remedies as coffee enemas, and in 1967 he wrote a book called *One Answer to Cancer.*

> I have uncovered and written this story, I've wished I could step back in time and offer some sound biblical counsel to Steve, the new believer, to help him discern between legitimate and illegitimate people claiming to be believers.

To Barbi McQueen, Kelley was "kind of a weirdo, a little off." Sure sounds like it.

"Naturopathic medicine wasn't as mainstream as it is today," she says, "and the whole thing had an underground feel to it. I didn't particularly care for Kelley, but this was Steve's choice, and I was there to support him. How I felt about the man didn't matter in the grand scheme of things. I just wanted Steve to get well."

Steve and Barbi flew to Kelly's organic farm in Washington State in April 1980 and listened to his presentation but returned to Santa Paula without agreeing to anything. Within a few more months McQueen no longer saw anyone. In late June he called Sammy Mason and asked him to take him up in the plane one last time. They made a date, but when Sammy got to the hangar, Steve wasn't there.

His condition was worsening. McQueen finally picked up the phone and dialed Dr. Kelley. "What can you do for me if I go all the way with your program?" he asked. Kelley made no promises but told McQueen every second was precious.

On July 30, two days after the premier of *The Hunter*, McQueen checked into Cedars-Sinai Hospital for another review of his case. "While he was under sedation," Barbi says, "the doctors pretty much told me he was going to die. I could hardly breathe," she added, misty-eyed.

"It was suggested I keep him sedated all the time, and when the pain got to be unbearable, bring him back and they'd make

> "While he was under sedation," Barbi says, "the doctors pretty much told me he was going to die. I could hardly breathe," she added, misty-eyed.

him comfortable until he died in his sleep. That's something a young bride should never have to hear."

When Barbi later told Steve what the doctor had said, he flared up. "I'm a fighter," he declared. "I don't believe that. I believe I can make it."

Then he picked up the phone next to his hospital bed, called ranch foreman Grady Ragsdale, and told him to get his Ford pickup truck ready for a trip to Mexico.

KNOCKIN' ON HEAVEN'S DOOR

By mid-1980 Steve McQueen was teetering on the rim of the abyss. When he looked into the mirror, death looked back at him through his own anguished and tired eyes. Jesus had entered his life and filled his heart with joy, and there was great peace and comfort in that, of course. But even the most committed Christian doesn't want to die. Plus, Steve had so much to say now and so much to offer to a watching world that held him in such high esteem.

The original bad boy, the King of Cool, was now doing the most rebellious thing he'd ever done in his life of nonstop rebellion. He was reading the Bible, going to church, fellowshipping with other believers, and following Jesus Christ.

He understood he had an unusual platform, and he wanted to use it—at the right time. He said he wanted "to tell people that I know the Lord, what I have to offer, what's happened to me." For the first time in his life, this man of few words really had something to say.

But to do that, he had to beat cancer.

It's one thing to calmly face and accept death when one is ninety years old and has lived a long, full life. It's quite another to do so, as Steve did, at only fifty. So he grasped at any straw that offered even the slenderest hope of extending his life. It wasn't weakness or necessarily even foolishness but just the life force we all have in us.

On July 31, 1980, Steve and Barbi secretly drove to Rosarito Beach, Mexico. The Plaza Santa Maria is located there, about twenty miles south of Tijuana. Originally opened as a tourist resort, now it was a clinic Dr. Kelley operated, where cancer patients written off as terminal by the medical establishment came for the "metabolic therapy program" that included strict diet, nutrients, tissue concentrates, enzymes, detoxification procedures, structural therapies, and psychological counseling.

> The original bad boy, the King of Cool, was now doing the most rebellious thing he'd ever done in his life of nonstop rebellion. He was reading the Bible, going to church, fellowshipping with other believers, and following Jesus Christ.

It's about a 120-mile drive south on Interstate 5 from Orange County to Rosarito Beach. Despite the name that sounds so tranquil, the Plaza Santa Maria has always summoned dark images to my mind. I understand what drove Steve to go there and submit to the last-ditch unorthodox treatments, but I can't help but think how confusing and horrible it must have been for Barbi and Steve's children to go through it—to watch his suffering go unabated while the tabloid press hovered like vultures for scraps of information to feed people's insatiable appetite for the sensational.

I had a personal friend, Arie, who found out he had cancer—advanced stage melanoma—and his doctor advised him to have surgery immediately or he would die.

Arie was cut from a similar cloth as Steve McQueen. He was a self-made man, quite a successful dairy farmer. Instead of opting for surgery, he decided to go a clinic in Mexico to get what some would call unorthodox treatment and others pure quackery. I was in the latter camp and pleaded with him to get the surgery. But Arie wouldn't hear of it, so I asked him at least to let me visit that clinic with him and see for myself what it offered.

We flew to the clinic in Tijuana. Everything I saw there made me wonder why in the world Arie would choose it for his treatment. The only answer was in the look of hope on his face.

Arie submitted to treatments that included drinking juices and eating natural foods. He also applied an ointment they prepared there directly to his cancer.

Despite the name that sounds so tranquil, the Plaza Santa Maria has always summoned dark images to my mind.

In time, the cancer disappeared. Arie made a full recovery.

Do I believe these treatments did it? I still have my doubts. But I know for a fact that many people prayed for Arie, and I know Arie had hope. Ultimately, it was God who touched him and extended his life fifteen more years.

It's easy to sit in judgment of Steve for going to the Plaza Santa Maria, but he never colored inside the lines anyway, so it's no surprise that he did it. He hoped it would work. One way or another, he knew it was ultimately in God's hands.

Steve's newfound faith kept him on an even keel through it all, and I'm going to Plaza Santa Maria myself to talk to someone who can personally attest to that. Teena Valentino was the "metabolic technician" who took care of Steve almost 24/7 for the last ninety-nine days of his life. She experienced his ups and downs and witnessed the transformation that Christ made in his life.

Steve's newfound faith kept him on an even keel through it all.

When Steve and Barbi arrived at the Plaza in 1980, uniformed guards greeted them at the large iron gate in front. Teena, who appears to be in her late seventies, greets me at that same place. The onetime cruise ship entertainer checked Steve into the facility and probably saw him more than anyone else while he was there.

No longer was he just Steve McQueen, the Christian; he was Steve McQueen, the *evangelist.*

"You probably can't even recognize me," Steve said to Teena that first day. "I don't look much like Steve McQueen."

"You look fine, Steve," she told him.

"He had a presence about him," recalls Teena. "He radiated an unusual combination of qualities: confidence, consideration, independence, and gentleness. I sensed he was a most unusual man in spite of the fact he was a movie star."

His very first night at the Plaza, he asked Teena if she was a Christian. When she responded affirmatively, he said, "I try to read the Bible every day. I've made my peace with the Lord.

Someday when I'm feeling better, I'll tell you how I found the Lord."

"I'd like that, Steve," she replied.

No longer was he just Steve McQueen, the Christian; he was Steve McQueen, the *evangelist.*

It didn't take long for him to rebel against the rigid diet of bland metabolic food on tap at the Plaza. Soon he was having a friend surreptitiously ship packets of his favorite foods in to him. Teena tumbled to it right away but looked the other way when Steve said, "I have very few pleasures in life right now; food is one of the few I have left."

"He would take one bite from each of the foods to get it out of his system," Teena recalls. "Eventually the taste didn't satisfy him any longer."

Barbi's constant presence, companionship, and tender support for her husband impressed Teena. "I saw a marriage that was innocent and natural. They had a childlike trust of each other," she says. "If Steve behaved disagreeably, he expected Barbara to understand and react impeccably. She did. To them, life and love were one inseparable act."

> "I love the Lord, and I just can't figure out why He let me get cancer," McQueen once said to Teena. "I took the Lord Jesus Christ as my Savior. That was before I got sick. I just don't understand. But I tell Him I'm willing to do whatever He wants. My life is His. If He wants me to die, I'll die. I won't fight it."

Still, and understandably, sometimes McQueen couldn't help but wonder why he was being put through such a crucible.

"I love the Lord, and I just can't figure out why He let me get cancer," McQueen once said to Teena. "I took the Lord

Jesus Christ as my Savior. That was before I got sick. I just don't understand. But I tell Him I'm willing to do whatever He wants. My life is His. If He wants me to die, I'll die. I won't fight it."

A moment later, he added, "But if He wants me to die, why did He lead me to Kelley? Why am I down here?"

Sammy Mason and Pastor Leonard DeWitt visited McQueen at the Plaza, and Steve asked Sammy to work up a Bible study program for him.

DeWitt told me Steve had lost a lot of weight and looked like he was knocking on heaven's door. Steve told him, "My only regret is that I was not able to tell others what Christ did for me."

Actually, he did. Teena has two cassette recordings with her, made by McQueen at the Plaza, and she plays them for me. The first one was a message and prayer he taped for fellow patients:

> We thank Thee, Lord, for all the kindness and understanding, and Your special way that You reach out to all the staff, the doctors, the nurses, all the people who are helping us be healed in this great, great experiment that we're all a part of. And for knowing in their times of anguish that You're here for them, as they are very tired and overworked and need the Lord's love too.
>
> And for the patients, all of us who have cancer, in our times of anguish and pain, knowing that the Lord

Jesus Christ is there for us. All we need is faith and the ability to reach out and to accept His love, 'cause He is there for us . . . Jesus Christ, our Savior. Amen.

This was clearly a vastly different Steve McQueen. His heart had changed. His compassion for others was strong. He knew what his fellow patients were facing because he was facing it, too, and he wanted to help.

On the second cassette recording, Steve's voice is weaker, but his message even stronger.

I really believe I have something—I think I believe, I'm pretty sure I believe, that I have something to give to the world as far as my relationship with the Lord, something I can teach to other people, something about a message that I can give. I don't know exactly where, but I've thought a lot about it when I'm by myself. I think that I should be here to do that . . . if not . . . and I've been in excruciating pain, and I've always tried to say that I've had faith and I never gave up.

I know now that I've changed a lot. I used to be more macho, and now my ass is gone, my body is gone, is broken, but my spirit isn't broken, and my heart isn't broken. I would like to think that I do have the determination to beat this thing, and they keep telling me they think I can, but there is a chance that I might not. Every day I go through this thing where my friends tell me I'm not dying, and they say I should take morphine and keep me happy because I get tired of the pain and

I wish it would go away. Even with my broken body, I want to go to Ketchum, where I own a place. Move everything. My planes, bikes, antiques, my wife, all my animals. To start living again. That's what I'd like, and to try and be able to change some people's lives. To tell people that I know the Lord, what I have to offer, what's happened to me.

These messages, taped for posterity, are a stirring, triumphant testament to the undeniable and unshakable faith of Steve McQueen and his unswerving commitment to the Lord as he faced his greatest crisis and endured such physical suffering as would plummet most people into utter despair.

He was no longer Steve McQueen the iconic movie star. He was Steve McQueen, man of God. He was not playing a part of someone suffering as he did so movingly in *Papillon*. He was living it. Steve's ultimate transformation was close.

Before it came, he would bear his heart to another messenger of God, a man who insisted everybody call him "Billy."

> He was no longer Steve McQueen the iconic movie star. He was Steve McQueen, man of God. He was not playing a part of someone suffering as he did so movingly in *Papillon*. He was living it.

SEE YOU IN HEAVEN

For good reason Billy Graham has long been known as "America's Pastor."

It's estimated that this tireless crusader for Christ brought a message of salvation to millions of people through the global crusades he conducted from 1947 up to his age-dictated retirement in 2005.

In the past century the world has seen a dizzying array of self-styled evangelists, gurus, cult leaders, new age teachers, and other false prophets come and go. Billy Graham has towered over and outlasted them all because he is the genuine article and has remained steadfast and true to God's Word. He is the gold standard of evangelists.

Presidents from Harry S. Truman to George W. Bush relied on Dr. Graham for spiritual advice and counsel on such complex issues as war, communism, race, morality, marriage, abortion, and, of course, spiritual rebirth. In 2016 he was named among Gallup's "10 Most Admired Men" in the world for a record sixtieth time. No other living human being has ever held that distinction.

I am proud to say that Billy Graham is also my friend. I've known him personally for more than twenty-five years and have served at his request on his board of directors for the past two decades. I can tell you from personal experience that the private Billy Graham is exactly the same as the public figure. There are not two Billys, just one.

In person he is warm, genuine, and considerate of everyone he speaks to. On one of our trips to his home in North Carolina, he took as much interest in my Cathe and our son Jonathan as he did in me, if not more.

He is the most godly man I have ever met.

Steve McQueen must have agreed and sought him out in the last days of his life.

Graham had been made aware of McQueen's illness through Leonard DeWitt. Steve had mentioned to his pastor how much it would mean for him to meet Billy, and as McQueen's condition worsened, Leonard picked up the phone.

"I made at least two phone calls," Leonard told me in Santa Paula, who had a connection to Billy through a member of the church. "The second time was to say that if Dr. Graham was going to come, it should be sooner rather than later."

By the end of October 1980, McQueen's body was wracked by cancerous tumors so large that his swollen abdomen made him look pregnant. At the Plaza Santa Maria, Dr. Kelley called in Mexico's most renowned surgeon, Dr. Cesar Santos Vargas, for a consultation. Dr. Vargas said McQueen's only hope was surgery to remove the tumors. It was scheduled for November 6 at Vargas's clinic in Juarez.

As Steve prepared for the flight from Oxnard to Mexico, his foreman Grady Ragsdale received a phone call from Dr. Graham himself.

"Does Steve still want to see me?" he asked.

"As soon as possible," Ragsdale replied. When Ragsdale told Steve Dr. Graham was on his way, he wept tears of joy.

They met on November 3, 1980. "Though I had never met [McQueen] before," recalled Dr. Graham later, "I recognized him immediately from his pictures, even though he had lost considerable weight. He sat up in bed and greeted me warmly.

"He told me of his spiritual experience. He said that about three months before he knew he was ill, he had accepted Christ as his Savior and had started going to church, reading his Bible, and praying. He said he had undergone a total transformation of his thinking and his life."

McQueen told Dr. Graham how Sammy Mason had led him to the Lord and said it was his faith in Christ that helped him deal with his illness. Dr. Graham read several passages of Scripture, and they prayed together.

In the small, private plane, they said a final prayer together, and when Dr. Graham got up to go, he handed his personal Bible to McQueen.

Graham then accompanied McQueen to the nearby Oxnard Airport, while Steve asked him questions about the afterlife. In the small, private plane, they said a final prayer together, and when Dr. Graham got up to go, he handed his personal Bible to McQueen. On the front inside flap he had written:

> *To my friend Steve McQueen. May God bless you*
> *and keep you always.*
> *Billy Graham*
> *Philippians 1:6*
> *Nov. 3, 1980*

Just before Dr. Graham exited the plane, Steve called out, "I'll see you in heaven!"

Referring to that visit, Billy later said, "I look back on that experience with thanksgiving and some amazement. I had planned to minister to Steve, but as it turned out, he ministered to me. I saw once again the reality of what Jesus Christ can do for a man in his last hours."

"Now look down a few entries," Mike says. That entry is dated November 7, when Mike brought Steve back in a casket. We ride in virtual silence for the next two hours.

Ever since I decided to undertake this investigation of Steve McQueen's spiritual conversion, I've been uncertain as to whether it was necessary to follow his trail to its very end in Juarez. We know what happened in that dank, depressing, dirty clinic. Would there be anything new to be gleaned there? I don't know, but now I feel compelled to see the place in which he took his last breath. It's become almost a hackneyed word, but for lack of a better one, I suppose I'm seeking *closure*—for Steve's story and also for myself.

Instead of driving the Bullitt, a friend with a plane is flying me down. My friend Mike Jugan, the pilot who flew Steve to El

Paso and later brought his body back from there to California, is accompanying me. As McQueen did three-and-a-half decades before, we leave from the Oxnard Airport and will fly to El Paso International Airport.

Upon reaching cruising altitude, Mike hands me a large black hardbound book. On the cover it says "Senior Pilot Flight Record and Log Book." He tells me to open to the first page bookmarked by a Post-it note.

"Look midway down the page," Mike says. "Notice the name of our passenger." It's Steve McQueen. The date in front of his name is November 3, 1980.

"Now look down a few entries," Mike says. That entry is dated November 7, when Mike brought Steve back in a casket. We ride in virtual silence for the next two hours.

It's around noon when we land in El Paso. Mike will stay at the airport while I take a cab to the US-Mexico border. It takes about twenty minutes for me to get processed at the US Customs Border Protection crossing station. Once on the other side, I grab another cab and hand the driver a paper on which I've written the address of Clinica Santa de Rosa.

> "As long as there are no patients waiting to be seen, I can show you the room," she continues. "And it looks like today is your lucky day, señor, as no one is in the waiting room. Please follow me."

Fifteen minutes later I step out at the intersection of Brasil and Guerrero Streets in front of a squat building of white and blue stucco that looks more like some kind of detention facility than a medical clinic. All the windows are barred—whether to keep people out or in, I can't imagine, and don't want to.

Inside, a middle-aged woman behind a counter asks, "Señor, how may I help you?" I tell her who I am and why I've come and then hold my breath, half expecting sirens to go off and guards to materialize and escort me off the property. But instead the woman says "Uno momento," and presses a button.

Moments later another woman appears and introduces herself as the clinic's head nurse. I repeat what I told the receptionist and again hold my breath. But she actually smiles.

"Many people come here looking for the same thing you do," she says. "My conditions are always the same."

How much, I wonder, *is this going to cost me?*

"As long as there are no patients waiting to be seen, I can show you the room," she continues. "And it looks like today is your lucky day, señor, as no one is in the waiting room. Please follow me."

McQueen's trusted aide Grady Ragsdale called Billy Graham to tell him the operation had begun, and Dr. Graham phoned Ronald and Nancy Reagan with the news. Everyone prayed for Steve.

As we walk, she explains the hospital has undergone several renovations since it was built sometime in the 1930s, and in fact the newer section we're passing through looks clean and well maintained. But the wing where Steve was operated on is virtually unchanged. It's on the south side of the building, where most of the light seems to come through a window overlooking an atrium garden. The interior is a combination of subway tile and aqua blue stucco.

We take a quick right turn and suddenly are in the room where Steve took his last breath. It has the same wood paneling, tile floor, sink, doorknobs, and lights as then. But it's spacious, and a receiving area adjoins the bedroom with a view to the atrium.

The nurse pats a metal-framed queen-sized bed. "This is where Señor McQueen passed," she says in a very practiced manner.

"I shall leave you for a few minutes," she says after a moment. "I need to go back to the front and see if there are any patients. I'll be back shortly."

I'm grateful to be left alone. I let my mind go back to what happened in this room starting on November 6, 1980.

"Hold my Bible and my watch," Steve told Teena Valentino as he was wheeled in just before 8:00 a.m. Then, to Dr. Vargas: "I want to live. I'm counting on you, doctor." Barbi, along with Steve's children Terry and Chad, arrived a few minutes later from a hotel across the street, prepared to wait in the adjoining room.

McQueen's trusted aide Grady Ragsdale called Billy Graham to tell him the operation had begun, and Dr. Graham phoned Ronald and Nancy Reagan with the news. Everyone prayed for Steve.

> The Bible given to Steve by Billy Graham—his most prized possession—was tightly clutched in Steve's hands on his deathbed. No one could explain how it had gotten there.

When Dr. Vargas opened up McQueen's abdomen, he was stunned by the amount of cancer he saw and exclaimed, "Oh, my God, where do I start?" For three hours the surgeon snipped and sliced. One of the excised stomach tumors was the size of a baseball and weighed about five pounds. When he finally closed Steve back up, Dr. Vargas literally collapsed from exhaustion.

Steve came out of the ether around two o'clock. His first words were, "Is my stomach flat now?" Cancer had clearly not infected his vanity. When Dr. Vargas checked on him later, McQueen gave him a thumbs-up and said, "I did it."

But it wasn't to be. Hours later, Steve suffered the first of two heart attacks. Staff worked furiously to revive him, but at 3:54 on the morning of November 7 he was pronounced dead.

"Do not feel bad, Señor," she says, reaching for a consoling tone. "You're not the only man who has cried leaving this room."

In her hotel room Barbi was jolted awake by the ringing phone. *That's it*, she said to herself. *He's gone.*

Chad McQueen went to the hospital at 6:00 a.m. Teena Valentino was there, and Chad asked for his dad's watch and cowboy hat. He noticed that his father's eyes were open, looking as blue as ever. The Bible given to Steve by Billy Graham—his most prized possession—was tightly clutched in Steve's hands on his deathbed. No one could explain how it had gotten there.

As I look down at that same bed now, I am gripped by a deep sorrow. I didn't know Steve personally, but researching this book and talking to so many people who did know him, I feel like I've lost a friend.

Know this: death is no friend to this world. In fact, the Bible refers to death as the enemy. It is so final and seemingly so cruel. But for the Christian who has put faith in Jesus Christ as Lord and Savior, death is not the end. For the believer, death is like passing from one shore to another. In truth, we live in the land of the dying and are headed to the land of the living.

The moment believers take their last breath on earth, they are taking their first breath in heaven.

I don't have a doubt in my mind how Steve's Bible got there. *He went right into the presence of God,* I think to myself. *Right into the presence of God.*

"Señor, is everything okay?" asks a voice next to me. The nurse has returned.

"Yes," I tell her, dabbing at my eyes as we turn for the door. "Everything's fine."

"Do not feel bad, Señor," she says, reaching for a consoling tone. "You're not the only man who has cried leaving this room."

There may be a hint of mockery there, but it doesn't matter because all of a sudden I'm laughing so loud the nurse looks alarmed. It's a joyful laugh of triumph and celebration because in this dingy place Steve McQueen finally was healed.

The Bible reminds us of God's power over death.

> Death swallowed by triumphant Life! Who got the last word, oh, Death? Oh, Death, who's afraid of you now? It was sin that made death so frightening and law-code guilt that gave sin its leverage, its destructive power. But now in a single victorious stroke of Life, all three—sin, guilt, death—are gone, the gift of our Master, Jesus Christ. Thank God! (1 Cor. 15:54–57 MSG)

Thank God, indeed.

Right then, right here, Steve McQueen had made the ultimate "Great Escape."

 **POSTSCRIPT**

GOOD NEWS IN A BAD WORLD

Juarez has approximately 1.3 million residents, but the city seems surprisingly still now at two o'clock in the afternoon. Sunlight greets me as I step outside the clinic, and its warmth is refreshing to body and soul. I wave for a taxi, get in, and head back to El Paso. Even though it's only been hours, it seems like days since I last saw Mike Jugan. And it's good to see him again.

Except for the din of the engines, the flight back to Oxnard is quiet. After a while I turn to Mike and ask him (only half kiddingly), to "tell me a happy story." Oh, how I needed a happy story.

Turns out, he's got a good one.

When the call came after Steve McQueen's death requesting that Mike and Ken Haas jet back to El Paso, he remembers while driving to the Oxnard airport, "All I could think about was how sad this would be for Steve's family. We had two Learjets—one for Steve's family and doctors, the other for

Steve's casket. I flew Steve's body behind the family plane." After departing El Paso, Grady Ragsdale entered the cabin and asked if Jugan and Haas could both do a "low pass" when they reached the Santa Paula Airport—an aviator's tribute. They said they'd be glad to.

"When we reduced speed, full flaps, gear down and were about a hundred feet off the ground, making our low pass along runway 22," Mike says, "a crowd of about fifty people had gathered outside, waving good-bye to Steve. Over the Unicom frequency I heard a voice say, 'God bless you, Steve.' Man, talk about goose bumps!"

> Earlier, Leonard DeWitt had conducted three services at Ventura Missionary Church, where McQueen's regular seat in the balcony was marked with a bouquet of roses and a small American flag. Barbi read the Twenty-third Psalm.

A few days later on Sunday, November 9, 1980, a private memorial service was held for Steve at the ranch. Earlier, Leonard DeWitt had conducted three services at Ventura Missionary Church, where McQueen's regular seat in the balcony was marked with a bouquet of roses and a small American flag. Barbi read the Twenty-third Psalm. The congregation sang the National Anthem in McQueen's honor.

The ranch service was more informal. Among the four dozen or so in attendance were his twenty-one-year-old daughter Terry, his nineteen-year-old son Chad, and Steve's former wives, Neile McQueen and Ali MacGraw. Pastor DeWitt spoke, and so did Sammy Mason.

"Steve operated at one speed—as fast as he could go," said Sammy, "and he never knew the word *quit*. He would always insist on flying as long as possible to total exhaustion. Yet he was always willing to take instruction."

Sammy's most important instructions of all were the ones that were lovingly delivered to Steve, the ones that saved his eternal soul.

This book has been an amazing journey for me. It's been a deep privilege to tell the salvation story of a true American icon. I had always been a fan and admirer of Steve McQueen, but along the way I've discovered lots of things about him I had not previously known.

One of the most surprising discoveries, and one that touched me in quite a personal way, was the eerie similarities of our early lives. I don't often meet someone else raised by an alcoholic mother who later searched for his real father. It happened to Steve, and it happened to me.

McQueen and I have another thing in common: we both put our faith in Jesus Christ. Steve is in heaven because of that decision.

It is no small thing that the number-one movie star in the world became a Christian at the peak of his success. The world was McQueen's oyster. The deeper he drank of her pleasures, the thirstier he became. But in the cockpit of an antique Stearman biplane, a seed was sown in Steve's heart that germinated in the balcony of Ventura Missionary Church, thanks to the gospel message presented by Pastor Leonard DeWitt.

Steve's conversion was absolutely real, and his faith grew stronger through the vicious onslaught of the cancer that ended his life. Today Steve McQueen is more alive than ever. Not just on celluloid but in heaven.

Steve's great regret in life was that he was not able to use his massive platform as an internationally known personality to share the story of what Jesus did for him.

That's why I wrote this book—to right that wrong.

One of the influential books Steve McQueen read when he first encountered Jesus Christ was *Mere Christianity* by Oxford professor C. S. Lewis. In his early life, Lewis was an atheist but came to a deep faith in Jesus Christ and used his scholarly mind to help others see how they could know the Savior personally.

Lewis confronts in that book the dismissive notion that Jesus was merely a good teacher, nothing more. "A man who was merely a man and said the sort of things Jesus said would not be a great moral teacher," he wrote. "He would either be a lunatic—on the level with the man who says he is a poached egg—or else he would be the Devil of Hell. You must make your choice. Either this man was, and is, the Son of God, or else a madman or something worse. You can shut him up for a fool, you can spit at him and kill him as a demon or you can fall at his feet and call him Lord and God, but let us not come with any patronizing nonsense about his being a great human teacher. He has not left that open to us. He did not intend to."

Steve McQueen made his choice.

He believed, and as a result his sins were forgiven and his past was put behind him. Many of the books and films

> Steve's great regret in life was that he was not able to use his massive platform as an internationally known personality to share the story of what Jesus did for him. That's why I wrote this book—to right that wrong.

about Steve's life tell the story that he came from one of the worst childhoods possible; clawed his way to the top of the Hollywood ladder; was an expert driver and motorcycle rider, a man's man and a charismatic superstar of cinema; then contracted cancer and died, leaving behind a legacy of cool.

> Steve was on a search his entire life. Yes, he wanted a father. But more than just his biological father, I think he was always searching for God Himself.

But there is so much more to his story than that. Yes, Steve did all of the above. But there was always a big hole in his heart, a gaping hole he tried to fill with possessions, accomplishments, fame, women, booze, and drugs. He was not unlike many others in that regard. Maybe this is you.

Steve was once quoted as saying, "I know I'm going to die early, so I'm going to have to grab a big slice of life." He got a bigger slice than most, but it crumbled to ashes. Steve was on a search his entire life. Yes, he wanted a father. But more than just his biological father, I think he was always searching for God Himself.

Every man, every woman is on that search.

What is the script Steve wanted others to read and hear and believe, the one that changed this Hollywood bad boy into a man who came to know God? The Bible calls this singular message "the gospel."

It comes down, again, to the definition of the word *gospel*—"good news"—truly good news in a bad world.

But before we can fully appreciate the Good News, we need to know the bad. The Bad News is that every man or woman who's ever drawn a breath has sinned. What does that really mean? The word *sin* has multiple meanings ranging from "missing a mark" to "crossing a line."

You and I have done both.

God gave us divine standards to live by called the Ten Commandments (not, as some would have us think, the Ten Suggestions). The commandments instruct us to not steal, lie, commit adultery, take God's name in vain, and more.

> Jesus came to pay a debt He did not owe because you and I owed a debt we could not pay.

All of us have broken those commandments.

Maybe you think, *Well, I'm not as bad as some people are.* While that may be true, you need to know that God doesn't grade on the curve. The Bible tells us if we "offend in one point" of the law, we are "guilty of all" of it (James 2:10 KJV).

God's mark for humanity is perfection.

"So, who can live like that?"

The answer is nobody.

That's where Jesus comes in. That's why He came to this earth, in fact. Like Steve McQueen chartering a jet to Mexico, it was really a rescue operation. But this operation was successful.

Jesus was God born in that Christmas manger in Bethlehem. God became a man and walked among us. God, the sovereign and holy Creator of the universe, had a face. He walked in our shoes; He breathed our air; He lived our lives; then He died our death.

No one forced Jesus to go to that cross He was nailed to. He did it voluntarily for you and for me. On the cross, He absorbed the judgment of God that should have come on you and me, and Jesus took it upon Himself.

Jesus came to pay a debt He did not owe because you and I owed a debt we could not pay.

But He did not stay on that cross.

Three days later, He rose again from the dead. And now, this same Jesus who lived, died, and rose from the dead is standing right before you as you read these very words, saying, "Behold, I stand at the door and knock. If anyone hears My voice and opens the door, I will come in" (Revelation 3:20 NKJV).

Jesus is waiting to come into your life.

As we've discovered in this story, Jesus was knocking on Steve's McQueen's door relentlessly throughout the years. And finally, when he had come to the "end of himself," he came to the beginning of God, and he believed.

I have good news for you—Jesus Christ can come into your life too. Right now!

But how, you may wonder?

First of all, you need to admit you're a sinner. Everyone has sinned and fallen short of God's glory, God's perfection.

Then, realize Jesus died on that cross for your sins.

Third, you must repent of your sin. Turn away from those things you regret. To repent means to be sorry for your sins and to change your direction, to hang a McQueen-caliber U-turn in the road of life. Instead of running *away* from God, you need to run *to* Him. He welcomes you with open arms.

Lastly, you need to ask Jesus Christ to come into your life. That is accomplished through prayer.

You can start right now by saying aloud:

"Lord Jesus. I know that I am a sinner. I also know that you are the Savior who died on the cross for my sin. Jesus, I am sorry for my sin and I turn from it now. I ask you to come into my heart and life to be my God and friend. I choose to follow you all the days of my life. Thank you for loving me and accepting me, in Jesus' name I pray. Amen."

If you just prayed that prayer, you can know with confidence that Jesus Christ Himself has come to take residence in your heart, just as He did for Steve McQueen, for me, and for countless others down through history.

If this book has changed your life or outlook, I would love to hear from you personally. You can email me at Greg@harvest.org.

May God bless you, my friend.